DEFINITELY MAYBE

A note on the author

Andy Bollen was involved in music from the age of fourteen. He worked in record shops, he was a DJ and he toured with Nirvana. He has written about football, sports and politics, as well as being a newspaper columnist and comedy writer for BBC TV and radio. His music books include *Nirvana: A Tour Diary* and *Labelled with Love: A History of the World in Your Record Collection*.

Also by the author

Nirvana: A Tour Diary

Sandy Trout: The Memoir

A History of Scottish Football in 100 Objects

Fierce Genius: Cruyff's Year at Feyenoord

A History of European Football in 100 Objects

The Number 10: More Than a Number, More Than a Shirt

Labelled with Love: A History of the World in Your Record Collection

Classic Derbies and Epic Rivalries: A Journey Through the World's Most Captivating Football Clashes

DEFINITELY MAYBE

The Birth, Death and Resurrection of Oasis

ANDY BOLLEN

First published in Great Britain in 2025 by Polygon, an imprint of Birlinn Ltd.

Birlinn Ltd
West Newington House
10 Newington Road
Edinburgh
EH9 1QS

www.polygonbooks.co.uk

1

ISBN 978 1 84697 719 0
eBook ISBN 978 1 78885 801 4

British Library Cataloguing-in-Publication Data
A catalogue record for this book is available on request from the British Library.

Typeset by Initial Typesetting Services, Edinburgh

Printed and bound by Clays Ltd, Elcograf, S.p.A.

To Sharon Murray (née Galway)
1965–2024

'I live for now, not for what happens after I die. I'm going to hell, not heaven. The devil has all the good gear. What's God got? The Inspiral Carpets and nuns.'

— Liam Gallagher

'What inspires me to write music? It's just what I do. And I'm fucking brilliant at it.'

— Noel Gallagher

'Those two guys are arguably the best comedians Britain ever produced. It's annoying how fucking funny they are.'

— Bill Burr

Contents

Preface

With Oasis, it is impossible to pen the standard rock book. They are a band like no other and their life a drink-and-drug-fuelled working-class fairytale. Forget any high-brow deconstruction of song structure, lyrical meaning or a detailed search for the artist's inner soul. No introverted navel-gazing or emotional heartache. No talk of vintage guitars and amplifiers or recording techniques and studio consoles. Oasis – both the band and their music – did not exist in a context of ambiguity. That's not them. However, if you want a band willing to run into a burning building to get you out, or maybe fit a kitchen in a day, they're your guys – or at least four of them are. They are a band best listened to loud and late, wham-bam thank you ma'am. The message is clear. Let's go for it, party hard, forget the misery and bleakness of reality and turn it up.

I was there on that quiet Bank Holiday Monday evening in May 1993 when Alan McGee of Creation Records offered Oasis a record deal in King Tut's Wah Wah Hut, Glasgow. My friend Ross and I were bored and remembered our pal, Derek McKee, DD, was playing in King Tut's and put us on the guest list. I was an eye-witness to something unspectacular which proved to be one of the most significant moments in British music history. I thought Oasis were alright and couldn't believe how animated Alan McGee became while watching them. During one particular song, he jumped with excitement as the lead guitarist played a solo. I eventually saw what McGee did and knew if I remained patient enough, the lads from Burnage would eventually return to the well.

I've watched their incredible triumphs and spectacular disasters from the moment they caught Alan McGee's eye in King Tut's to T in the Park and Knebworth. Their meteoric rise to fame, explosive fallouts and those key moments where it went spectacularly wrong. Not just slightly wrong but the musical equivalent of a friendly-fire attack, a self-inflicted omnishambles of enormous proportions. This was a band encouraged to be themselves, to bring excess and disorder, and they delivered. Yet when the elements were stable, and they kept it together, Oasis played groundbreaking shows.

I grew to respect Oasis. As they developed and bloomed into this globally famous and successful band, I looked on with pride at every achievement, every obstacle, the first TV appearance, their first single, like a nervous uncle. How uncool is that?

I've walked around shaking my head in disbelief for over three decades at their music's inconceivable impact on so many people. Every time I see Liam in the news, even now, I can't believe he's the same guy I saw on stage that night. When I watch Noel chat on a BBC4 documentary about Britpop, I smile. I bought into their story. I saw behind the façade and sensed the vulnerability under the bravado, the five working-class lads from a housing estate, the lucky guys who made the grade.

It turned out Oasis had songs, and songs are important to us: they are our lifelong friends, as constant as the stars. Here was a band capable of producing songs like 'Live Forever', 'Don't Look Back In Anger' and 'Wonderwall'. There was sensitivity, but it was mixed with volatility, frustration and passion. Oasis not only had songs, they had classics that connected across a huge demographic. At times this does read like a surreal fairytale. The concept of this seemingly rough-and-ready band playing a random gig in Glasgow after acting on a casual invite from a mate and ending up with a record deal and global success is extraordinary. That didn't happen any more, did it? In my experience record deals were the result of months, sometimes years, of chasing, of hard graft.

What McGee witnessed did not register with me. I was standing beside him. He was bouncing off me. Oasis played four ordinary songs and McGee was drunk and high (by his own admission, not mine). Speaking to the Guardian in 1993, on the tenth anniversary of Creation Records, Alan McGee was already smitten with the band's demo: 'The music is a cross between The Kinks, Stone Roses and The Who, and the cover of this tape, which is incredibly rare, only ten ever made, is important because it's a Union Jack going down the toilet. That sums up our country at the moment. I don't want to herald them too much, but they're already one of my favourite groups. Seeing them is what seeing the Stones must have been like in the early days. Brutal, exciting, arrogant.'

Time has shown how McGee called it right. He had an eye for the shape and sound of a band. The look, the dynamic. I thought they were another baggy Manchester band. And although, for the opening act in a four-band bill, they were loud, I could never see it becoming a pivotal moment in British rock and pop history. One thing is undeniably true: at that moment McGee was far better at his job than Oasis were at theirs.

The rumours about Oasis and McGee at King Tut's spread like wildfire across the city. No one in their right mind believed he'd offered this band a deal without knowing anything about them. Yet, according to McGee, it was sheer luck. It was a Bank Holiday and he thought the venue would be closing earlier than usual. His friend was also in one of the support bands so he thought he'd show up unannounced and surprise her. That's how he accidentally caught Oasis.

While everyone scratched their heads and got on with life, Oasis were uncharacteristically off-radar, keeping quiet, recording, rehearsing and getting it together. Many assumed their classic debut album *Definitely Maybe* was an effortless project. It was far from it. Noel, Alan McGee and their manager Marcus Russell found it a stressful experience. They got it right eventually by doing what they did best, recording live as a group. 'The demos Noel had given me were better than the studio recordings,' McGee says in his autobiography. 'They were trying to record the instruments separately, something that never works for our bands. It was another of our links to the 1960s; our bands worked best when recorded live.'

Despite splitting in August 2009, Oasis still had this lingering aura. It turned out their music was generational. The kids of the original fans grew up loving the songs. Oasis had enormous TikTok and Spotify figures. When it was announced in August 2024 that they intended to get back together, the world went mad. On Saturday 31 August 2024, tickets went on sale and Oasis officially broke the internet.

This book tries to understand how it panned out from that night in May 1993 in King Tut's by leading up to the night and looking at those behind the band who steered their career, from record deals to developing their stagecraft. We look at the musical backdrop of the time and discuss what drove the band, what made them tick and what pushed them on to become one of the biggest bands in the world. We also try to understand why their legacy is such that after witnessing them live, Dave Grohl said: 'That's the greatest rock band I've ever seen in my life.'

11 August 1996: Set List

The Swamp Song
Columbia
Acquiesce
Supersonic
Hello
Some Might Say
Roll With It
Slide Away
Morning Glory
Round Are Way (ending with Up In The Sky)
Cigarettes & Alcohol
Whatever (Octopus's Garden at the end)
Cast No Shadow
Wonderwall
The Masterplan
Don't Look Back In Anger
My Big Mouth
It's Gettin' Better (Man!!)
Live Forever
Encore
Champagne Supernova (with John Squire)
I Am The Walrus

1

Knebworth & the Media Turn

The bass drum hits you like a cannonball to the solar plexus. The drum tech is over-eager. He's out of time with the pre-gig music playing through the PA. The stinging orange smoke catches your throat. You feel like you're an extra in a Vietnam movie. The scene shifts to a slow-motion shot. Events become confused. It all starts to become surreal. Every movement and thought process is framed, like a jarring reel-to-reel in a movie projector. Sky becomes ground. Ground becomes sky. The horizon changes and is blocked by a mammoth electric pylon. There's something bizarre but enjoyable playing with and mixing up your senses.

Distinctive smells: the countryside, the stink of diesel, fried onions. Electricity. There's a deep, powerful humming of generators and seismic vibrations. The carnival's in town. Guitar music on a loop; playing backwards. Booker T's 'Green Onions'. Booker T frying green onions. Beautiful girls in denim shorts run with impractically attired men, plastic Mods. Onions, fried onions. A moment caught in time, a photograph, a snapshot, frozen forever. You immediately sense its significance; this is something you will always remember. The distinct noise of huge helicopter blades, whip-crack-thud-whip-crack-thud, pound directly above you. The sound is in stark contrast to the motion; you smile at the stylish ease and grace, the precision of the engineering of the helicopter itself. Leonardo da Vinci was some man. Then you catch a glimpse. Yes, it's them, they're only fifty feet above you. There you see the unmistakable faces of Oasis peering down. You can see them point and shake their heads and see the genuine concern on their faces. They are worried about your predicament. Don't be. We will see you on the other side, brother. Sooner than you think.

Hours later, and with only a few feet of movement in the queue, the fifth band are on. The band in the chopper were correct to be concerned. In a few hours, to huge applause and a whirling engulfing cacophony, Oasis stomp on stage, and you can hear the noise coming through the trees. You're stuck on a tiny country road, in a traffic jam to end all traffic jams. The only thing you can see for miles and miles are cars. The best new band in the world were playing through the trees in a field and, for many, this queue was the story of August 1996, when Oasis played at Knebworth.

Knebworth was more synonymous with major label artists and often disdainfully referred to as *Knobworth* thanks to the acts who played there. It was a festival for those who moved millions of albums, a vacuous, hubristic statement. For some reason, there was an establishment acceptance that to play in the shadow of Knebworth House out across the estate to thousands of fans was an achievement. A field of dreams for former public schoolboys and now music business bosses, basking in the glory of their charges. A self-indulgent folly for millionaire rock stars, flying in for the open-air rock concert and ticking every sorry cliché in the book along the way. But then Oasis played there. It didn't seem so bad.

Many fine bands have played Knebworth but for every Rolling Stones, I'll give you Queen. For every Who gig, I'll talk about Genesis. For every Devo show, I'll ask you about Jefferson

Starship. There's a peculiar music industry doff of the cap to those who make it and find themselves playing there. So, take a bow, Santana, Status Quo, The Darkness and so many more.

In May 1996, 2.6m applications were made for the 250,000 available tickets. Blenheim Palace and Castle Donington had been considered before Marcus Russell decided Knebworth was the best option from the fans' point of view. Most music fans were miffed when it was announced Oasis, a Creation band, were to play there. When I heard there was a guest list of 7,000 and an individual trailer for each band member I sensed that something felt wrong. And that was before I heard security was so tight the man who offered them a recording contract in a club in Glasgow less than three years earlier took three attempts to get in to see his band's crowning glory.

Joining the band, and the quarter of a million who assembled for the two shows, was a specially selected mix of dance and rock acts. Bands who would keep the party going nicely till the kings of Britpop strolled on stage. Playing the first gig, on 10 August, were Ocean Colour Scene, Manic Street Preachers, The Bootleg Beatles, The Chemical Brothers and The Prodigy. The second gig had Cast, Dreadzone, Kula Shaker, Manic Street Preachers and The Charlatans (who had lost keyboard player Rob Collins a few weeks earlier in a car accident). Admittedly, these bands were an improvement on Knebworth's usual major-label buy-on bands and heavy metal groups. It was an unusual decision to play there but it was chosen, despite the traffic jams getting in and out, as it was the most realistic venue that could come even close to satisfying ticket demand; plus, it was also one which matched the band's uncompromising ambition.

Knebworth is a vast, sprawling estate near Stevenage in rural Hertfordshire. Historically, it was the perfect place for the

Rolling Stones, Queen and Led Zeppelin to rock out. Yet Oasis naturally embraced the landmark gigs with their accustomed haughtiness, shrugging their shoulders as if to say, 'Well, what did you expect?' Now Oasis were like them, behemoths – giants of rock. This was the key. This was the journey; from King Tut's to Knebworth, in three years. With a colossal, towering PA and gigantic video screens, nothing matched or beat the sheer size and scale of the Oasis shows. To be fair to the band, it was only £25 a ticket, not bad considering the number of decent bands on the bill. Touts could squeeze you in for anything between £250 and £300, and that's what it cost those city types beside friends at the gig. You even got to see a terrific fireworks display at the end too. (More about that later.)

There was nowhere else big enough for Oasis, and it was seen by McGee, the band and Marcus Russell as a true statement of the band's popularity at that specific moment. It also feels symbolic that Oasis had reached their peak by the time they played Knebworth. Perhaps it was the scale and magnitude of the event. If it was a movie (a documentary movie was released twenty-five years later in 2021), it would be the perfect end, chapter over. If it was my band, I'd have walked away from it at its peak. Say thanks for the ride, but we can't beat this. We're quitting while we're ahead. Two groundbreaking albums and two landmark live shows. 'It's over, thank you Knebworth.' I wasn't alone in thinking this. Guitarist Bonehead told the *Guardian* in 2009: 'I always thought we should have bowed out after the second night at Knebworth.' Then again, Noel was under pressure with the third album already written, and a recording contract to honour.

As the money came rolling in, Oasis were enjoying themselves. Not exactly seduced by the fame and fortune, but certainly living it large. You've got to accept that guys who grew up where they did, who had a tough time, are going to flaunt it a bit. Why should we be modest? We deserve it. When Noel became famous and made some real money, he bought his house in Primrose Hill and christened it 'Supernova Heights'. And until 1999 it was infamous for its bacchanalian excesses. He then went on to buy even bigger and better houses in the country and abroad and spent freely on the cars, guitars and all the usual trappings. You could always tell Noel was a working-class hero because one of the first moves he made when his ship came in was to have his teeth done. And they are tremendous teeth. He suits them. He doesn't have that look some celebs have when they get new teeth and come back from Turkey looking like they're breaking gnashers in for a horse.

Oasis played the gigs with unwavering assurance and confidence. Their assuredness only served to make it appear that playing these career-defining gigs was an everyday occurrence. Nonchalance and self-belief were the order of the day. The band and management's decision to play Knebworth split Creation staff. Some were unhappy about the gig's corporate nature and the band's change. To some, it was a crass corporate rock event, a million miles away from the spirit of what the true indie ideal was about. Others remained more pragmatic, thinking if it wasn't for the Sony money they'd be dead and buried by now. For many, the Knebworth shows were a step too far, especially if witnessed as part of Creation's natural arc. You go from the beginning, see Alan McGee's journey from The Living Room, those first club nights and gigs above pubs in London, from The Legend! to The Television Personalities, from Primal Scream to My Bloody Valentine, from Teenage Fanclub to Oasis – the continuation of a sequence of remarkable events.

By August 1996, millions wanted to see Oasis. Some at the label also took a more practical point of view: this was the only kind of show that could satisfy demand by playing to 250,000 people over two days. With demand for tickets hitting the 3-million mark, the band would've had to play twenty-four separate shows at Knebworth to satisfy all those who desperately wanted to see them. Having reached the pinnacle, the subsequent problem that inevitably followed for the band, and Noel in particular, was – where do we go now? And how could he continue writing exciting songs with an edge, when they were so outrageously rich and successful?

Noel had written most of the songs on *Definitely Maybe* while working in a building site storeroom or unemployed, in his early to mid-twenties. That's what gave them such vitality and desire. How do you write songs that connect with your audience when you are beyond wealthy, and worse still, now enjoy telling people how rich and successful you are by rubbing it in their faces? That's how it felt in 1996. Noel in particular, once with a keen internal barometer of how to keep the man on the street onside, was acting way above his station; it had gone straight to their heads. They were heading for a fall.

Always clever enough to carry off playing the part of the cheeky rock star, Noel wouldn't take those who supported the band for granted. He was always aware the fans put the band up there. He'd always kept it real, playing it perfectly, part confidence and part charm, but he was now turning into a caricature of a Loadsamoney type. The drugs do work, allegedly.

The show at Knebworth was as much about the band's celebrity status as it was about the music. Oasis had reached this weird place in society where everybody, their mum and their granny were aware of them. They were hanging out with film stars, supermodels and all kinds of famous people and were protected by a ring of security more fitting for a visiting head of state.

Those present spoke about two things. The backstage marquees bigger than festival tents. No one's arguing with the success and how much the band deserved it considering where they started from. What their fans and Creation staff who put in the hours working for them couldn't buy into was how much this obsession with celebrity turned their heads. You also have to remember this feeds both ways. They were the band of the moment and Noel and Liam were the men to be seen with. They had moved on from being favourites of the *NME* and *Melody Maker* and were now prime targets of *The Sun* and *The News of the World* (the latter now gone; how sad, oh my).

The second issue raised was the fireworks. How it felt there was something symbolic afoot as they watched explosions and rockets crack and flash across the sky. Powerful blasts and cannon fire everywhere, whizzing, banging, snapping, hissing, a circling, cascading cacophony, a crescendo of noise. This sonic spectacle felt like a closing chapter and out of place for an Oasis gig. While promoting his autobiography around 2013, Alan McGee mentioned the fireworks and that moment too. It had a significant effect on him; it was out of character, maybe the noise shook him and made him realise he was growing apart from the band.

The tabloids now lauded Oasis. They talked up the shows. Suddenly the band had transcended from being a Manchester band with a couple of decent singles into this entity or commodity who shocked and thrilled with their behaviour. The press excitedly proclaimed that Knebworth was the fastest sell-out in history. Some papers decided to go as far as calling it the gig of the century. I would have plumped for Led Zep at Madison Square Garden, New York in 1973 or The Beatles at Shea Stadium or Candlestick Park or a random gig by the Ramones in CBGB's in the East Village. I have an A4 poster in a drawer promoting The Cramps and The Fall at Glasgow

Tech in 1980, which always sounded like fun. (I was too young, aged 13-ish at the time, but the idea of seeing Kristy Marlana Wallace, AKA Poison Ivy, in the flesh would have been too much to take.) What about Jimi Hendrix at the Isle of Wight or Woodstock? The Who live at Leeds? Nirvana at Reading in 1991, Killing Joke at Glasgow Barrowland in 1985 or how about Primal Scream at Hanger 13, Ayr Pavilion, 1993? I could happily do this all day.

The reality was that Oasis had become far too big. They towered over Creation and suffocated the development of bands attempting to come through. Creation had now become Oasis. The major problem was that the band's popularity had grown exponentially. Those in favour of them playing Knebworth could say, well Oasis are produced and distributed by an indie in the UK, but the truth is they were seen by most at Creation as a worldwide Sony band.

From performing as The Rain, then changing their name to Oasis, then Noel joining and their relentless rehearsals in The Boardwalk, the Oasis story is genuinely mind-blowing. The same band had gone on this rare and remarkable odyssey. From being another average Manchester-sounding band with a soft spot for The Stone Roses to walking onto that stage at Knebworth. (There was a symbolic moment, a passing of the torch, as the band were joined onstage by The Stone Roses guitarist John Squire to play 'Champagne Supernova' during the encore.) The same band I was nonplussed about at King Tut's were playing Knebworth. They were now one of the most famous rock bands the UK ever produced and in the process went on to sell well over 22 million copies of *(What's The Story) Morning Glory?*

These sales figures made it tough for any artist to remain level-headed and the press quickly flipped, demonising Oasis and ridiculing their wealth. Noel was an easy target with his house 'Supernova Heights', his chocolate-brown Rolls-Royce – which he couldn't drive – and his newly immaculate teeth. At first, everyone was rooting for the band, but once they achieved so much success, it seemed that they rounded on them. The tabloids were brutal. But the people they were attacking were from Burnage. They didn't give a toss.

Where were the reports in the press about Blur's country houses and wealth? A competent tabloid editor can twist, manipulate and nuance anything they want to get their side of the story across; after all, it's their job. Perhaps Oasis liked to flaunt it whereas Blur were a little cuter about it. The line always read something like, 'Well, they're working-class northerners who've got lucky and can't stop bragging about their good fortune and wealth.' The situation was polarised and oversimplified and on many occasions inaccurate. Blur were chess-playing, cricket and cheese-loving cads. They weren't. Oasis fans wanted the shocking, lurid leanings of *The Sun* and *The Mirror*.

The fact that Oasis made it so big – and connected with the masses – still takes me by surprise. I never envisaged such a vast swathe of the general public looking to Oasis and tuning into their music. They appeared accessible, looked like the common man, acted like the common man and spoke for the common man, so when the common man thought they were getting too big for their boots they enjoyed seeing them self-destruct, they relished seeing Liam lose teeth after the nightclub fracas in Germany. There was a definite change towards them, slowly controlled by the music press and the media in general. To the newspapers, they were a busted flush. From 1994 to 1997 they had their fun with the band and then moved on. Apart from the Rolling Stones, I can't think of a band before or since who generated so many column inches.

The continued concept and ploy of 'any publicity is good

publicity' had eroded and diluted the public's opinion of the band, and Liam in particular. Now it was so clichéd and predictable. Liam would act up, retaliate first, then strike out without thinking. It was hardly news if everyone was waiting for it to happen. There they were, splashed across the newspapers, in another drunken brawl, getting into slanging matches with the paparazzi. Liam, especially, always took the bait. No matter how tough it was for him to turn the other cheek, the reporters and photographers knew how easy it was to goad Liam into a reaction and provoke him into flying off the handle. What if Liam was in on it and knew that, say, if he headbutted a *Sun* photographer, the free publicity would secure a sell-out show and another 5,000 albums that week? All by getting his brawling mug on the front cover of the tabloids.

Despite not knowing it at the time, Knebworth, perhaps by default, was the end of a chapter and the end of the Oasis we'd grown to love. Or at least it was the end of the beginning. Playing there was a statement. In playing to such colossal crowds, Oasis were saying, OK, look at all these people who are into us. Let's see if we can get the same reaction in Rio, Barcelona or Sydney. Creation may have enjoyed the ride up until now but Sony must have been thrilled.

Of all the goings on, the debauchery, the coke, my abiding memory of the Knebworth shows were those reports of Liam driving about the VIP area in a golf buggy trying to hit famous people, including Ant and Dec. Sounds too funny to be true. It appears it was true. Here's what caterer Alex Vooght, speaking in the documentary, *Oasis Knebworth 1996*, recalls: 'I remember standing at the front of the marquee I was working in, and Liam had spotted Ant and Dec. He clocked them and drove straight for them in his golf buggy, and they had to dive out of the way like cartoon characters.'

2

King Tut's 31.5.93 (Part 1)

'One Night in May 1993' was one of many titles for this book. Here's what I wrote in my diary:

> *Boyfriend/18 Wheeler gig, 31 May 1993.*
>
> *Standing beside Alan McGee, he was excited, practically going nuts, animated watching one of the support bands, a Manchester band called Oasis. They were loud, a bit aggressive, and angry, the singer and the guitarist stood out. The frontman snarled, had that nasal tone and sounded like a Stone Roses/Manchester-type band. They were workmanlike, tense and angry, but nothing too remarkable. They were very loud. Their songs were long. They slaughtered 'I Am The Walrus'.*

Clearly, my A&R skills are rusty. I kept a diary at this time because I was involved in bands. It seemed important then, to keep notes on what was happening with other bands and gigs I'd been to. With hindsight, I could've changed it and eulogised about witnessing the future of rock 'n' roll in Oasis and predicted they would go on to play iconic gigs, write generation-defining songs and make classic albums that would resonate through the ages. In the brief passage, I repeat two words twice, *loud* and *angry*, and that's how I would describe Oasis on that night. (I also repeat *Manchester*; make of that what you will.) Later, downstairs, when asked at the bar what had just happened with Oasis, I was mocked when I said Alan McGee had just offered them a deal. I saw him and the guitarist shake hands on it. I wouldn't have offered them a pint never mind a recording contract. I honestly felt a bit sorry for them; to me they sounded a bit dated.

People constantly ask me what it was like to have been there. What were Oasis like? The clearest and most consistent memory I have about one of the most talked of moments in UK rock 'n' roll history was how unremarkable it was. I usually smile and shake my head when I think about it. I remember a rigid, workmanlike band on stage. They were well-drilled but performed like a band who rehearsed far more than they gigged. They needed to relax more on stage. Sometimes it's easy to rehearse the soul out of a song. One gig is better than three rehearsals.

There was little interaction and what there was came from the lead guitarist. He was the boss. It's outlandish to think they became this major sensation. That's the real Oasis story. How a band could go from the one we witnessed in May 1993 and transform into a group that would play such a significant part musically and culturally. They became central figures in politics, football, fashion and the whole phenomenon of Britpop. I normally finish by saying McGee was either a genius or lucky. In truth, probably a bit of both.

It was so unspectacular. There was no way you could envisage it becoming such an iconic moment. I was not thinking, wow, in decades to come, millions will regard this a momentous and significant night. It was anything but. We were hanging out at a gig waiting to watch our mate's band and then friends of support band Sister Lovers ambled on stage and played loud, long songs.

The night Alan McGee offered Oasis a deal at King Tut's has become fabled. There's a self-perpetuating aura around this evening in 1993. It's now one of those nights that has drunkenly meandered into the realms of mythology. It's surreal to consider it's up there with the most talked about moments in rock and pop history. That's a lofty position when considering the many noteworthy moments rock 'n' roll has thrown up. Is it up there with 9 February 1964 when The Beatles played the *Ed Sullivan Show*? Dylan being called a Judas at Manchester Free Trade Hall in 1966 for going electric or the Sex Pistols swearing on the *Bill Grundy Show*? Is Oasis at King Tut's Wah Wah Hut that momentous? The gig is now afforded a similar eminence. But its ordinariness continues to amaze me.

The myths and rumours of the night have grown to such an extent that if you believed them, Oasis would've been playing to a crowd the size of Knebworth. Other than the main players in the drama, the bands, crew and staff, there were around fourteen people present to watch the band perform. I know, because it was one of the lowest crowds I'd ever seen at King Tut's. It was so quiet you could do a rough head count. The history books and detailed, exhaustive research have given us a figure of sixty-nine paying punters in total, for the night. I've played sold-out shows at King Tut's and it's a beast of a place to perform in when it's full. When filled to its 300-capacity, it's a hot and lively venue. That night, I was surprised at how quiet it was.

For the romantic dreamers among us, this only added to the band's enduring appeal. This story, from near-empty venue to being lauded by millions. That figure of sixty-nine doesn't include the guest list, which wouldn't be too big if the crowd was so small. But, remember, they weren't upstairs at the venue. When Oasis played, most were still downstairs in the bar. But that's OK. That's what happens when a night like this occurs. Those present stay quiet, while those who stayed at home watching TV get to have an opinion and lie about being there. Those who were nowhere near King Tut's add their partial truth to the legend and, by the time the anecdote reaches you, Oasis were about to bomb the venue down if they didn't get to play and when they did, they performed like rock messiahs. They were Led Zep, Bowie and The Beatles but with bigger and bushier eyebrows. No, I'm sorry, they weren't.

I could name most of the people there. Alan McGee and his sister, Susan, were to my left. Eugene Kelly, to my right. Then behind us, my friends Ross Clark and Derek McKee and a few other guys from Boyfriend. There was also a Japanese couple, friends of 18 Wheeler, who I remember thinking, poor kids, coming so far to see this band on a Monday night in Glasgow. Paul Cardow and Murray Webster were there, members from the other bands were scattered around, though not many. Most of the bands playing were in the dressing room tanking into their rider or downstairs chatting in the main bar. There were two or three from the Oasis crowd dotted around the seating at the back behind the mixing desk and on the bench down the side of the venue. There were staff, busy running around. I see Frankie, Gerry Love's girlfriend at the time, working at the upstairs bar, and William Fyfe the bar manager, who was busy earlier keeping an eye on the Manchester crew while working betweeen the live venue and the downstairs bar. You get the idea. It wasn't lunchtime in the Cavern in 1962.

3

Birth of Britpop, the Creative Evolution of a Scene

It's a wet Thursday evening in March 1991. Aren't they always? I'm heading to London on the overnight bus. I find my Tufty Club badge, which I thought I'd lost in the lining of my biker jacket. It's a sign. It's fallen through a small hole in the pocket. Fortunate moments occur when I wear it. 'Lucky Badges' became a song that never saw the light of day with the opening line: *sometimes I feel like I've fallen through a hole in my pocket.* The Lucky Badges were also the name of a fictional band in a short story I wrote at school. One teacher loved it and she sought me out to tell me. Ellen Hughes her name was – Mrs Hughes. It was someone in Nirvana who explained to me that, in America, a badge is called a pin.

Every time I wear the badge, it brings me luck and love. I'm visiting a friend who lives down in London. The original idea was to see Blur play at The Venue in New Cross, but my friend's shifts get in the way. I'm befriended by Morag and Gill – because, I'm told much later, 'You know how to wear a biker jacket and we love your Tufty Club badge.' I'm still not entirely sure what knowing how to wear a jacket means but from the moment they got on the bus in Glasgow, we just clicked and got on immediately. They're a cool mix of indie rockabilly with a slight edge of Goth. It turns out we share a few friends. We are acquainted with people from bands and have several mutual friends who attend the Glasgow School of Art. It's a small world.

They share their considerable carry-out (booze bought from an off-licence) with me and because of roadworks the normal eight-hour journey becomes almost eleven hours. I know my friend was on his last nightshift and probably still sleeping, so I suggest we go and get a bit of breakfast from a greasy spoon. When I see how cheap it is, I insist on buying as I want to return their carry-out generosity. More coffees and teas are ordered and after a few hours of exchanging stories, addresses and phone numbers, it's almost lunchtime, 12.30-ish, and now we aren't hungry, we're thirsty. Gill suggests we go to this cheap little boozer she knows with a marvellous jukebox, the name of which escapes me.

I can't believe my luck, as if it's another sign, and by one o'clock we were in this small place right across from where I was staying, close to Great Ormond Street. It was beside the Celtic Hotel on Guilford Street, at Russell Square. I remember it from an album cover by the Battlefield Band from my record shop days. I went over to check and my pal was sleeping. I could hear him snore and so I left my bag with a beautiful Irish nurse across the way who knew him. She kindly gave me a notebook and pen to leave him a note. If she wasn't heading for duty she joked, she would've loved to come and join us. She loved the badge too.

I'm convinced back then people were warmer and nicer to each other, especially if you liked music. Few had a mobile phone and if they did, they were so big you would look like a total lunatic carrying it around, so no one bothered. It's still 1991, remember, so we don't have texts, or emails on our phones, no X (Twitter), WhatsApp, Facebook or TikTok. The internet had only just been invented. It was still two guys with electronic paper cups and a bit of fraying string between them but it was called the internet. If you were going to meet someone, you'd arrange to meet them at a given place and a certain time and wait till they showed up, and in the old days they usually did. This was a time before phone boxes became toilets or non-existent; instead, they were used as crucial modes of communication. So when someone gave you a phone number or an address, you wrote it down and kept in touch, maybe you even wrote a letter.

They, the girls, want to go to their friend's place who they are staying with, get a sleep, change and head to this club above a pub, near the Post Office Tower, which, they excitedly explain to me, was run by Alan McGee years before. By now he was running a record label and dealing with Teenage Fanclub, My Bloody Valentine and Primal Scream. That always stayed in my mind. As if it was some kind of indie music shrine, or maybe a guarantee of a cool and tasteful indie night. He hadn't been near the place for years. I can't remember if it was the Adams Arms in Conway Street where the first Living Room club nights were held. But Alan's presence or maybe the attitude of an upstairs night above a pub close to the Post Office Tower always reminded me of the seminal birth of Creation – and the opening titles of *The Goodies*.

The girls don't make it to their friends: we all stay out. I get lazy, see a phone box and instead of running over the road, I wake up my friend who is knackered and content to let me do my own thing. Before we know it, we're into happy hour, then the next thing it's late and dark and we're heading to this club. I'm in a small, tight club above a pub and something is happening. You can sense it. There's a distinct look and sound, a nod to the classic Mod, R&B and 1960s garage rock. A cool club, full of people in bands, some who would eventually have a role in the Oasis story. Members of Blur and Ride casually mingle.

The place is packed to the rafters. There's a Mod look and style to the fashion as if the kids have just jumped off their scooters. Smart jackets, striped T-shirts, tight-fitting tops, hipster trousers. Think pictures of The Who circa 1968. Crucially, however, it doesn't feel like they're trying too hard. There's no snobbery. You would expect with everyone so cool and hip there would naturally be an element of exclusivity but it's the opposite. It's mainly full of music fans contributing, DJing, organising and running things, and punters who seem to love the music.

Each song powers through, the drumming has a driving backbeat. The girls are beautiful, cool, and some have bee-hives, wear miniskirts, bright colours, and sport high hemlines. There's also a punk aspect to their fashion. The guys are in drainpipes and wearing Chelsea boots with their hair modelled into a Bobby Gillespie circa Primal Scream 1987 fringe. This is a scene. This is what it's like to be at the start of something. Let's bottle this. We could make a million. This could happen. The sounds are fantastic. They follow a direct line, there's a natural flow as each song overlaps into the next. There's music from one of my favourite eras, the 1960s. Garage, Mod and psychedelic punk pop. There's The Yardbirds' 'Over, Under, Sideways, Down' and then The Kinks' 'You Really Got Me', then we're off with The Kingsmen's 'Louis Louis' and the hipsters and beatniks pick up the pace as The Litter's 'Action Woman' and The Haunted's '1-2-5' kick in. Bam!!! There's a Mod nod to Motown, with The Marvelettes singing 'I'll Keep Holding On'. There's an energy, a happening feel. We move to northern soul and Betty Everett sings 'Getting Mighty Crowded', and it is; the place is jam-packed and musically it's all converging and making perfect, rhapsodic sense.

Is this just a random group of cool young people coming together for a night out? Yes. But are they conscious of the fact they're cultivating a scene? Is it a concerted effort or is it all happening naturally? Is this the beginning of a movement? Here in a small club, in London in 1991? I thought it was so cool, so hip, so bang on the money that I came out of my shell and danced to the bar. Two cider and blackcurrants for my friends and a Jack and Coke for the man who knows how to wear a biker jacket.

In a few months' time, Nirvana, Sonic Youth, The Smashing Pumpkins and The Pixies were welcomed from the edges into the UK mainstream. Suddenly, having played small clubs across Europe to pockets of faithful fans, all these bands seemed to come through. Sonic Youth had been playing festival shows across Europe and had invited label mates Nirvana to tour with them. Then Nirvana played Reading in 1991; if you'd like to see it in action, this period is chronicled in Dave Markey's movie *1991: The Year Punk Rock Broke*. All these bands brought their brand of punk and independent music into the mix from across the Atlantic. Some thought they were far too commercial. I just thought they were professional, seemed well-managed and knew exactly what they were doing.

Pubs would open the dusty function suites upstairs and give small club nights a chance and soon there'd be nights on a Tuesday, Wednesday or Thursday and there was something of a backlash across London. In a few years, Blur were the first band to actively question the credibility of those same American bands. Albarn was especially vociferous around this time, although by 1997 he was more relaxed. He eventually embraced Graham Coxon's love of lo-fi underground American bands like Pavement. Songs like 'Beetlebum' and 'Song 2' yielded hit singles and a return to form on their critically acclaimed album of the same year, *Blur*. But in 1991, he chose to champion British bands of the 1960s like The Kinks and The Small Faces and deliberately adopted a pro-British anti-grunge stance. Ironically, the friction created by the emergence of American bands acted as a catalyst to the UK music scene at the time.

In the same year, this time in December of 1991, on a Thursday, I was in a club called The Syndrome on Oxford Street. It was a similar gathering of hip bands and tasteful indie people. This time the music was more from British-based indie bands. The Television Personalities and tracks from My Bloody Valentine's *Loveless*, which had come out around this time, were also playing. Again the vast majority of the sounds were based on garage punk and 1960s Mod groups.

Cool people, wearing cool jackets, with cool badges, and some are so cool that while the music is pumping they're reading a Penguin classic; I can't help but notice one coquettish hipster reading Virginia Woolf. A couple in front of me read a fanzine and I overhear them talking about Calvin Johnson of Olympia's Beat Happening. They smile as I nod approval at mentions of Sub Pop and their chat about bands like Mudhoney and Nirvana. I was drummer of the band Captain America, and we had been invited to open for Nirvana on their *Nevermind* tour. We had just played the last night of the UK leg at Kilburn National. If I may be forgiven for a monumental piece of name-dropping, by coincidence it was the end of tour party and we left a free bar and headed to this club. I was standing with my friends Kurt Cobain, Krist Novoselic and Dave Grohl.

So there you have it. Two different clubs in London in the same year, with the same feel and influences. People are exchanging ideas, forming opinions and they are mostly fans of independent music. Bands, music fans and dreamers are standing shoulder to shoulder with one of the hottest bands on the planet at the time, Nirvana. All together in a small club at the start of something. You can tell these people had an artistic spirit fundamentally aligned with the central values of being independent. Not only in music but in film, literature and art. They were adopting a slightly left-of-centre, anti-mainstream, aesthetic take on popular culture. There's the love of lo-fi indie rock acts like Half Japanese, The Vaselines, The Pastels and The Television Personalities. The groups who preferred primitive recording techniques, a lack of gloss, and championed bookish introspection and reticence.

These were the kind of bands who avoided rock 'n' roll cliché and posturing while writing songs that were poetically eccentric and shunned musicianship. Bands who maintained that independent spirit, stayed anti-corporate, recoiling from the machine and commerciality. Bands that at some point in their life had to decide when offers were made, and there were ones who rebuked major deals and advances; they remained true, their principles should be applauded. Artists from these bands kept day jobs and worked in record shops, bookshops or did bar work, they still had an authentic creative output. On the other hand, bands like Nirvana found themselves being lauded by the masses and drowning in what they felt was hypocrisy, as they played corporate rock songs to an audience full of Guns N' Roses and Metallica fans.

This is a crucial factor in the way Oasis handled their success when it came in 1994. When they broke through, they made no apologies for wanting it all. They wanted the huge fuck-you houses with the swimming pool and the Rolls-Royce. They didn't care about indie sensibility; they didn't want vintage clothes and quirky, hand-me-down decor. When Kurt Cobain found fame with the masses it sat uncomfortably with him. Uneasy lies the head that wears the (clichéd grunge rock breakthrough) crown.

As much as Cobain initially wanted to write songs that would effect change and thus wanted to share his songs and his art with the world, when he got there it quickly lost its appeal. It's interesting how much Kurt despised it, yet Oasis would eventually love it. It's funny how artists can either be so cool about their ambition or become so hung up about it. Kurt Cobain seemed troubled by the dichotomy of maintaining a true indie spirit while at the same time benefiting from and enjoying the kind of major label funding that would get their music out there. Oasis didn't care about being a true indie-minded band; they had no desire to stay up late to personally colour in hundreds of record sleeves, fold singles into them, box them up and phone the distributor to collect the latest releases. McGee has since revealed he was never too into his label's image and the indie thing. He was always about rock 'n' roll and that meant being about the money – and power – too.

In 1991, we're back at the beginning of something. Amid the embryonic spark or the evolution of a scene. So, if you take the independent shambolic style, add in 1960s garage, Mod and soul, and include a cool fringe, then you're creating a pop photofit. It's the 1960s haircut, the late 1980s and early 1990s rock and pop meets the Madchester dance culture of The Stone Roses. It's the creative white heat, energy and arty scene of The Velvet Underground mixed with the love of British psychedelia. It's also post-punk girls with edgy hair and fringes like Gill and Morag who we met on the bus last

March. It would take a few readjustments and some minor tweaks, but in a few years, the people running the nights or attending them were forming bands and, with the help of some A&R people, influential music journalists and pop enthusiasts doing fanzines, they created an irresistible buzz. The bands became the forerunners to the next significant sea change in music. This was the art school Mod 1960s scene that evolved into Britpop.

4

Back to the Future

It's essential to get our bearings. We need to look back at the story before we can go forward. Liam Gallagher has joined a band called The Rain, along with Paul Arthurs (Bonehead), Paul McGuigan (Guigsy) and Tony McCarroll and he is wondering why the world hasn't cottoned on to how astounding they are. The early struggle with The Rain and Bonehead's importance in the history and shape of Oasis was overshadowed by the way the band signed to Creation. Their story is viewed as a rags to riches one, the classic overnight sensation, yet like millions of bands before them and countless after them, they worked hard to overcome many obstacles to get there. Before the romantic side of that night in King Tut's was reimagined by Creation, pre-Noel, they were toiling.

I've never heard or witnessed The Rain, so I wouldn't think to comment on a band I know nothing about. However, you can assume with Liam singing, they wouldn't be short of self-confidence. Bonehead formed The Rain in the late 1980s and when their original singer, Chris Hutton, left, he asked Liam to join. Seeking to transform their fortunes, Liam immediately demanded a name change. The Rain, thank god, became Oasis.

It was August 1991, and Noel was at a loose end, having returned from the US, where he'd been working with Inspiral Carpets. His mum said Liam was in a band and had a gig.

She encouraged Noel to go and check out his brother. Out of curiosity and boredom, Noel went with some of the Inspiral Carpets to see them support Sweet Jesus at the Boardwalk on Little Peter Street. He was shocked his kid brother could sing and had something of a presence. Noel didn't know Liam could sing. He had shared a bedroom with him for the first nineteen years of his life and didn't know he was interested in music, let alone in being in a band. So imagine his shock when he witnessed Liam on stage giving it plenty. Noel would have been unsure what to expect, but he was pleasantly surprised. The band were OK, but he was secretly most impressed with Liam if not their songs.

Liam was impatient and his dreams and ambitions didn't align with reality. They were playing infrequently, weren't rehearsing enough, they needed more than a name change. Noel's journey up to this time was more meandering if still productive and focused. He was quietly developing his craft and already had songs: one in particular called 'Live Forever' marked the start of Noel Gallagher's elevation and evolution to one of the greatest songwriters of his generation.

The story is even more unbelievable and impressive when you consider Noel never had a guitar lesson. He was self-taught and had learned how to play chords on an old guitar that had sat behind the door in the living room for years. It was bought by their errant father, Thomas. A positive amid little that was good. His father's violence created a troublesome period for Noel. For most of his adolescent life, he was in trouble with the police. He would play truant in the morning, then show up for lunch because his mum was working as a dinner lady in the canteen, then dog off in the afternoon.

At thirteen, Noel got caught robbing a corner shop and was placed on probation for six months. It was at this time he picked up the guitar. Three years later, he famously saw The Smiths performing 'This Charming Man' on *Top of the Pops* in 1983 and wanted to be Johnny Marr. Marr would go on to play a crucial role in the Oasis story. If there was a rock family tree based on the band, it would feature Johnny Marr of The Smiths. He'd probably be the roots, branches and leaves such was his early support for Noel.

We should be thankful Noel was curious enough to try the guitar. He played along on one string to the bass lines of Joy Division and the Sex Pistols. Then he moved on to learn chords, then on to the first standard for most guitar heroes good or bad, as constant as the North Star: The Animals' 'House Of The Rising Sun'. The guitar was rickety and the strings rusty. They were so high off the fretboard that he'd need fingers of steel to hold them down. These were small character-building moments that added purpose and fortitude.

When Noel was in that front room in Burnage, who could've imagined what lay ahead for him? I wonder if he ever used to dream then that Johnny Marr would give him his favourite guitar. That's what happens when dreams come true. Now you are on stage, with your guitar tech, placing your favourite guitar of the week, the red Epiphone Riviera over your neck, as 50,000 of the faithful wait for the opening chords of the next anthem.

Noel learned new songs, listening to The Beatles, copying them, working out the chord changes and progressions, learning little lead parts and those bewildering, unconventional chords Lennon and McCartney skilfully placed in their songs. Slowly it started to come together, though you have to wonder how a boy with nothing but intuitive instinct and determination reached a point where he was writing era-defining songs. That is the real story. The journey of an artist from the first untutored spark, going from nothing to achieving an astronomical level of success.

Growing up, Noel stood out from the rest of his mates because he loved going to gigs. It didn't matter if it was a big show like The Stone Roses or three bands on the bill and a pound a pint on a Tuesday night. He was at his happiest going into town on his own to see any bands that were playing. He watched, learned and took it all in. Noel swears that out of everyone he grew up with in Burnage and Levenshulme, he was the only one who played a musical instrument. 'It was far too weird to want to sit in a bedroom. You should be out robbing and enjoying yourself. So I kept it a secret that I played guitar.'

It's difficult to believe but Noel was quite shy, or at least quiet. He also must've been thinking his chance had passed him by. When he saw Liam and Oasis play and knew the songs he had, he clearly thought, he's a great frontman, decent voice, the band are alright, they need loads of work but this could be my chance. He wouldn't let on, though. It was up to Liam and particularly Bonehead to convince Noel to join.

We should flip back a bit and introduce someone. In life, luck and a few chance meetings can often seal your fate. That moment when you bump into someone and connect. You may not know it at the time but when you look back at that chance meeting, that accidental decision you made, you realise the profound significance of that simple choice. At a Stone Roses gig, Noel approached a guy who was bootlegging the show to ask if he could get a copy. They hit it off. He turned out to be the guitarist of Inspiral Carpets, Graham Lambert. They became mates and when Inspiral Carpets were looking for a new singer, Noel famously auditioned on 21 December 1988 (the same day as the awful tragedy of the Lockerbie bombing). But he didn't get the job.

The band liked Noel though, and offered him a job as a roadie and guitar tech. We should be grateful that Inspiral Carpets found his singing too weak. The job meant Noel could get out of Burnage, get on the road and earn a decent wage from the music industry. Road crew and techs are paid handsomely for doing the unglamorous work of gigging. He was able to learn at close hand, by observing how bands perform on stage. Learning all the technical aspects, how to tune guitars, getting a guitar sound right, the best monitor levels and, most importantly, the attitude. How to deal with interviews in the press, radio and TV and learning about stagecraft and the type of professionalism needed to perform at this level.

While working with Inspiral Carpets he also befriended their monitor engineer Mark Coyle, who would later become Oasis's soundman and producer. As they set up for soundchecks, if they had a spare five minutes when the band were late, or doing interviews or having dinner, they would work through Noel's songs on stage to get the levels right. So the astonishing journey is right there, from humping gear to being driven in a blacked-out limo heading for the airport before jetting off first-class for an appearance on American TV. It's hard to believe the songs he was writing then would yield such a rich harvest and encapsulate and reshape the mid-1990s. Noel couldn't play for Man City but he could play guitar.

Unbelievably, as Noel watched the fledgling Oasis gig at the Boardwalk, he still hadn't played a gig. Liam asked his brother if he would help them, maybe even join them: he had songs, he could maybe manage them or use his contacts in the music scene to help. Noel was nearly five years older than Liam and, despite not having any live experience, had witnessed during his time with Inspiral Carpets how much hard work and graft was required to get a deal. Noel took his time before joining. It wasn't till he invited Liam, Bonehead and Guigsy to the India House flat he shared with his then-girlfriend, Louise Jones, to hear his songs, that he would eventually join. This was when the others heard 'Live Forever' for the first time. Liam, Bonehead and Guigsy must've been amazed. Not only were the songs well crafted, arranged and structured, but one sounded like a hit single.

As far as Liam was concerned, Noel was the missing piece of the jigsaw. He must've been blown away. He was convinced if Noel joined, then Oasis would make it. Noel believed in his own ability but he needed something too, he needed a band. When Noel watched Oasis he knew Liam would eventually be the frontman in his band. Noel also knew how much work they'd need to get close to being ready to play. Liam was smart enough to know he needed his brother's music industry experience, discipline, contacts and, most of all, his songs.

It was Bonehead who was keenest to get Liam to secure the services of Noel. Bonehead was slightly older than the others, perhaps wiser, and he recognised that there was some magic in Noel's work. With Liam singing those songs they had a chance. Eventually, Noel joined and this is where the myth about him being a control freak probably started. He made it clear that if he did come in, they all had to take it seriously and focus on it. If they were going to make it, there had to be some tough ground rules.

At this time (though not for much longer), Noel had an excellent job with Inspiral Carpets; he knew how good they were and saw at close hand the effort required to succeed. He also saw how much Oasis loved to party, especially the drink and drugs part. They had to seriously curtail their excesses. They all had to commit to the project 100 per cent, no one could miss rehearsals or they would be out. And here's my favourite rule: even when Noel was away working with Inspiral Carpets the band would still report for rehearsal. Six days a week in the Boardwalk, missing big football games, nights out and, on one occasion, a wedding.

Noel also brought in his pal Mark Coyle to set up the gear and help get their sound right. This was unheard of at this level in the local scene. Rehearsals kicked in and the band worked hard, learning Noel's songs. Coyle arranged the band so they faced Noel and could see what he was playing. It was loud and exciting and Liam had to work twice as hard to toughen up his voice to compete.

This was when the band's on-stage presence and style was created. The way they looked on stage, unmoving, unemotional, expressionless, just playing. It almost looks as if it came effortlessly to them, but they slogged to make it look easy. It was with Noel and Coyle at the helm that the music came together. This is when they learned their craft, understood their parts, played them to perfection and instilled the professionalism which saw them emerge at the forefront of the British music scene.

Noel starts 1992 in a positive frame of mind. With the latest demo in hand, he feels the band are ready to secure a deal. He seeks out the ear of Tony Wilson at Factory. The label says no to the band on the basis that they sound 'too baggy' (a reference to the fashion, wide jeans and loose-fitting sweatshirts, and the sound, funky wah-wah rock with acid-house dance music, epitomised by The Happy Mondays). When I saw them at King Tut's, I thought the same. This is where I would've placed them in a record shop, under 'Manchester', with a similar vocal feel to The Stone Roses but with less of a dance edge; more rock and guitar-based.

They play their first gig outside Manchester at Dartford Poly on 19 April 1992. It didn't go too well, as the audience was made up of construction workers. Seeing the gig more like a Man City away day brawl than a bona fide show, Liam delights in winding up the crowd so much that they are chased from the venue. They continue to play locally in Manchester, building up something of a reputation. They support more established bands like The Ya Ya's, record a new, better demo and manage to get tapes to Caroline Elleray, manager of Intastella, and also Northside's manager, Macca. Both like what they hear and use their contacts to organise a session on BBC Manchester's *Hit the North*. In an early portent of what was to come, Liam started slagging off the stand-in host, New Order's Peter Hook. Liam was just in the door and was already giving it out. They manage to secure a support slot at The Venue in Manchester at the In the City music seminar, but blow that too by fighting on stage.

When Inspiral Carpets were preparing to head to the States and were particularly nervous about their road crew's drug taking and the problems this could create getting visas, the crew found themselves out of work. Now Noel and Coyle were even more determined to make it happen with Oasis. Demos were widely issued, and the frequency of rehearsal increased. They invited the Griffiths brothers, from Liverpool-based band The Real People, to watch them at the Boardwalk on 5 January 1993. At the gig, Tony Griffiths was standing beside a former Sony colleague, who was now at Warner Chappell Publishing, and he loved the band. Tony suggested that Warner Chappell organise some studio time and his brother, Chris, could produce it. Nothing came of it though, so both Tony and Chris ended up recording the band themselves at their eight-track studio. They recorded over twelve songs, eight of which made the demo Alan McGee eventually heard.

The Real People connected with Oasis and the two bands got on well. They would work hard and party hard. The drummer of The Real People was a huge music fan and would play Captain Beefheart and then Slade. He always had Slade on, so if you're looking for a source of that loud, towering guitar, blame him. Tony and Chris also introduced Oasis to their cousin, Digsy.

During this period the band played, rehearsed, recorded and found themselves. Noel is writing and his peers are taking notice. They are still playing gigs in front of thirty people, but also learning and gaining invaluable studio time with The Real People in Liverpool. From August 1991 to May 1993, their graft and perseverance brought them to this moment, where Alan McGee had shaken hands on a deal but the band still needed an experienced manager to help navigate the business side. In fact, what they needed was an advisor.

The plan was coming together. Noel gives Ian Marr, Johnny's younger brother, his demo tape and Ian eventually pins down Johnny and makes him listen to Oasis. He loves it and begins badgering his manager Marcus Russell to come and see them live. They were supporting Dodgy at the Hop and Grape on Friday 19 June 1993. This was always a hot, sweaty venue with a great atmosphere and a convenient but small bar at the back, in Manchester Academy. By this time, under Noel, Oasis were a tight, professional and well-rehearsed outfit. Russell was visiting Johnny Marr in Manchester and, with Johnny's pal, the hairdresser Andrew Berry, drove into town. Once he saw them live, he was captivated, yet Russell was canny, he stayed cool and kept his counsel.

His immediate impression would've been one of relief. The word on the street when it came to Oasis was not positive. 'Johnny's younger brother, Ian Marr, kept banging on about this band Oasis,' said Russell, speaking to Wales Online. 'I'd checked them out with other people in Manchester and they said, "Nah, they're not going to make it." Tony Wilson, at Factory, said he had passed on them a year before. The word around Manchester was they were "Stone Roses wannabes". Nobody was interested in them.'

Russell was a seasoned music business figure and, like McGee, he recognised something. They had a power, energy and stage presence and suddenly with this set of songs they were blossoming into serious contenders. 'I liked where they were coming from – Slade, the Pistols, The Kinks. There were hints of it all there but I didn't think, these are going to be mega!'

The situation changed when Russell returned to London the next day and received a phone call. Noel had heard he was at the gig and had enjoyed it. 'Back in London the next day, I got a call from Noel Gallagher. He said he'd heard I'd seen them and that they were looking for a manager. Noel was very charismatic. He said, "Manage us." I said, "Woah, that's a big conversation." He replied, "Well, I'm up for a big conversation. You get my train fare and I'll be with you in two hours." I said OK. Three hours later, he's sitting in a cafe in Marylebone.' The two hit it off and it was this phone call and meeting and the effort made to get to London which swung it. Russell continued: 'We got on really well. He gave me a cassette of demos. It had "Up In The Sky", "Whatever" and "Married With Children" on it. I met the rest of the band and that was it. That's how Oasis came to be managed by me, and the rest is history as they say.'

Marcus Russell eventually became the manager of Oasis in summer 1993, and after getting the nuts and bolts of the Creation/Sony contract sorted, the next problem he, McGee and the band had was the quality of what had been recorded for their debut album. Noel was unhappy, and McGee was concerned. Marcus Russell approached Johnny Marr's former Electronica producer, Owen Morris, and asked him to have a listen. He stripped back, mixed and cleaned up Noel and Mark Coyle's recordings and generally saved the day with *Definitely Maybe.* Russell took over when the band needed him most. They needed guidance, support and advice in the fickle music industry.

By the end of 1993, they were garnering loads of press, their reputation was growing and Radio 1 enhanced the buzz with the white label of 'Columbia'. When I heard that for the first time on Radio 1, I had goosebumps and started laughing. I was amazed and delighted. Then events changed gear again. All these little strands of fate and luck started to collide, to weave together and take hold. But let's not get too far ahead of the story.

5

Noel Joins, Made in Manchester
& *Top of the Pops*

I've always loved Manchester and have a genuine warmth towards the city and its people. I put it down to Manchester having the same light as west central Scotland … and the rain. Apart from the rain, and growing up in and around postwar, working-class areas outside major cities, surrounded by a shared backdrop of unemployment, hopelessness, violence, alcoholism and crime, it wasn't always terrible. Just don't give us your sympathy. Don't get all clichéd and liberal about it. There were always areas of calm and safety, love and warmth, good people with a strong sense of decency and community. Many families came through unscathed and went on to better and brighter things. Thousands more continue to live and thrive and are simply getting on with life. There was a harshness, a tough reality, but genuine love and kindness too.

For people like Oasis and many others, growing up on the periphery of a city, that distance is what makes you. You almost feel as though you're forced to look on from the outside while everyone in the city is partying. It may only be a few miles but it feels like a world away. Oasis hail from Burnage, four miles south of the city centre. It's not the worst of places; to some it might even seem pleasant. It's not Moss Side or Longsight;

their upbringing was rough and ready, it was hard, but they were resourceful. It's never easy, especially if your mother's left to contend on her own and has to work as a dinner lady and raise three sons.

The problems start when you want to be an artist, a filmmaker, a writer, a photographer, a journalist or, god forbid, form a band. Priorities change, expectations are stifled, any spark or genius is dismissed and extinguished. Then kids were not encouraged to be famous or to be creative or express themselves, nor did they have showbiz parents determined to help their dreams of pop stardom come true. No. All you have is an imagination fired up from books, annuals and children's TV and *Top of the Pops*. Debbie Harry said it and she meant it: dreaming is free.

When we watched *Top of the Pops* and the fading glamour of 1970s acts, this show made the dream of being a musician accessible and tangible. You watched *Top of the Pops* and realised that David Bowie, despite claiming to be from a different planet, had guys in the band that no matter how hard they tried to look glamorous in glitter jumpsuits, looked like horny brickies. He and Marc Bolan were writing and performing songs, and if you had read your sister's *Jackie* magazine or your brother's *NME* you would know that they'd had a dream and they had worked hard for years – and they weren't as young as they looked.

Bands like Sweet and Slade looked like bin men and labourers in fancy dress and, despite the lip gloss and eye shadow, if you laughed at them they would kick your head in with their platform boots. Their music exploded into your living room, leaving you spellbound. They were working-class guys. They were all stars but the whole point of pop music, at least at that time, was that you could do it too. Just dare to dream big. Most of the musicians in these bands, apart from posh, over-educated ones like Genesis and Queen, were normal people from a similar background as you. And they became pop stars. Even then you knew that there were two ways you could get out of the situation at home, in the streets around you. Be a footballer or a pop star. One is tough, the other almost impossible, and, either way, anyone who manages to get out deserves their reward.

Then suddenly, from that fading glam of the late 1970s, there seemed to be more possibilities. You didn't have to be a cross-dressing alien from outer space to get a deal, have a hit and be on *Top of the Pops*. Punk rock soon eclipsed glam and evolved into new wave, which adopted the attitude of punk and the melody of glam, but in doing so offered more accessible and commercial music.

From America, you'd have bands that were less punk and more song-orientated and radio-friendly, such as Blondie and Talking Heads. The UK's new wave remained challenging to define as it evolved from a mix of groups and artists, parti-cularly in London, honing their skills playing the pub circuit and emerging from post-punk bands. This meant we had a broad church with artists like Eddie and the Hot Rods, Nick Lowe, Dr Feelgood, Ian Dury and Elvis Costello and the Attractions. Then Siouxsie and the Banshees, The Jam, XTC, The Undertones, The Cure, Joy Division, U2, Echo and the Bunnymen and The Smiths: all these bands were formed by friends and like-minded people at school or university or someone who lived across the road with a cool haircut, a guitar and some decent records.

They were doing something. They were getting record deals, releasing singles and albums, gigging at venues near you and being played on the radio. They seemed to be getting the breaks. Never underestimate the power of dreaming big. It's such a huge part of the Oasis story, that working-class northern thing. Sound familiar? 1963? Cheeky chappies from the northwest of England kicking in the doors and changing the landscape of the music industry forever? With The Beatles, it was fresh youthfulness and unabashed charm and cheek. With Oasis, it was two crazy brothers, who didn't like one another or anyone or anything for that matter, except The Beatles.

Noel and Liam could never be two-faced; if they didn't like a band, they said so. Journalists would suggest it was refreshing; inside they were loving their scattergun rants knowing their interviews made fantastic copy. Oasis were not thinking it through or worrying about how what they were saying came across in print. They behaved like a quarrelling family while someone was visiting, the guest sitting there with a cold cup of tea, arse cheeks clenched in full nutcracker mode and uncomfortably watching on as it all unfolded – inevitably ending in punches. The visitor, in this case, was usually a gobsmacked journalist. The brothers had no internal editor or anyone telling them to calm it. John Lennon may have suggested nothing was real, but with Oasis everything was. Just pure northern grit and you couldn't take your eyes off the car crash. The Beatles may have asked the people in the rich seats if they would rattle their jewellery – Oasis looked like they would come into your house, kick your head in, steal your plasma, laptop, collectable vinyl, eat what was in your fridge, do a shit on the rug and then steal your jewellery. All this masculine instinct and authenticity was a huge part of the Oasis character and can't be underestimated. There it was, right on our TV screens, in the music papers, swaggering along with fantastically crafted songs, a mix of vibrant confrontation and great rock 'n' roll melody; all familiar yet sounding new. This is Manchester: this is real.

6

Marcus Russell & The Deal

Marcus Russell was another essential character in the Oasis story. He was central for several reasons, including his ability to handle the innumerable problems linked to the intense fraternal relationship central to Oasis along with the business and logistic side. Despite a full and varied roster of acts, he was determined to find an artist who matched his ambition to rival his managerial hero: Led Zeppelin's Peter Grant.

Russell had established his credentials while managing Latin Quarter (his friend Mick Jones from the band also came from Ebbw Vale); he then managed The Bible and The The. He was finally carving out a niche as a respected, hard-working manager, but also felt he needed that challenge. He was after the artists who would elevate him to the level of someone like U2's (then) manager, Paul McGuinness, who was in effect the CEO of a big organisation.

Russell, as we've learned, didn't rush in either, wary of reports that the band were just another baggy 'Madchester' band. He took convincing before finally going to see Oasis live. They weren't established and needed managed at every level. He'd have to formulate a detailed strategy and bring in the most suitable booking agents, promoters and lawyers. He was reluctant to add to his list of artists, who he was already fully committed to. Were Creation and Sony even suitable labels at this stage? Would they allow Oasis to nurture their talents and develop musically? Then he would need to hammer out a beneficial and fair recording and publishing deal, organise and coordinate every detail and then find producers to record them. He couldn't see it working. But, like Alan McGee, once he saw them live, he was hooked, immediately recognising a band that matched his hunger and drive.

Sensing their commercial appeal, Russell instinctively knew where they would fit in. He loved their sound, their look, attitude and these songs, with influences that read like a compendium of all the great British bands. So many contradictory components and elements were coming together in this one moment: he loved their power and swagger, which merged into a modern contemporary sound. If they wanted him, he'd love to work for them. Then when Noel spoke to him, it was job done.

There's the touch of the quiet hero about Russell and his role in the Oasis story; something that makes you respect him without ever knowing him. Maybe because he had started out as a blast furnace operative for a British Steel plant at Ebbw Vale and had a spell working in an open-cast mine for the National Coal Board at Waun-y-Pound. Jobs fraught with toil and danger were the perfect preparation for managing Oasis, making the role a stroll in the park.

He left Ebbw Vale in 1974 to take up a teaching course at Middlesex Poly and, while there, put loads of punk bands on, most notably some upstarts named the Sex Pistols. Before getting into the music industry full-time, he worked as an economics teacher and became Head of Economics at Royal Liberty School in Romford, Essex by 1983. As an economics teacher, he needed to be an effective communicator and handy with numbers. His heart wasn't in it, though. By day he was the mild-mannered economics department head, and by night he was out promoting and managing bands. Eventually, he grew so dismayed with teaching that he quit and decided to go full-time in the music business by securing Latin Quarter a record deal.

Following the break-up of The Smiths, Johnny Marr needed a manager and his lawyer referred him to Russell; he got a call from the guitar legend and they hit it off straight away. Soon he was handling Marr and Bernard Summer's career. Marr informed him about this group, Oasis, and this unbelievable demo his brother Ian had given him. Johnny Marr's instinct was true: within a few months, Oasis had a deal and Johnny was on the phone again asking Russell if he could recommend a lawyer. He suggested a chap named John Statham. Coincidentally, another fateful moment – Statham then rang Russell back and suggested what the band needed was a manager and that he, Russell, should take them on.

Marcus Russell understood how to handle Liam, when to push and congratulate and when to berate him for his behaviour. We can only imagine that his teaching experience, taking a pick to a coal seam and perhaps the perils of dealing with molten steel had come in handy. He had to be part disciplinarian, part mentor, father figure and businessman – and, whatever he was doing, Liam trusted him. He also learned quickly when to step back and let the band, or more precisely Noel, make the critical decisions. Noel may have been the band's creative driving force (no doubt with some serious mentoring and instruction on when to mix it up a bit from Alan McGee), but it was Marcus Russell who advised and made it run smoothly, like the director and producer. When asked what it was like to manage the band, Marcus

Russell's response surprised many: 'Both of them very much allowed a manager to get on with managing. They understood the demarcations very well. They were great to manage. They weren't control freaks at all. They were very street-smart. Most of the time, it was an absolute pleasure and privilege. It was a great time.' As I've said, he knew when to let Noel go with his gut instinct and trust in his intuition. It was thanks to Noel's insistence that the band signed with Ignition soon after supporting Dodgy at the Hop and Grape on 18 June 1993.

The choice of the first single was a great example. Most assumed it would be 'Live Forever' but Russell didn't want this. He believed releasing 'Live Forever' as a first single would be a mistake. Where would you go after that? No, you had to build it up gradually. The band would have to be watertight and confident live. They weren't ready to release that single yet and their unpreparedness would set them back. So there was a deliberate pick-up in the pace of gigs. You would think, this early in the band's now professional career, that Alan McGee or Marcus Russell chose the singles, but it was Noel Gallagher who wanted a track he'd recently written and recorded, entitled 'Supersonic'.

So Russell's management company, Ignition, took over the band's strategic development. They arranged for Oasis to play loads of shows and support slots with established acts. They wouldn't be glamorous headline gigs, but they would help build up a fan base through word of mouth. The band, who even at this stage weren't short of self-confidence, played some dates and support act slots alongside bands like BMX Bandits and The Verve and shows supporting Dodgy, Saint Etienne and Milltown Brothers. Both Noel and Marcus Russell were adamant that the most important thing for the band at this time was their stagecraft. They had to get out and play live, learn how to interact and perform in front of an audience. This way Oasis would learn quickly and reach a place where their ability matched their confidence.

They would play their own shows, but the idea of playing support slots would mean performing in reputable venues with established acts, and with a professional backline, monitor and stage set-up. Despite being first on the bill and dismayed at playing to empty halls when they were sometimes better than the headline act, it was essential for the band to gain stage time, perform, tweak and hone the songs while gaining invaluable live experience. According to some of the bands they opened for at this time, they were tight and organised and played some of their best gigs, always performing like they were the headline act. These shows in 1993 were an effective learning curve, preparing them for the onslaught of the following year when they would hit the road, playing 107 shows in 1994.

Oasis had still not physically signed to Creation, but a deal was eventually hammered out by Marcus Russell. As soon as Russell had left McGee's office after their first meeting on 2 July 1993, Noel was on the phone to McGee, wanting to know what he thought about their manager. McGee said he was one of the best he'd ever dealt with. Straightforward, and even though his opinions were honest and would effectively cost Creation, Alan McGee respected his thoroughness and unwavering intention to look after the group's affairs. The band were fortunate to have both a manager and, more unusually, a record label boss who, as he always had done, despite it possibly hurting his business, (mostly) looked after his artists as if they were his mates.

The main issue for Creation wasn't the UK but their licences everywhere else in the world. Russell made it clear he and Noel, and therefore the band, wanted to sign to

Creation in the UK and that deal would be watertight. However, he refused to sign if Oasis were released on the underperforming and much-pilloried American label, SBK. Creation had a contract with SBK to release their acts in America, or at least to give them first refusal. McGee realised Russell had a point but was desperate not to lose the band. If McGee could sort out his end and make guarantees that they could work in the States without going through SBK, then a deal could be done and Oasis would put pen to paper. It was complicated, as Alan McGee couldn't second guess on behalf of SBK and had always maintained a professional relationship with the people there. How would they react to hearing they weren't doing their job well enough to get first dibs on Oasis?

Creation were once again desperately in need of cash as their income from worldwide licences had just about run out. They were close to going bust. Sony were becoming irritated with Creation as they had run to the well too many times, and their credit line, as well as patience, was running out.

McGee understood he would need cash to offer Russell and Oasis a five-figure deal. If Marcus Russell wanted, he could go elsewhere and find a label willing to pay up for the band. McGee knew he was perilously close to losing them. He had fallen in love with Oasis. He couldn't stop listening to the demo, had connected with the songs and couldn't believe how impressive they were. Losing the band now would be devastating. Here he was, though, with a label in America incapable of providing the necessary support for the band and the cold hard fact that they had no cash to offer Oasis. Also, some of the staff at Sony didn't share McGee's enthusiasm for the band. Alan McGee needed a miracle.

The call came from Marcus Russell and played out

something like this. Oasis were signing with Sony, were going with Sony-owned Epic in America and would be prepared to license Oasis via Creation for the UK. Russell then asked McGee if he wanted to be involved. The answer we now know was a resounding yes. By the time Oasis officially signed on 22 October 1993, few, if any, realised the negotiating and political manoeuvring which had occurred to get the deal done – in effect, to sidestep SBK's involvement in America. SBK could have sued but thankfully they didn't, realising if they took it further, their frailties and weaknesses would be highlighted.

Oasis received an advance of £40,000, a pittance in comparison to what less talented bands were being paid. Marcus Russell, by structuring the deal, obtained financial security and Sony's major backing while maintaining the cool indie kudos of Creation. In his book *Creation Stories*, Alan McGee drills into the level of detail that was being discussed: 'I had to talk them [Oasis] up in LA to get Sony to come in internationally. Marcus Russell and Noel believed in me, but getting the wheels in motion for Sony was a reminder of how much autonomy I'd lost in the partnership.' McGee continues: 'But we got them on board eventually and Marcus was more impressed with them than any of the other American labels who wanted them. Sony's label Epic signed them for the world, we signed them for the UK. Marcus trusted me to do the business for them in Britain and I was determined not to let him or the band down.'

Still, Alan McGee had left colleagues at Creation a bit miffed. He had signed this band from Manchester based on their attitude, the guitarist's volume and the stage presence of their lead singer. He'd accidentally heard them perform four songs while out of his face at a low-key gig in Glasgow. In an attempt to win everyone over, in early November, Oasis played a showcase gig at the Powerhaus in Islington. It was set up so the staff of Creation, Sony and Epic could see the band they would be working with. Despite Oasis playing a blinder, instead of galvanising the troops the gig appeared to divide more than it united. The band's signing split Creation. Suddenly there were two distinct factions: staff who got it immediately, could see their promise, and those who felt they weren't an appropriate fit for the label. Some think they have this presence, confidence and ambition which will blaze the charts and capture the country's imagination. Others don't get what the fuss is about and can't understand why the boss has signed them on a hunch while label favourites My Bloody Valentine had been dropped the previous year. (The recording of MBV's *Loveless*, their 1991 masterpiece, is worthy of a book in itself. They almost killed off Creation by taking two years to record the album. A mix of Kevin Shields' perfectionism, continuous takes and endless experimentation came with astronomical costs. The tambourine played on 'To Here Knows When' famously took a month to record. Forty-five engineers and nineteen different studios were used. Creation claimed *Loveless* cost £250K, Shields argued it was closer to £140K. If you split the figure around £200K that would be the equivalent of well over half a million in today's money.)

Oasis critics pointed to the problems finding the correct producer for their debut album and the way it was salvaged and patched together as proof McGee had made yet another serious error of judgement. Despite the problems, McGee and Russell instinctively believed the band had something, an indefinable quality and unshakeable self-belief, a punk rock attitude that could send the country crazy. McGee and Russell also had the advantage of having heard the extraordinary new material Noel had written. The band, for their part, had to keep playing gigs and work on finding consistency in their live performances.

Oasis liked working with McGee and Russell. They were straightforward and uncomplicated. The band hated bullshit, deceit and anything fake. They liked people to be upfront and honest. So, for example, when Noel said to McGee he would sign for Creation, despite bigger and better offers and interest from a few majors, Noel stuck to his word. Despite recognising Oasis were a more commercial-sounding band than their label mates, McGee's enthusiasm and belief were genuine. It would do their indie credibility no harm to be on Creation.

For their part, both Russell and McGee quickly grasped how much Oasis stood out from the crowd. In 1993 there weren't many British bands freely admitting their desire to scale the heights of hedonism. A band who loved football, drugs, women and rock 'n' roll. Bands didn't go around declaring their brilliance either, not then. So they stood out by wanting to be famous and longing to live out every rock 'n' roll cliché in the book. They were honest, refreshing and unapologetic and theirs was a stance that related to millions.

Despite hardly being short of self-confidence himself, McGee's is – I believe – more a misplaced bravado. That is down to his Scottish upbringing. Scots aren't encouraged to think they're something special. It's passed on to us from an early age that it's a crime to become big-headed. It's drilled into us that self-praise is no honour. So if Scots find success and receive plaudits we aren't used to it and there's a self-defeating tendency to become alcoholics and drug addicts or die. What amazed McGee about Noel Gallagher was his self-belief. He wanted fame, fortune and success and openly admitted to it.

In some way, that is what sets the Manchester scene apart from most other UK cities. When Noel writes a song like 'Live

Forever' and implies that his words and music are so special he'll be remembered and his songs sung throughout eternity, Manchester says, 'Yeah, we hear you, man.' In Scotland he'd most likely get a kicking and his band considered a laughing stock.

Leading up to the release of 'Supersonic', they were out on the road again. They co-headlined a three-week tour with Greenock's finest, Whiteout. Oasis had gone on first at the beginning of the tour, which started in the Angel, Bedford, on 23 March 1994. They were paid the standard fee for the gig, £100, and they invited the fans back to the Moat House Hotel, got the guitars out and partied into the night before being barred from the place. The tour started in high spirits and didn't relent. Oasis were evolving into a compelling band. The band's reputation and reaction became such that Whiteout quickly realised not too far into the tour that it made more sense to switch and for them to go on first. After their appearance on Channel 4's *The Word*, the band's profile ensured droves of new Oasis fans were coming to check them out to see if the hype was merited.

And so, although both bands were at the same level, Oasis suddenly gained momentum. At this time, Whiteout were cool indie hipsters. They were seen as the band most likely to make a breakthrough. The music press loved them and they had recently signed to the same label as The Stone Roses, Silvertone. Bonehead was still the road manager and driving the van for Oasis. They would pile into their van, while Whiteout would head off on their fabulous tour bus.

It's important to highlight Whiteout were an accomplished band who could play. They were a tight outfit, with Eric Smith on guitar, Paul Carroll on bass and the energetic Stuart Smith on drums; they also had a charismatic frontman in Andrew

Caldwell. They had the songs, cool hair, and were influenced by similar groups, like The Faces, and by the same 1960s and 1970s sound. For a Scottish group especially, they weren't short of self-confidence either. Whiteout were pitched closer to the pop end of the market, more capable of reaching the cover of *Smash Hits* as well as the *NME*. But at the time, they were expected to do well. It was unfortunate that they were on the road at a time when Oasis were hitting such blistering form. Oasis were continually improving and the ever-present music press were with them every step of the way throughout the tour. The reports of their exploits weren't doing any harm with publicity, leading up nicely to the release of 'Supersonic' on 23 April 1994.

This would also be a time of reckoning for Alan McGee and Marcus Russell. Soon their faith in Oasis would be judged. From the moment Alan McGee signed Oasis, the best he'd hoped for was that they'd maybe sell a few hundred thousand, maybe do as well as Primal Scream or The Stone Roses, but when he heard a demo of 'Live Forever' he must've thought, this band could take on U2 or REM and possibly start to sell on that spectacular life-transforming scale. McGee thought they could be the best band in the world and suddenly a mainstream breakthrough was possible. Something Alan McGee always does is credit the management team Ignition for nurturing the band properly and harnessing Noel's ambitions to be bigger than The Beatles and to emulate his heroes by releasing a single every three months.

They did the previously mentioned *NME* interview with John Harris where they started a full-on argument about nothing. At that point, it was hard to believe how far they'd come in under a year and their sheer bravado when they still hadn't released their debut single.

Then, in April, the moment so much energy had built towards: that super-charged debut single was launched upon the world.

7

King Tut's 31.5.93 (Part 2)

King Tut's Wah Wah Hut is on St Vincent Street in Glasgow. The name is nicked/borrowed/shared from an 'Egyptian-themed' experimental theatre space and venue in 1980s New York. Our version is a cool, well-run venue with an illustrious reputation, but it's most famous for the night in May 1993 when Alan McGee from Creation Records offered the Manchester band, Oasis, a record deal. Loads of bands have played there at the start of their career, and it's such a popular venue that many established bands and artists often come back to play one-off gigs or warm-up shows there.

It's 31 May 1993. Ross Clark, my friend and bass player in our band, Boomerang, rings to see if I fancy getting out of Airdrie and going to watch our mate Derek McKee (DD) play with his band, Boyfriend. He's put us on the guest list for his gig at King Tut's. So we both agreed to 'jump into town' (go into Glasgow) to see Boyfriend and another local band, 18 Wheeler, play this show at King Tut's. Also on the bill was a Manchester band, who were friends of Boyfriend, called Sister Lovers. They had said to their mates Oasis to come up and play on the bill too, but more about that later.

Ross and I meet DD downstairs at the bar. As we wait, we chat but, based on intuition, I can sense a bit of restlessness. Something was brewing. It wasn't about to kick off as such, but the situation was fraught; there was an air of apprehension. There were a few Manchester accents and a crowd of maybe a dozen or so had gathered downstairs around the pool table. (Ah, the mythical pool table. There was a detailed debate about that. Staff at the time are adamant there was no pool table in 1993. But there was a table, where there's now a pool table. Clarity, or lack of, is everything.) They had feather haircuts, looked useful with their fists and appeared out of place in King Tut's. They acted and dressed like football casuals. Their tough-guy vibe and attitude made them stand out in a laid-back indie venue.

I meet Eugene Kelly from a previous band, Captain America, and we head upstairs and continue to chat. Those who prefer the more cynical take on the story think it's far too fanciful for McGee to show up at King Tut's and sign Oasis. One thing is certain, though; he was there. Accounts as to how and why he was there have varied over the years. In classic McGee style, as someone easily bored, he has offered diverging reports as to how he found himself there. He didn't know Oasis were playing. The most likely story is that he showed up on the night in question to meet his sister Susan and one of her friends and head off to an Italian house night at the Sub Club. (I'm basing that on the red Gucci loafers he was wearing.)

One story I've often been cynical about was that Susan, who was standing to my left, had tried to fix him up on a date. Sadly, the blind date couldn't make it. I often wonder what would have happened if she'd shown up and Alan McGee was captivated by her beauty and patter? Would he have noticed the first band on the bill? Imagine if he'd been distracted and hadn't signed them? Another story is that he'd missed his train down to London and decided to jump around to King Tut's to see 18 Wheeler and Boyfriend. 18 Wheeler were on Creation while Boyfriend were on my friend Dave Barker's label, the

Creation subsidiary, August. He also thought it would be fun to surprise his friend Debbie Turner, whose band Sister Lovers, from Manchester, were third on the bill. Boyfriend headlined that night, promoting their album, *Hairy Banjo*.

McGee arrived early, expecting the place to close at 11 p.m. But, as this was a Bank Holiday, the venue was open later, which gave him time to start on the double Jack Daniel's and Cokes. So he was there to meet his sister and catch 18 Wheeler and Boyfriend, but Debbie Turner's part in the story shouldn't be understated as it adds more weight to the random nature of fate.

When McGee got into clubbing, ecstasy and acid house – let's euphemistically call it his Manchester clubbing phase – he lived between the Creation offices in Hackney and spent three or four days a week in a rented flat in Manchester. These were four-day parties and blowouts. It was here he befriended The Happy Mondays, particularly Shaun Ryder. He famously recalled: 'It was one big party. I wrote myself a prescription of ecstasy, speed, acid, coke or Jack Daniel's every day.' It was during this period he also became mates with Debbie Turner. So there were many reasons why McGee might have been there on the night.

I finally managed to catch up with Debbie Ellis (née Turner) in December 2024. She's a happy mum of three, carving out a career as a photographer. She speaks with warmth, humour, common sense. Despite being one of the most important people in the Oasis story, she modestly refuses to accept her place in the evening at King Tut's while remaining immensely proud of what her old friends have achieved. Her band Sister Lovers split up around six months after Oasis were signed.

We laugh at the many versions and takes of the King Tut's evening, and discuss some of the far-fetched conspiracy theories, like the singer from a famous Northwest band claiming Sony ordered Alan McGee to immediately check out

Oasis at King Tut's. Definitely not. Most importantly for our story, for the dreamers and romantics, Debbie scotched the myth that it was planned, confirming Oasis didn't know Alan McGee was coming to the gig nor did McGee know anything about her mates Oasis coming up to sneak on the bill. Debbie was unequivocal about the idea of McGee showing up based on a tip-off about Oasis. It was all just fate: the stars aligning. Karma. 'They definitely didn't know Alan was coming. There was another band called Sister Lovers on his mate's label, and Alan called and asked if it was their band playing at King Tut's or his mate Debbie's band. When he said no, he knew it was us. So that's why Alan was there, he showed up to do my head in, stand right in front of me, scare the shit out of me and freak me out at my first gig. So no one knew he was coming.'

For the few in the venue at the time, there was a frisson of excitement with the label boss around. Not for Debbie though: 'I wasn't like, oh, Alan McGee of Creation is here. It was like, fuck, my pal's here and standing right in front of the stage.' Now in fits of laughter, she recalls how 'I was just mortified. I don't even know how to work my guitar pedal.'

There's been some wonderfully imaginative spinning of how events unfolded at King Tut's with Creation setting the tone. It ties in with the band's image and attitude. Better still, over the decades the story has stood strong. Everyone thinks Oasis threatened to trash the place, burn it down if they didn't get on stage. Many elements of the tale are true. Oasis showed up in a van with their gear in the back. They also brought along a minibus full of mates. But there's the adage that the lie told often enough becomes the truth.

Oasis did show up with friends who had travelled for four hours from Manchester to see them play. When the band were told no one named Oasis were on the bill and the door politely but firmly shut in their face, a few of the guys with the band had some choice words. There was talk of one particular beast among them who wanted to take it further, who may have suggested in a distinctly forceful fashion that arson would be deployed if the doors weren't opened and the geezer in charge let them in. The bravado and machismo soon subsided when the guys from Manchester realised they were dealing with experienced staff who'd been through this before with bigger, harder and scarier bands and their mates.

Here's the King Tut's side of the story. According to them, the rep in charge of the gig, Ali Murdoch, phoned his boss, Geoff Ellis (who was through in Edinburgh on business and missed the whole thing), explaining that another band had shown up claiming to be friends of Sister Lovers. Ellis was more concerned about the logistics (of having four bands on one bill) and the budget. He asked if they could cope with another band. Murdoch said yes. Ellis gave Oasis the go-ahead. However, as they hadn't budgeted for four bands they couldn't pay them, so he suggested they offer them some beer.

Geoff Ellis remembers the evening: 'To say I feel gutted at having missed the gig would be a bit of an understatement. But I had a prior engagement in Edinburgh. The first I knew about Oasis was when the gig manager Ali Murdoch phoned to say an extra band had turned up.' Ellis continues, 'He wanted to know what I thought about letting them play. I said no problem, as long as they didn't want money. So they agreed to play for a few free beers.' Ellis sheds some light on the band behaving like they were about to wreck the joint if they didn't get in; he remains dismissive: 'The whole thing about them turning up and demanding to play is one of the biggest myths in rock 'n' roll history. They were cheeky and a bit wide but there was never any sign of trouble. The stories of them threatening to wreck the joint only came out months later. They were pure invention – all part of the band's laddish image.'

It doesn't sound as dramatic as the Creation version of events, does it? Compared to a wonderful tale about threatening to torch the venue if they didn't get on the bill? Eventually, the band won, and they got to play. But it was down to the gig manager, a bit of common sense and the other bands on the bill being willing to give up some stage time. Easy does it, in other words.

8

Creation: How Does it Feel?

Alan McGee has a Glaswegian directness. He finds it hard to suppress his emotions; delight, anger, joy or rage. This always made for first-rate copy. Whether acting as a musician, music executive, manager or later in his career as a cultural commentator and blogger for the *Guardian* or his many other projects, he always had a keen understanding of how to manipulate the media, particularly the press, to break or promote a band, his label or an event. He seemed to live on energy and sheer instinct. He always believed the music would save him, or at least his label. He trusted in the music and had faith that at least one of his artists would come along and pull him out of a hole.

I remember a *Glasgow Herald* interview in the mid-1990s. By then McGee was a millionaire many times over thanks to the Sony deal and the phenomenal success of Oasis. He was riding on a commercial and creative wave and buoyed with his customary self-confidence. But he kept talking about money, property and swimming pools. I'm sure he was most likely bored and taking the piss, but there was an unusual side to him. The keen McGee watchers detected a change. It sounded like there may be trouble ahead. You sensed he was practically over-compensating; he was legitimising how cool the Creation and Sony deal was. He pronounced they could now compete with the big boys and, with the Sony money, could sign anyone they wanted. He boasted they were in the position to put down a million to sign New Order.

Back in the late 1980s and early 1990s, Creation Records were the label many wanted to sign with. If given a choice, around 1991-ish I would've preferred DGC, Sub Pop or Virgin's American imprint Caroline. Food EMI had a creative energy and were home to Blur. Though, if I could personally pick a label from any era, I would sign to Elektra. Imagine hanging out with The Stooges, MC5, Love and Tim Buckley? Engaging company if they happened to come round for coffee and cake. They were the quintessential pop benchmark.

I also have a soft spot for Buddah Records, perceived as the best bubblegum pop label of the 1960s. They were formed in New York City in 1967 by Kama Sutra boss Art Kass. He became frustrated with owners MGM's lack of support and distribution despite The Lovin' Spoonful's success pumping cash into MGM's coffers. The label was a balance of radio-friendly bubblegum and album-based experimental acts and operated a highly profitable distribution arm with bands such as The Lemon Pipers, Ohio Express, The 1910 Fruitgum Company, Salt Water Taffy, Melanie, Captain Beefheart and Gladys Knight and the Pips. We could play fantasy record labels and talk as much as we want about cool labels with first-rate artists but, I hear you, what's this got to do with Oasis? Not much, but it has loads to do with Creation.

I was never besotted by Creation's bluster and coolness. That's despite loving the Creation bands and the message, the label's ethos and spirit, that fuck you, we're mad punk rock pirates on a sinking ship. I did get that. When Alan McGee speaks now, as a sober, drug-free man given a second chance at fatherhood, he displays the brutal honesty of a cleaned-up addict thriving in his sobriety. His interviews make for even better reading. Speaking to Kenny Gates from PIAS, the Belgian-based independent label, distributor and service provider, McGee revealed what he truly felt about record companies. 'No! I like people, not companies. I used the indie thing to my own advantage. I was indie when I wanted to be indie, and I was major when I wanted to be major. I only did it for completely self-serving interests. I'm not an indie guy. People think I am, but I'm not.'

At the time, it was a brave decision for Creation to take a chance on Oasis, especially when you consider Suede were the darlings of the music press. They were the band they'd be up against at the time. In terms of look, attitude and sound, Oasis were pretty much the polar opposite. Creation had influential bands like Primal Scream, My Bloody Valentine and Teenage Fanclub, but they didn't have that consistent commercial act who could regularly sell albums on a major scale worldwide. One which suited the 49 per cent of the company Sony now owned. This was a major departure for the label, but McGee's instinct was there. He was going on a hunch based on the singer's look and attitude, which matched that of the two JLs – Lennon and Lydon – and the catchy commerciality of the songs.

The honest McGee continued to be blunt, especially about the night at King Tut's. When asked in the same PIAS interview if he immediately thought Oasis were amazing, McGee responded: 'I didn't think they were amazing – I thought they were really good. I thought I could nick in and steal The Stone Roses' audience for one record, so I signed them. I had no idea I was signing something bigger than The Stone Roses. It was an incredible few years. The maddest thing was me,

Noel and Liam thought it was going to go on forever. It wasn't to be!' While discussing the essence of Creation and Oasis, McGee is forthright: 'Creation was, in my head, always punk rock meets psychedelia. And that's what Oasis were. It was the same aesthetic all the way along.'

McGee came to London from Glasgow as a purist and a fan of music but he was always rock 'n' roll, schooled in the classic bands. It was always The Beatles, the Rolling Stones, The Kinks, Pink Floyd, The Velvet Underground, Led Zeppelin, the Sex Pistols, The Clash and Joy Division. In 1978 he got hold of a bass and joined Andrew Innes's band, The Drains. This band later evolved into Captain Scarlet and the Mysterons with McGee's pal Bobby Gillespie on vocals. They rehearsed every week for six months but never played a gig. He then found the ambition to up sticks. It was Andrew Innes who was determined to leave Glasgow and offered McGee an ultimatum: 'Come to London, McGee, or you're out of the band.' So they headed to London in 1981 to attempt to make it with their newly formed band The Laughing Apple.

He started a fanzine *Communication Blur*, then *The Communications Club* in 1982, seeing a niche for disciples of 1960s psychedelic underground music, Pink Floyd and Syd Barrett. He progressed to open the Living Room, a tiny function suite above a pub, the Adams Arms (now known as the Lukin) on Conway Street, then in 1984 they moved above the Roebuck on Tottenham Court Road (now named the Court). The Living Room featured gigs by bands like The Television Personalities, The Pastels and The June Brides.

It was here, at the second incarnation of the Living Room, where McGee signed the Jesus and Mary Chain. It was Bobby Gillespie who insisted he book them to play. Gillespie had received a tape from Nick Low, a friend of Andrew Innes, and he'd begged McGee to get the band out of their bedroom and down to London to play.

McGee claimed that the JAMC infamous feedback was an accident, caused by the lowness of the ceiling and bands using a vocal PA; normally guitarists had to turn down so they could hear the singer. Speaking to Tim Jonze of the *Guardian* on 21 September 2010, he explained: 'The guitars were too safe. There was no feedback then. That all happened by default. They played the guitars so loud they all fed back. It was incredibly violent. At the soundcheck, they did "Upside Down", "Never Understand", "In A Hole", "Vegetable Man" and the best version of Jefferson Airplane's "Somebody To Love" I've ever heard. The Mary Chain summed up what me, Joe Foster and Bobby were into, namely garage psychedelia. This was May 1984 and I signed them at the soundcheck.'

From there, McGee would eventually form a record company. He was always about instinct and gut feeling from the start. In a Q&A in 2019 on *Beffshuff*, a lifestyle blog, McGee repeated his mantra. 'I still will go off a gut instinct. If I like it, I sign it. The only reason that I don't want to change that is that it's always worked for me quite well. If I feel it, I'll sign it.' It was intuition, the band's attitude, an ear for a tune, and an eye for record sales. He would often get it wrong, get over-enthusiastic about a band he loved, and he wouldn't care what anyone else thought. Let's ignore the ones he got wrong and focus on the successes. The Jesus and Mary Chain, Primal Scream, My Bloody Valentine and Teenage Fanclub. Now that's only four bands. What connects them? The Velvet Underground? The songs? Again, they also have a unique indefinable quality.

McGee is entertaining and has always had that certain self-assurance. His biggest asset was his enthusiasm; allied with a similar line of attack to the US Svengali and impresario Kim Fowley, or the UK's Andrew Loog Oldham and Malcolm McLaren. It was about promotion, shaking it up, having the eye for publicity or spotting the next cultural change before it hit the masses. To be there in the middle of it, a mover and shaker, armed with a quote, often deliberately belligerent, at times irritating, often annoying but rarely boring.

McGee is also an excellent communicator – and again this was before social media. It meant putting posters up on bus shelters or handing out flyers outside other indie clubs. There's always this recurring theme of mass communication, with a punk rock activist attitude (seen even in the name of his fanzine and club). When you look back now, there was an inevitability that he'd become a high-profile and controversial player in the music business.

The Creation mantra was *doing it for the kids*, finding and seeking bands that would appeal to teenage indie-pop fans. Those with intelligence, taste and an element of sensibility. Those who understood 1960s psychedelic culture, cough syrup, fanzines and garage punk. If you give this a British twist, you incorporate something close to a Dadaist approach when you embrace the eccentrics and the nonsensical into the label. If you add that to the undoubted formula in McGee's mind like MC5, The Stooges, the Rolling Stones, The Velvet Underground, Syd Barrett-era Floyd, Big Star and The Faces, you will have a clear understanding of the Creation ethos and prototype. This might sound oversimplified, but he signed bands he liked. If they sold a thousand or a million, were popular or not, it didn't matter. He had to buy into what his artists were doing and genuinely always did.

Before Oasis ever came into Alan McGee's life, Creation Records were struggling financially. The label didn't have much in the way of business acumen, but what they lacked in accountancy skills and legality they made up for in energy and enthusiasm. They were music fans and punks and guys who played in bands. Creation at the time were verging on bankruptcy and, as we have seen, were brought to their knees by the cost of recording My Bloody Valentine's album, *Loveless*. They may have had cool and popular bands like Teenage Fanclub and Primal Scream but financially they were a train wreck.

Alan McGee sensed that through fanzines, he could communicate with indie-pop fans. Over in America in 1980, Bruce Pavitt, who would eventually set up Sub Pop with Jonathan Poneman, was doing the same. He started a fanzine *Subterranean Pop*, which focused on US independent record companies in the Pacific Northwest and punk, pop and early hip hop. As it became more popular he would release tapes with the magazines and this approach evolved into Sub Pop. McGee started in the fanzine scene and quickly realised that money made by putting on indie club nights could be reinvested in a label which featured bands he liked.

In 1983, McGee formed Creation with Dick Green and Joe Foster. The Jesus and Mary Chain became a sensation when Creation released 'Upside Down' the following year. High-profile, controversial, mired in fights and riots, seldom off the front of the music papers, they were the perfect vehicle for McGee and Creation. Already you can see it. The warring brothers, riots, loads of controversy and its subsequent free press. If you include the shared love of The Velvet Underground and Pink Floyd when it featured Syd Barrett, scorching white noise feedback and the volume of a jet fighter plane, it is easy to see why McGee invested so much energy in them. When the Mary Chain signed for Warner Brothers, McGee spent the money he'd made as their manager on signing Primal Scream,

The Loft and Jasmine Minks. The label kept growing bigger and bigger.

McGee was sharp and intuitive; he would learn from his mistakes and keep improving, but there were horrendous problems with cash flow. Creation were always stacked to the max on their credit cards, always on the phone extending their credit or phoning up distributors to take a few per cent off their fees. Their very existence was often hand-to-mouth. There was also a continuing concern over the label's predisposition to sign bands McGee loved but who didn't sell. As someone with the gift of the gab, an eye for the story and an instinct for manipulating the music press, most of the Creation bands gained critical acclaim and a loyal fan base, thanks to his ability and skill at creating a scene.

It was about promotion, shaking it up and being on the case when it came to publicity. Instead of shying away, it was about living up to the reputation. It was about cultivating relationships and connections with half a dozen key journalists who would give his bands a favourable review in the music press. Again, it's important to frame the story and lay out the backdrop to what was happening.

When McGee arrived in London in 1981, the UK and the world in general were screwed. Politically, musically and creatively, it was a trying time to consider doing anything positive, especially between 1981 and 1983. Punk had evolved into new wave and no one had any money and everybody seemed to be beyond fed up with it. So much so that they started rioting in Toxteth, Liverpool.

In 1981, McGee would find the first London Marathon running by his bedroom window with the soundtrack of Bucks Fizz and the latest reality TV show winner Sheena Easton blaring from Radio 1. Simon & Garfunkel were playing their reunion show in New York's Central Park. In the UK, synth bands like Depeche Mode, OMD, Human League and Ultravox were successful. The music industry had come up with a slogan – *Home Taping Is Killing Music and It's Illegal* – while the TV showed Charles and Diana getting married. Both Ronald Reagan and Pope John Paul II were shot. At the cinema, the big movie was *Raiders of the Lost Ark.* If it was a quiet night in, the first ever series of *Only Fools and Horses* was being aired, or there was *'Allo 'Allo!*, *Bergerac*, *Bullseye*, *Tenko* and *Wogan.*

By 1982, if gritty drama and the harsh reality of life in Liverpool were more your thing, then there was always *Boys from the Blackstuff* or the era-defining soap opera *Brookside.* Mark Thatcher (erstwhile arms dealer son of the prime minister) disappeared in the Sahara, blown off course during the Paris–Dakar rally; we had the launch of Channel 4 (adding a dash of edgy independence to the existing offer of three, yes, just three TV channels) and the then sexily aerodynamic Ford Sierra. *The Tube* started on Channel 4 with one of McGee's favourite bands, The Jam, headlining. (For pop fanoraks, the first ever band on *The Tube* was The Toy Dolls.) It was also the year of the Falklands War, the sinking of the ARA *General Belgrano* and IRA attacks on London's Hyde Park and Regent's Park. Joe Strummer disappeared and The Clash's tour was cancelled. (Strummer showed up later in Paris.) John Belushi was found dead in the Chateau Marmont hotel in LA. Michael Jackson's *Thriller* was released and Madonna released 'Everybody' on Sire Records. Italy won the World Cup after beating Brazil 3–2 in one of the best finals ever.

In 1983, Thatcher was re-elected, and that became the year of the *Hitler Diaries*, Reagan's Star Wars and Alex Ferguson's Aberdeen winning the European Cup Winners' Cup against favourites Real Madrid. The charts were full of corporate pop – just take a listen to Michael Jackson's 'Billie Jean', Culture Club's 'Karma Chameleon', David Bowie's 'Let's Dance' and The Police's 'Every Breath You Take'. Top comedy shows at the time included *Blackadder*.

Amid this cultural backdrop, we had a crazy guy from Glasgow selling The Television Personalities and making a living as a record label boss. When you consider what he was up against and what was happening around him, you can't begrudge Alan McGee a penny. There were disappointments along the way, the failure with Rob Dickens and Warner Bros indie project Elevation, for example, but he returned to Creation and tasted real success with The House of Love and My Bloody Valentine.

Fast forward to 1992 and the word was out. Alan McGee was actively having meetings with a view to licensing or maybe even selling a controlling interest in Creation. As always, the label needed money. Sony LRD may sound like a space-age laptop these days, but in 1992 they became a crucial part of the Creation story. The LRD part stood for Licensed Repertoire Division and it was run by Jeremy Pearce, an experienced and respected music publisher and lawyer.

For some time, Sony boss Paul Russell had been looking to make inroads into the independent scene. They knew their roster was heavily weighted with established artists. Their track record in finding relevant indie bands had been poor. Having licensed Suede's singles for Nude Records and the Farm's Produce label, they were in the market again and had Creation in their sights.

McGee now realised he would have to speak to majors or Creation would go under and jobs would be lost. Russell was aware of the financial situation at Creation; he had bumped into

McGee who as ever was upfront and conveyed the label's woes to him. McGee had a lot of time for Paul Russell's non-fussy and common-sense approach. Russell had always respected McGee's maverick style, though he sometimes found his mercurial nature infuriating. However, if they could get into a meeting together without the presence of lawyers and accountants, they would have a reasonable working relationship.

Eventually, a meeting was set up in the Groucho Club. The proposal was straightforward. Russell and Pearce suggested Sony LRD would provide much-needed funding and international licensing without meddling with McGee's bands. In the UK, he could continue to be Creation's creative force.

Sony were now buying acts like Primal Scream, Teenage Fanclub and Ride, which they would deal with internationally. To put the deal into some kind of timeframe and context, Primal Scream were the big attraction for Sony. They were the band expected to hit pay dirt in the US and sell, baby, sell. Sony were convinced world domination beckoned. But then drugs intervened and the mega-stardom mantle was picked up by Oasis.

The jury remained out on Oasis at the start of their career. The band were a 'Marmite' group; people either loved or hated them. Around this time, in 1993, there was a scathing and now infamous *NME* review by Johnny Sharp (aka Johnny Cigarettes). It appears in full in his book, *Mind the Bollocks: A Riotous Rant Through the Ridiculousness of Rock 'n' Roll*. He wasn't too enamoured by the band. He mentions, in none too glowing terms, their version of 'I Am The Walrus'. This is the review where the line that Oasis were 'too well versed in old records to do anything new' was picked up. It begins with 'If Oasis didn't exist, no one would want to invent them . . .'

and then gets worse. In the book, to give credit to Sharp, he includes it under the heading of rock journalism getting it wrong. Later, at the end of the year, in their annual 'ones to watch' selection, when the magazine uses its cunning and sticks its neck out and takes obvious punts on the band they think will break through, *Select* picked Whiteout; Oasis didn't get a mention.

Another stumbling block with the Sony deal was the previously discussed agreement with the label SBK to release any Creation acts in America. Sony had bought 49 per cent of the label, so as to allow Creation to retain creative control. McGee shocked his contemporaries in the music industry by leaving a meeting with Sony boss Paul Russell on 31 May 1996 (three years to the day after witnessing Oasis at King Tut's), having renegotiated the contract between Sony and Creation.

The record industry expected a buyout but they were wrong. The move meant a five-year extension on the existing deal of £2.5 million for 49 per cent, signed in 1992. There was an improved royalty rate on Sony's sales of Creation bands outside the UK. Alan McGee faced Paul Russell with the confidence of knowing Richard Branson was keen to have him run his fledgling record label, V2. He also had one of the hottest bands on the planet at the time, Oasis. The renegotiated deal made McGee and Dick Green millionaires. McGee celebrated in full sobriety; he was getting clean. He bought a bigger, nicer flat in Bickenhall Street in Marylebone, where his neighbour was BBC newsreader Michael Buerk. This might be a good time to remind ourselves that Alan McGee started Creation Records in 1983, with a bank loan of £1000.

For spotting Oasis's potential, he deserves all that came his way. That is sheer, instinctive genius. McGee may have got lucky but he took a chance. You have no idea how much talent and skill it took to unearth or even see anything resembling potential in the band that played in front of us both that night. The idea of them being offered a record deal is inconceivable. But, again, I'm genuinely happy to admit I got it wrong.

9

The Lost Art of A&R

When music fans go to gigs, it's to see the band play their favourite songs, relish a bit of excitement, get drunk and maybe fall in love; whatever happens, it's better than being stuck at home watching TV. When A&R staff go to gigs, they think in an atypical manner. They don't see the balding rhythm guitarist or the plodding bass player. They don't care about the drummer with the one loud beat almost hiding behind his hi-hats. They see beyond all that.

McGee looked at the scenario unfolding before him and was instantly convinced he would sign this band. I looked at Oasis and saw football casuals out of Manchester for an away day. He looked at them and saw the future. He placed a bet on the way fashion would – and did – turn out over the subsequent years. He recognised that specific street look. He saw the feathered haircut like Paul Weller's. At King Tut's, Alan McGee looked on at Liam like a talent spotter. The songs and the music were secondary. It was the kid's presence, his sneer, his attitude. In some ways, his decision was based more on the way a 1960s Svengali would look at him. He understood girls would want to shag Liam and boys would want to fight him.

The Mod look was important, crucial in fact. Like northern soul, both its sound and fashion have become commonplace. These days, everyone's an aficionado. They never used to be. It's the same with people wearing Ramones T-shirts and claiming to be into them. Have you noticed the millions of people who wear those T-shirts? They weren't standing beside my friends, brothers Keir and Davey Morrison, when they showed up for every Ramones gig when they came to town. (I mean, they couldn't be; they weren't born yet.) Those brothers would show up in hail, rain and snow and be there for shows that weren't exactly full to the rafters. Where were those Ramones fans when they played gigs in Glasgow? People follow the style and fashion, mainly because they see others do so and they think it's cool. Fair enough.

As for the actual word Mod, it's from the word 'Modernist', which was the name for a group of cool stylish youths in London, who in the late 1950s took to dressing well, with parkas only there to protect their slimline, sharply tailored outfits, while turning their back on traditional jazz, preferring modern jazz. They were a select group at first, but that's where the Mod subculture began. Whenever you bump into a Mod, ask them.

With Oasis, McGee recognised similar elements. That look from the street. The idea of lad culture, the smartly dressed look, influenced by magazines like *FHM* and later *Loaded* and *Maxim*. The sound would fit the fashion, be as much a cultural trend as a musical one and be earmarked for the type of football fan who embraced rock 'n' roll and dance culture. Millions would buy into that. They were, you might say, up for it. Oasis were the ideal band, the perfect fit, willing and more than able to be moulded into the next big breakthrough band. Liam, at that moment, looked like he could be the face and personality to carry it off. That's what McGee meant when he said he'd made his mind up about signing them. It was as if the songs were secondary. Then when they played their songs he loved them too, his instinct kicked in, and even though he has subsequently confirmed he was drunk, he just had to sign them. As he stood beside me, he must've been analysing the way they looked, the contemptuous singer with the attitude which matched the band's sound and songs. Maybe he thought Liam had that star quality; it could be his decision was as tenuous as that.

Oasis were a brief anecdote among the gossiping, unsigned bands, part excited, part jealous, part amazed that bands were still offered a deal. (They weren't signed that night, a deal was offered and agreed but it was still based on a handshake. The contract was not signed until October.) That this could still happen was old-school. Bands were rarely signed without managers and agents and expensively produced demo tapes. The chat among the mostly unsigned bands was about the way Oasis looked, not their sound.

At the time, Liam and Noel stood out. Liam was tall, and had the look of the wayward footballer or snooker player with drink or drug issues. Like the star of a movie when the dreaded leader of the pack falls for the posh, beautiful girl. The boy from the wrong side of the tracks who would break into the manor, shag the hot girl, then shag the wife, then punch the husband and drive off in their car, that kind of look. Noel looked like he'd be there too, directing the movie, controlling the scene and writing the soundtrack. Noel at least was less intense, but he was the boss. He was self-assured with a confident style and an insightful presence. The rest of the band looked like normal guys who liked football and a pint down the local. Guys who would happily fix your roof, be able to rewire the house, build a wall, turn their hand to a bit of plumbing then fix the van's fan belt.

In 1993 there was still the perceived wisdom among bands that you had to have a certain look to get a deal. A stylised rehash, a look that has been tweaked and slowly modified since Elvis, Gene Vincent, The Beatles and the Rolling Stones. You had to have that defined look. The compelling lead singer whom you can't take your eyes off, with his cool hair, classic features, preferably with an element of danger, but also a great name. Your lead singer can't ever, in fairness, be called Nigel or Trevor. (Pop quiz prize if you can think of any.) The band name similarly has to be slick, branded, memorable, and the band has to be able to deliver live. After bands like The Pixies, Nirvana and Teenage Fanclub came on the scene, the focus changed. That's not to say they weren't cool or handsome but the focus shifted to music and songs. To vibe.

Kurt Cobain was an enigmatic presence with a uniquely powerful yet tortured voice who photographed well but, for him, it was always about melody and the songs. When they broke through from the independent scene via Sub Pop, Nirvana loved bands like Beat Happening and The Melvins. They eventually took alternative music into the mainstream by pitching their sound somewhere between The Beatles, Sonic Youth, The Pixies and REM. By the time *Nevermind* hit big, no one cared about how they looked.

Teenage Fanclub were inspired by Postcard and bands like Orange Juice and The Byrds. They were indie but pop and pop was cool. They were lauded for their songwriting, harmonies and being unafraid to admit their lineage back to Big Star, Gene Clark and Neil Young. Both bands continually acknowledged a debt of gratitude to The Velvet Underground, the off-the-charts energy of The Stooges and the 1960s garage punk scene, mixed in with bands like Dinosaur Jr.

So there was a change. For the successful bands it was less about image and more about charisma and songs. For millions of people in bands like me, the rejection letters or phone calls usually ended by being reminded you sounded too much like The Pixies or Teenage Fanclub. I didn't take that as a criticism; I was chuffed and often had to be stopped from writing back to thank them.

Oasis's appearance – their image – was undeniably an important factor in their success. If the Jesus and Mary Chain spoke to thirty indie kids in leather jackets in the local university union who shopped in Oxfam, Oasis spoke to millions of football supporters, office workers, electricians and builders who liked to spend their hard-earned cash on designer casual gear from Stone Island to Burberry via Kangol and Fred Perry. The band, from that night in King Tut's, if not being primed, were slowly being manoeuvred into a position which would allow them to connect with millions of music fans. I understand that now. It's easy to see it now. I don't understand how on the night Alan McGee could see Liam blossom into such a captivating frontman, someone who would sing anthems in stadiums and festivals throughout the 1990s. Someone with the charisma and attitude to lead a band who merged the sound of the great 1960s bands, the attitude of punk, the fashion and look of The Stone Roses, all from that night at King Tut's and those four songs.

Bands can get their break based on more than the music, of course that's always been true. It was also about the band's distinct chemistry; one of anger, annoyance and menace. It had an appeal which set them apart. The Beatles were signed because of their personalities. George Martin liked their charm, their humour and George Harrison's cheek in questioning his tie. He thought they were OK musically, could play regular standards, and were fairly typical of most of the bands he auditioned. However, with the group as a unit, he could sense they had magic, something enthralling and appealing that created an indefinable quality when they were together. That's what won him over. Even as he conversed with them, he could sense something special. They were unique as individuals yet fitted together as a group in their nature and personality. This insight held true well before he got to unearthing and unleashing their phenomenal musical talent.

So in Alan McGee's mind, as Oasis came on stage and as soon as he realised the guy in the middle of the trouble earlier was the singer, the band as a musical unit merely had to be OK. In May 2011, while promoting the DVD release of the Creation film *Upside Down: The Creation Records Story*, McGee confirmed that when he first saw the band, he thought Liam might play another role among the Oasis party: 'I was up in Glasgow seeing my dad and I wasn't sure I'd even go to the gig. I got there early by mistake. Oasis were on first before most people arrived. There was this amazing young version of Paul Weller sat there in a light blue Adidas tracksuit. I assumed he was the drug dealer and that Bonehead was the singer. It was only when they went on stage I realised it was the lead singer. I knew I had to sign them.'

I know I'm repeating myself but I do so for effect. I want people to know that it's staggering how the Oasis I witnessed that night would in two years become one of the biggest rock 'n' roll bands in the world. How the same band I watched could ever go on to achieve so much is so far-fetched it is ludicrous, in fact, it's mind-blowing. Alan McGee saw them that night in King Tut's and was already thinking, planning how, in the hands of a reputable manager, a sympathetic and patient producer and some well-orchestrated PR to market the singer's attitude and football casual style, they could just about pull it off. If that didn't work, revert to Plan B: that is, create some anarchy, throw in some class As, loads of booze and riots, fighting at gigs and, with the music papers on their side, they could grow into a rockier, messier alternative for fans of The Stone Roses; after all, securing even a fraction of their sales would still be a success for Creation. This was all before he heard them play. After the first two songs, he would have a rough idea of the albums they would sell. Most of us don't think like that at a gig. Our main concern is whose turn it is to get to the bar, the time of the last train home and why the tallest person in the venue always stands in front of you. Always. Ironically, the only time that hasn't happened to me was at this gig. There was no one else between us and the stage.

We should make it clear that the mindset and logic of the average A&R representative is at odds with most people. They don't care about songs or the band. They sometimes see the singer's cheekbones or the guitarist's fringe and think girls will love them and boys will want to be like them; they can learn to write better songs. They don't see what you or I see. They might see a band with a fabulous drummer and tip off another band they're chasing who need a better drummer and hook them up. They don't care about sensibility; only product. It's about the package and this mindset means they don't tend to judge bands like we do. You might have an outstanding band, with accomplished musicians, but they will, unfortunately, always look like scaffolders or farmers. You can get skinny art school punks with attitude, with the edgy hair, ones who've got the gear but no idea. The A&R guy will think, *now, if only we can get the songs from the scaffolder and farmer's band and teach the skinny arty band to play them.*

Does that make sense? It might be easier to explain like this. Imagine it's the 1980s. You're in Danceteria, in New York. A girl is singing to a disco backing track, most people in the club are ignoring her, she's struggling but she's giving her all. You might think there's something about her but you would return to your conversation and your ridiculously overpriced beer. An A&R man sees a star, they speak to her and learn she's come to New York to make it. Technically, she isn't good. She doesn't sing too well, she's nervous, dancing out of time and struggling with the PA. That can be fixed and worked on because when she speaks, she has something. She has this drive and energy and there's something about her. Sexy, the high school babe all the guys and girls fancied, but she was more interested in the older guys with motorbikes and was so much cooler than you could ever be. Again she has an indefinable quality about her. You and 700 others are ignoring her but people like McGee see her and mentally they are already working out the hit albums and stadium tours because they are watching Madonna Louise Ciccone, fresh from Rochester Hills, Michigan.

Fast forward thirty years and you're in the same city; an unusual-looking singer is hammering out songs on the piano in a wine bar in the East Village. Most of those present find her irritating. Her brash style puts people off their conversation. Alan McGee would be spilling his drink over revellers because he's spotted Lady Gaga while others in the crowd are blethering about the weather. He's already offered her a deal. Something divides the average gig-goer from the A&R man and the music business mogul. The latter have a finely tuned radar and are intensely familiar with the cultural vibrations, 'the word on the street', way before mere mortals like us.

In 1993, Alan McGee is also there with a slightly different business viewpoint. He will still have the eye, ear and intuitive shrewdness for a band and have his A&R mojo running at full tilt, but apart from his usual instinct for seeking out artists he loves, he's now there as a record company owner looking for a band that will be 49 per cent Sony owned. He's looking for a band who do not fit the perceived notion of a 'Creation' band. The label was in so much debt that he had to sell. As he told the *Guardian* in 2010, 'A few times we were actually begged to stop by the accountants. We were fucked, man, for years. We never made a penny for the first ten years. When we did the Sony deal in 1992 we owed over a million quid. Without that, we'd have gone bankrupt. Bobby Gillespie was talking about doing a benefit gig for the label in a football stadium. I told him you'd better do a tour of football stadiums to pay our debt off.'

The minds of A&R people are off-kilter, their logic normally misguided, the victories celebrated and their many epic failures buried. You would've been part of the latter. Whatever fraudulent promises and lies one label was offering you, other labels were offering even more convincing promises and lies. You're the songwriter and singer and aren't that desperate to speak for a generation and sell millions. All you want is a cool new guitar, and a record in the shops to irritate some ex-girlfriends and previous bandmates when they see it in a record shop on Byres Road. Those interested, though, have been two-timing you from the start and signed your biggest local rivals. Now labels have gone cold on you, and you're back to the harsh reality of bar work or the call centre. That's how it happens in the real world. People like Alan McGee don't fall downstairs (upstairs for King Tut's!) like Leggy Mountbatten from *The Rutles* and stumble upon Oasis, do they?

Once Creation set in motion the process of signing Oasis and those involved at the label heard their demo, for some, it was a no-brainer, while many were deeply unsure. Based purely on their show at King Tut's, I would argue that most A&R reps would've wanted to come back for a second hearing.

They may have seen something in the frontman but would've needed another few gigs to be convinced. Even if the venue had been packed full of A&R people, McGee would be the only one who spotted something – and acted on it with such surety. Label scouts tend to act in pairs. The psyche of A&R people is such that even if they hate a band, they suddenly become interested because someone else is. The first one is genuinely intrigued by something, the other is playing the averages, and fear of missing out looms large in their world.

By September 1993, with the band still unsigned, they played at the In the City Music Seminar in Manchester. In the Canal Café Bar, they played 'Supersonic' for the first time in public and 'Live Forever'. Despite the city heaving with A&R reps, no late bids were made. Perhaps they assumed it was all done and dusted with Creation but companies were uncharacteristically shy. The industry was still ignoring them. Even the *NME* didn't carry a review of the gig. The labels had set their sights on the same three acts: Whiteout, Tiny Monroe and Elastica.

10

Gestation Period

Shortly after the King Tut's gig, Liam, Noel and Bonehead were invited to Creation's London offices to meet the staff. Even so, it took a while for Oasis to eventually sign their contract. The band were locked away rehearsing what became their debut album and their live set for the following year. They would spend hours endlessly rehearsing the same set. The same eleven songs, unremittingly playing them again and again and again. Noel was now in charge and known by the others as The Chief while Mark Coyle was shaping and organising the sonic mesh and disorder into something resembling a coherent sound.

Both Alan McGee and their manager Marcus Russell became involved with Oasis on the strength of their live shows and without hearing a demo. They must've been delighted when they finally got to hear songs like 'Live Forever' on tape. The problems began when the band entered the studio to start recording the album. McGee, Russell and Noel didn't think the production and recording was good enough. They wanted to capture the dynamic of the band's live sound; the energy, excitement and power that matched the quality of their songs, and transfer that exhilaration onto the album. They understood that if they got the album sounding as vital and alive as a live performance, they'd be sitting on a successful breakthrough.

Meanwhile back in Manchester, there were many still undecided about Oasis. Loads of bands, agents, promoters and the local press were unconvinced. McGee was still head over heels with them as were Sony America, particularly for some reason, for the song 'Columbia'.

By July, Alan McGee was telling everybody he met that he'd found *the* band he'd been waiting for. He meets Nathan McGough, manager of Happy Mondays, who shares his excitement and enthusiasm until he realises McGee is talking about Oasis. McGough famously met Noel in Manchester shortly after and congratulated him on signing with Creation and Noel, rarely one to mince his words, told him straight that they hadn't signed yet. So he could've nicked them but didn't, showing some uncharacteristic music business integrity. He now also has a stupendous 'I could have legitimately stolen Oasis from under Creation's nose and made millions but chose not to because I had some integrity' future anecdote as a highly paid guest speaker at a music seminar.

McGee installed Johnny Hopkins as head of press to steer the band's PR. He was their spokesman for the following seven explosive and hot-tempered years. Sensing that the band were already viewed as trouble by the press, something he actively encouraged, he figured Hopkins was better placed to control and harness that ever-present 'it's-all-kicking-off' potential. He got the band's attitude and understood what was required. Someone able to manipulate the media and navigate the band through the impending onslaught. McGee's decision to appoint Hopkins as the band's publicist instead of the expected Laurence Verfaillie sent ripples through the label and ended up with her being marginalised and eventually leaving. Andy Saunders, initially reluctant about Oasis, took over her role in charge of press. The reason given for Hopkins getting the job ahead of Verfaillie was that he immediately got what the band were about. He shared McGee's excitement and vision of the band whereas Verfaillie remained uncertain and made the mistake of questioning McGee's judgement over Oasis. She disliked Tim Abbot and had also openly slagged off the band. Saunders, like Abbot, saw them when they visited Creation and immediately took to them. The good-looking gallus singer and the acerbic, sharp-tongued songwriter with songs that could change the label's fortunes. Hopkins bought into the band's chemistry and ambition, something McGee believed was essential to their success. McGee also knew it was crucial whoever took over the band's PR had to 100 per cent believe in Oasis to present them as a mix of indie rock 'n' rollers with a punk attitude.

In his 2013 autobiography, *Creation Stories: Riots, Raves and Running a Label*, McGee didn't pull any punches with regards to those at Creation who didn't like the band: 'I probably sound like a cunt when I say running a label is like a dictatorship, but you've got to remember how few people at Creation at that time liked Oasis. James Kyllo didn't rate them. Laurence [Verfaillie – the then-publicist] hadn't. Andy Saunders didn't think they'd work. If I hadn't seen the business as a dictatorship, if I hadn't had absolute faith in my judgement, Creation would not have put out the records of the band who became the biggest in the world.'

It had been a while since the music industry had this type of band who didn't give a fuck, who were quick to anger and react, who didn't care what people thought. An act that attracted loads of sensationalist press. The sort of group who would make the front cover of the *NME* and the tabloids, whether through drunken fights on ferries or smashing up hotel rooms. Soon the press picked up on the hedonistic side of Oasis, and the incendiary sibling rivalry between Liam and Noel. The PR had to be harnessed and worked through. But attitude means profile, means notoriety, means publicity – and sales.

Things looked as if they were finally coming together for McGee. That is until Sony started sending in accountants, particularly one – a certain Mark Taylor – to look closely at how the company's financial affairs were doing. And he couldn't believe the shape they were in.

It's to Creation and Ignition's credit that they handled the band so well during this time. Oasis were desperate to get the album released but both their record company and management wanted to make sure they controlled it in such a way that they wouldn't turn out to be yet another flash in the pan. They were carefully introduced to the appropriate promoters and journalists; they would play only a few select gigs and the build-up would be measured. This was a long-term project, one that required consideration and forethought. There was plenty of time for disarray and disturbance. If it took time to find the most suitable producer, then it would take time. They had something truly special in their favour; both McGee and Russell had heard Noel's songs and they understood with absolute clarity that the production of the band's debut had to be of the same quality.

Their biggest issue wasn't handling Noel and Liam's public outbursts and the band's freewheeling self-indulgence, it was finding the appropriate producer, capable of capturing that energetic, raw power and excitement on the album, something inexpressible and vital that would deliver the message to an as yet unsuspecting public. Russell and McGee had to keep the process in check, release slowly, and allow the music to do the work. Indie purists knew Oasis were not a bona fide Creation band; from the start the band were primed to bring in fans of The Beatles, The Jam, The Smiths, The Stone Roses and Nirvana. They needed to make a record that sounded good enough in this sort of company. Then, if they were marketed correctly, they could start to sell big.

Even though their sound is typically British, their message is unfiltered. Sixteen-year-old kids and middle-aged men got it. They shared the same frustrations; those of being held back in a job they hated with a boss who is a prick. Maybe they don't even have the ambition to ever want a job because they know they have a better chance using their cunning to get out there and face the world with some hope, some street-smart instinct instead of a life in a factory. Well, it used to be a factory; now I suppose it's a call centre, or, worse still, a zero-hours food-delivery contract. That's true globally, I think: an all-encompassing passion to improve yourself, to make it happen, to better yourself. Daring to dream is a universal theme.

During this gestation period, in less than a calendar year, between the show at King Tut's on 31 May 1993 and the release of 'Supersonic' on 11 April 1994, the improvement was unbelievable. Was this even the same band? In hindsight, those eleven months were probably the most important of their career. The progress was extraordinary. They had undergone this metamorphosis from a nervous, strained band into an accomplished, confident rock 'n' roll group.

From May 1993, they'd been working flat out, rehearsing then recording their debut album. The only recorded material released was 'Columbia', which was purely for radio and collectors on a limited-edition white label. It received a fair amount of airplay on Radio 1 and was slightly unusual as it didn't truly represent the more direct, in-your-face sound the band would eventually be known for. 'Columbia' was a slow burner and its sound was more like their Manchester compatriots, with that distinct vocal, guitar sound, groove and a melody you gradually grew into. But it was on the nation's main music station and it was on a lot.

By now, the hype around Oasis was such there were rumours they'd recorded an album and every song on it was a hit single. The more Marcus Russell reined in expectations by getting a grip on the mounting hysteria, the more the excitement around the band rocketed. It was apparent, as we watched on from afar, like many bands and artists before them, that Oasis were being primed and that those around them were expertly preparing and setting up a pop onslaught.

Some hoped the band would falter; there was jealousy and that continual element of snobbery. People refused to buy into the unremitting turbulence. It was as if the band's nihilism had overtaken their songwriting ability, and to some they lacked subtlety, an element of good grace. Their songs were hardly full of lyrical genius or wit. They weren't cool enough to deliver and meet expectations. The band's response – or indeed their opening salvo – was anything but nervous or faltering. They released a confident, blistering call to arms in 'Supersonic'. Oasis had officially touched down.

Looking back, those working with the band knew how untouchable *Definitely Maybe* was. Their management were aware of the songs Noel had in his arsenal. So many songs that they'd be able to adopt a strategy where the first album would reap a commercial harvest of singles and terrific B-sides. They also were privy to some of the material held back for the second album. Noel had openly let those close to him know that most of *(What's The Story) Morning Glory?* was written, arranged and organised and he was looking forward to recording, producing and sharing its brilliance with a growing public, keen to hear more.

Their marketing structure focused around the two albums. Singles were drip-fed, then the first album, more singles, second album, more singles. The idea was to release a single every few months (as noted, just like The Beatles), building up the band's profile while they worked on and established their live reputation on the road.

The release of their debut single came at a dreadful time for music fans across the globe. April 1994 saw the death of Nirvana's Kurt Cobain. In the months leading up to his death, the signs were ominous. Despite the shock when his death was announced, there was a dreadful, tragic inevitability about it. Musically there's a whole raft of difference, but Kurt and Noel have more in common than you'd imagine.

They were both born within weeks of each other. One in Aberdeen, Washington, in February 1967. The other in Longsight, Manchester, original home of BBC Manchester's *Top of the Pops* studio, in May of the same year. Both working class, both obsessed with The Beatles, both loved punk and new wave bands, both had troubled adolescences, dabbled in drugs, dope, mushrooms and glue. Both would love music more, though. They had this unquenchable thirst for music, for listening to records, for working out, learning and copying songs, listening to the radio and going to gigs. Both would have this yearning, desire and passion allied with an unstinting ambition to leave their mark.

Kurt Cobain was right-handed and taught himself to play guitar left-handed. Noel was left-handed but plays guitar right-handed. Both would write songs that would redefine their generation. One killed himself after a brief and tortured time on earth. Days after his suicide, the other would release his first single and so, to many, would reluctantly fill the void. Nirvana would write anthemic rock hits 'Smells Like Teen Spirit', 'Come As You Are' and 'In Bloom'. Oasis would release 'Live Forever', 'Wonderwall' and 'Don't Look Back In Anger'. Songs of breathtaking power and urgent, unparalleled quality. That moment in April 1994 was seen by some as the passing of the torch. The beat goes on, Kurt is dead and here comes Noel a few days later. Oasis didn't have the same global reach and impact as Nirvana but they left an impression. Kurt is no longer with us; Noel is. Noel found fame at 27, the age Kurt took his own life. Maybe that's a small part of the difference. If it's handed to us when we're not ready, able or willing to handle it, it's really tough.

Kurt Cobain's death also overshadowed what was, up until then, the music press's preoccupation with Primal Scream's much-anticipated follow-up to 1991's critically acclaimed landmark, *Screamadelica*. (The focus centred around the challenges involved in recording *Give Out But Don't Give Up*.) The arrival of Oasis in the same month with their debut single 'Supersonic', followed in June with 'Shakermaker', then 'Live Forever' and the release of *Definitely Maybe* in August, placed Creation at the forefront of the music industry. It was the label of the moment. Both albums dovetailed and positioned Creation as one of the major players in the British music scene. It was a surprise at the time but it was Oasis the media and the public craved and wanted to hear from.

Despite singles like 'Rocks' and '(I'm Gonna) Cry Myself Blind,' the reviews of *Give Out But Don't Give Up* were lukewarm. The critics found it hard to handle the country-blues Stones riffs and Allman Brothers harmonies. However, around this time, the music press changed focus on Primal Scream; it was no longer about their music but an ill-fated US tour with Depeche Mode.

In 2018, Bobby Gillespie told *Record Collector*, despite the reports of debauchery and hedonism, that the tour was tedious: 'The reality: it was boring. There was excessive drinking to kill the time. Every night we were playing what they call these huge sheds: they were thirty miles outside the city and all looked the same.' Gillespie compared it with his previous US tour. 'The *Screamadelica* US tour had been an adventure, the first time for Primal Scream in the States. We were playing theatres in town, we went to record shops, clothes shops, met kids in the street, went to clubs after the shows. [On Depeche Mode tour] We went on at 7 p.m. for forty minutes then had to hang around until the bus went at 4 a.m. and then it would be a ten-hour drive to the next show. The Depeche Mode tour wasn't rock 'n' roll. People got fucked up, but not in a fun way.'

Primal Scream were still producing solid rock 'n' roll records, but fans and critics wanted another *Screamadelica*. The people wanted more of Oasis, too. It was their tunes that resonated and connected with millions. Primal Scream were overshadowed by Oasis fans wanting songs filled with confidence, self-belief, arrogance and working-class attitude. They loved their honesty, self-indulgence and that we-want-it-all-and-we-want-it-now defiance.

At the time, their unstinting self-belief was no doubt fuelled by being out of their trees on coke. However, it did make them and their music stand out. It was unusual for bands around this time to be so fond of themselves. They genuinely had a high regard for their music, their look and their whole vibe, and enjoyed taking this to an almost comedic level. They got away with it because it wasn't conceited or vain or stuck up, they genuinely believed what they were doing was wonderful. They trusted in their ability and didn't care what you thought about them. They were like a musical Manc version of Muhammad

Ali. When they said they were the greatest, you bought into their arrogance and drama. You believed them.

Usually, when idealistic bands speak in their first noteworthy music interview there's talk of how lucky they are to be in this situation. There's thanks and gratitude to the fans for putting them there. There's a hope they might try their best to reward them by recording albums worthy of their newfound fame and elevated position. But not Oasis. They tell you without even a shred of subtlety they want to be famous, do drugs, shag as many hot women as possible and make loads of money. Plus, Noel wants a Rolls-Royce even though he hasn't got a driving licence. This energy attached itself to football supporters, clubbers and the lads who bought *Loaded* magazine, which hit the shelves days after the release of 'Supersonic' in 1994. Suddenly Oasis made sense to millions of guys who wanted to be in a band with them and hundreds of thousands of young women who wanted to sleep with them. Me? I still couldn't believe what I was seeing.

In 1994, the press and media started feeding into the same branding. TV shows celebrated laddism, drinking was great, shagging was better. Hedonism was back with a flashy vengeance; everything was about excess. It was cool to mock feminism, magazines like *Nuts*, *Zoo* and *FHM* were a roller-coaster of big-boobed soft porn, starring glamour models who were famous for bedding footballers. Punters couldn't get enough of fashion, style, grooming and even more big boobs. It was branded, it was about football, sex and music. Once again, rock 'n' roll was cool. It had, well, it had become the new rock 'n' roll.

11

Definitely Not, Amsterdam, *The Word* & NME

In January 1994, the band headed for Monnow Valley Studios near Monmouth in Wales. They are excited, positive, and ready to rock. The countless hours spent rehearsing, fine-tuning and preparing should reap dividends as they begin recording *Definitely Maybe*. By now, we recognise the pattern. We know this is Oasis. When the story finally makes sense and comes together, and the band gains momentum, they will soon encounter the first of many hurdles.

Dave Batchelor, the album's initial producer, was familiar to Noel. He worked as a soundman for Inspiral Carpets and Noel was convinced Dave was the man for the job. He may have liked Dave and his work as a soundman, but recording and playing live are two separate disciplines. Batchelor was more of a traditional producer who had worked with Nazareth, The Sensational Alex Harvey Band, Dr Feelgood and The Skids. He was the singer in the early 1970s Glasgow band Tear Gas. They recorded two albums before evolving into The Sensational Alex Harvey Band. They are worth checking out, by the way: their records have a lovely warmth, an early 1970s charm, similar in feel to Procol Harum. His process was the tried and tested recording technique of having the band record their parts separately. He wasn't bad at his job; he recorded his way; his approach was more traditional. But Oasis needed a record that would thrill, exhilarate, one full of power and excitement. The best way to sum up the saga with Dave Batchelor is that Noel picked the wrong man for the sound Oasis needed.

Instead of accepting and embracing the impetus and momentum which Noel wanted to capture, Batchelor's method did the opposite. The truncated nature of his process prevented the energy from coming through on the initial recordings. It wasn't wrong, it just wasn't what the band needed at that specific time. *Definitely Maybe*? Definitely not. Speaking in John Harris's excellent *Britpop!: Cool Britannia and the Spectacular Demise of English Rock*, Bonehead was perplexed. 'Batchelor was the wrong person for the job. We'd play in this great big room, buzzing to be in this studio, playing like we always played. He'd say, "Come in and have a listen." And we'd be like, "That doesn't sound like it sounded in that room. What's that?" It was thin. Weak. Too clean.'

Alan McGee and Marcus Russell were both concerned. Rock 'n' roll was about capturing the moment. The excitement and edge of the band's live sound. Oasis, at least in their limited studio experience to date, set up as they rehearsed. They played the songs until they got a take that worked, and later added vocals and guitar overdubs. This was how they worked in the studio. Dave Batchelor's approach of recording individually meant the collective energy the band naturally created was lost. Still, Batchelor was the producer and was entitled to remain stubborn with his way of doing things. He assured Oasis they'd better get used to his way of producing proper grown-up records.

McGee and Tim Abbot were disappointed but remained

pragmatic about what they had heard from Monnow Valley. It was Noel, who was too close to the songs and the material, who was most concerned. Was it the band's fault? Were they too nervous? Was it him? It cost £800 a day to record there and the decision was made to end the sessions with Batchelor. It speaks volumes for Creation's belief in the band that they made that call and accepted the loss if it meant getting the sound Noel wanted. It also shows how much Alan McGee believed the band's sound had to capture their spirit and edge.

*

On 8 February 1994, the band headed for a gig at the Paradiso in Amsterdam to make their European debut. Having already drunk copious amounts of Jack Daniel's and ingested more powders than a Beecham factory on the way from Manchester to the ferry, the band and crew continue partying on the boat. On board, there's a scuffle and fight with West Ham fans, a real battle royale and they are accused of stealing champagne and Jack Daniel's from the duty-free shop, and using forged money to pay for whatever they did buy. Security is brought in and it becomes frenzied. As they stagger to their rooms, Guigsy sees a guard about to hit Liam with a truncheon and punches him, then it's bedlam as a team of security guys wade in and beat Guigsy up badly before taking him down to a cell. Liam is then taken down, too. Later their passports are confiscated.

Noel wakes up oblivious to the previous night's carnage. The first thing he witnesses are the perpetrators passing by, handcuffed. He must've shaken his head and wondered what the fuck he'd let himself in for. The others are shipped back home and the gig in Amsterdam cancelled. It's an early example of the way Liam and Noel are poles apart in their perception and approach to what it means to be in a band. Liam claims the incident and their behaviour is being rock 'n' roll, a reaction to Noel's domineering style. Noel thinks it's unprofessional and shows a lack of discipline; he thinks it's clichéd, immature and stupid not to turn up for a show you're booked for. Noel thinks you're letting people down who have bought tickets for the gig. Liam thinks he's a rock 'n' roll star, it's his job to be unreliable; his attitude is if you want me, then expect the unexpected.

Witnessing his band being escorted off the ferry, Noel immediately rings Alan McGee. 'I called McGee and I'll never forget this and this is another reason why I love McGee, I said: "Are you sitting down? I've got some news. Everybody has been arrested." The only word he said was [adopts Scottish accent] *brilliant*.'

Maybe out of a sense of guilt from failing to even make it to Amsterdam for their first European gig, the band reconvene, this time in Sawmills Studio, Cornwall, with Noel and Mark Coyle producing in a second attempt to record *Definitely Maybe*, their way this time. Drums, bass and rhythm guitar are recorded together without soundproofing so the sound would take over the room. Then Noel recorded loads of overdubs. The band might have thought it was going well, but the grown-ups didn't. Creation and their management at Ignition could see it wasn't working and two key things – money and time – were now being wasted. They had to make a decision. What was in the can and recorded from the various sessions somehow had to be salvaged and made into an album.

Marcus Russell had spoken to Johnny Marr about his producer, Owen Morris, and Johnny said he was keen to have a go. Morris was given carte blanche to salvage anything he could. By the Bank Holiday in May, Morris had moulded, stripped back, finished and organised the album we know today. He understood what the band were trying to achieve and sensed from what he was listening to that Noel had become too engulfed in the process. Morris started by losing any guitar parts that were surplus to requirements and bravely adopted a 'less is more' approach. He stripped it down, enhancing the parts he thought worked and chopping out parts that made it sound too hefty. Noel had become lost in his music, a common situation for most artists, and the project had veered off track and lost focus.

Owen Morris brought a much-needed fresh ear. He wouldn't be precious; his job was clear: strip back the album and conjure up something from what was already recorded. His background as a live sound engineer helped crystallise the project, distilling, tidying and editing the songs into the restless, aspirational sonic narrative that became *Definitely Maybe*.

Before he was given the job of working on the album, Owen Morris was convinced Marcus Russell wanted to test him to see if he was able to work with Noel and Liam. They were booked in to re-record the vocals and then mix 'Columbia' and 'Rock 'n' Roll Star' over a weekend with the brothers at Loco Studios in Caerleon, Wales. Morris felt that this was his audition, to see if he could keep the brothers on side, which he did, by telling Liam he sounded like John Lennon and impressing them both with talk of Phil Spector production techniques. Morris passed the test. He further impressed Noel by telling the singer to fuck off when he wouldn't stop talking, allowing Morris to concentrate on the music. He was in. Alan McGee is a fan too: 'Owen Morris is a genius. He single-handedly saved *Definitely Maybe* and at the same time created the Oasis full-on, gigantic rock 'n' roll sound. I'm proud to call him a friend.'

Oasis released a demo version of 'Cigarettes & Alcohol' on a free compilation cassette, *Mutha of Creation*, on 12 February 1994. In March they performed an excellent version of

'Supersonic' on *The Word*. As I've said, Channel 4 didn't start broadcasting until 1982. They had a show called *The Tube*. I remember coming in from school and watching *The Gong Show*, then *The Munsters* and, at last, from 5.30 p.m. until 7 p.m. *The Tube*, a ninety-minute show dedicated to live music and interviews, would come on. I remember sitting with my brother's Betamax video and taping these incredible bands: Killing Joke, Japan, Echo and the Bunnymen, REM, U2, The Smiths and The Cure.

After *The Tube*, it was on to BBC2 for the *Oxford Road Show*. There was also *Whistle Test* (which used to be *The Old Grey Whistle Test* before moving to a mid-evening slot with its abridged title). There was a surfeit of music shows which showcased emerging talent and featured established bands. These TV performances were scheduled to promote their current album and tie in with the UK tour they would likely be undertaking. By the time Oasis made their national TV debut, there was only one show in town who fitted, and that was *The Word*, again on Channel 4. (*Later . . . With Jools Holland* emerged in 1992, but when it started, it mainly featured established popular acts.) It was odd waiting for Oasis to appear on *The Word*. It was the first time I'd seen them since the now infamous King Tut's gig in May 1993. The one thing that annoyed me about *The Word* was that although many bands delivered legendary performances like Nirvana and L7, the sound was always poor. It was as if the bands had shown up with their gear and plugged in somewhere, any old where. Then the presenter would link from chatting to that week's vacuous airhead celebrity or pissed soap star and cut to a band playing badly for two minutes.

As I nervously waited for Oasis, I feared the worst but I shouldn't have worried. Their sound was superb and, more importantly, they performed like they belonged there. Liam had a Super 8 camera which he pointed at groovy people dancing around. Again the drumming and bass playing were solid, reliable and on the money. Noel and Bonehead were locked in and they seemed focused and ready. That's what I remember; they looked like it was their time to shine. I was left shaking my head again at this band. Why was I worried? What was it to me if they fell flat on their arses and blew it? I had changed, though. I had gone from a bitter and twisted cynic to becoming a believer. I now felt this strong connection to Oasis and I wanted them to succeed and go on to bigger and better things. I was, as they say, invested.

I had followed the hype and the gigs and the fights and the rants and I honestly expected them to monumentally blow it and fail. Most music fans watching on felt the same. I wanted them to prove me wrong and they did. They sealed their reputation with an expectant studio audience waiting for the arrival of five guys now set to be one of the leading rock 'n' roll bands of that era.

With this appearance on *The Word*, Oasis proved they were in shape and making giant strides. There had been a quantum leap from when I'd seen them last May, at King Tut's. The most noticeable change was the improvement in Liam's singing. It was still the same guy obviously, but the snarling growl was even more pronounced and intense. Visually he had more of the cool swagger and attitude of Stone Roses' frontman Ian Brown, his singing now that classic sheer pop, punk and rock hybrid of Lennon and Lydon. He had taken these iconic singers and moulded their vocal style into his own.

It was also noticeable how the women in the crowd were ogling Liam. The band aren't necessarily the best looking – though it's surely churlish to suggest that Liam in his heyday was anything but smouldering – but no one can deny that they made up for any shortfall in star quality. The attraction of the bad boy was ever thus, especially when they scowl and pout in that super-confident, disdainful style. Liam had become better at being the frontman. He looked like a star. Now he had the whole cool 1960s Mod look. When I saw them at King Tut's, Liam was wearing a tracksuit top and looked more like a football casual – or to some eyes, a drug dealer – than a pop star.

In early April, before their debut single's release, Oasis did their infamous 'Wibbling Rivalry' interview with John Harris of the *NME*. The band were on tour to promote 'Supersonic' and the interview became a watershed moment in the nuanced branding of the band's career. It's noticeable that the *NME* were claiming and championing Oasis. I would be surprised if Johnny Hopkins, their publicist and confidant of both McGee and the band, had picked one major music publication over the other. The skill was to surely keep all the major pop publications in the loop. Hopkins sought out journalists sympathetic to the band's cause. One member of the *Melody Maker* staff, Paul Mathur, was a fan. Mathur would become part of the band's inner sanctum having championed their cause before their breakthrough and he would later write the critically acclaimed *Take Me There: Oasis the Story*. The music press as a whole, however, remained split over the band. They were hardly singing from the same hymn sheet. Even some of Mathur's *Melody Maker* colleagues were non-believers. In his *Melody Maker* review of 'Supersonic', Peter Paphides dismissed the song as something Blur would've done four years ago and criticised Noel's lyrics. So maybe he was the one who planted the seed of hatred, particularly in Liam, towards Blur. In his review of the same song, the *NME*'s Keith Cameron raved about it. Noel always received criticism over his lyrics but are the words to 'Shakermaker' or 'Supersonic' any worse than those of 'Paperback Writer' or 'Ticket To Ride'? Pop music at its most effective should celebrate, captivate and heighten the human condition and shake you out of your slumbers. It's about primitive feelings and emotions. At its most basic, it can be a compelling force, as evidenced by the energy and excitement of bands like the Rolling Stones, MC5, The Stooges and the Sex Pistols. It should be evocative and take you back to that moment. When we listen to Oasis now, they still pulsate like they did in 1994 and 1995. They still have a resonance and importance that feels uniquely their own. The work from this peak period still stands the test of time, the jukebox test; it elevates them into that timeless bracket.

After a few mentions and a one-page article in the *NME*, John Harris from the same paper was sent to Glasgow's Trust House Forte hotel to do an in-depth follow-up. He interviewed the brothers in what became one of the funniest rock interviews ever, although it wasn't meant to be. It's one of the few rock 'n' roll interviews to be released as a single, 'Wibbling Rivalry' (released on Fierce Panda, 1995). You can hear it or read the transcripts online.

Harris, by default, has done more for the Oasis sibling rivalry than any fight on a ferry or pub brawl in Camden ever could. Everyone knew Creation's press people would love this. The timing couldn't have been better; it was set up to coincide with the release of that first single, 'Supersonic'. Rarely had any newspaper article gotten to the heart of the issue so quickly and effectively. These guys were unhinged and the interview would take its place in the annals of rock 'n' roll history. It was at times hilarious, shocking and muddled. It also bordered on chaotic, frenzied and confused.

Harris was aware of what he was doing. He was an experienced music journalist and lit the touch paper and left Noel and Liam to get on with it. There was no way a band would go into an interview and be so candid, stupid or naive. The *NME* was the home of shy vegetarians and angst-ridden former art school rockers, melancholic fans of The Smiths and Suede. The type of artists who were everything Oasis were not; diffident and well-read. Johnny Hopkins was present and let it unfold when he could've jumped in and whispered to calm it down a bit. Though why should he? If it was a case of branding, marketing and setting out the band's stall and reputation, it was a PR masterstroke.

They spoke about getting thrown off ferries; Liam thought it was cool, it matched the persona they wanted to get out there. They were shouting, ranting and continually interrupting each other. Noel is trying to be the clever one and Liam is hysterically funny without meaning to be. It worked because Creation hadn't sent them to do a course on media training. The closest they probably got to any mentoring would be from McGee, and he'd just be telling Noel how amazing he was. He was also most likely prompted to go for it, get some momentum going, think Sex Pistols, think controversy, don't hold back. If you think it, say it. We want disarray and rampage. Fights mean column inches and publicity, leading to sales, bigger and better gigs and money for one and all.

I always felt their outbursts were primarily due to the availability of the highest quality white powder you can imagine, partying full-on, drinking, shagging, and none of your cheap street Manchester bicarbonate soda here. They were encouraged to take it to the brink. That's how to create a scene and court the press. Get fired up, push on, create stories, don't hold back, don't give a fuck. This was their first major interview. There's a moment when the interview passes from being funny and edges closer to being cruel, hurtful and raw. OK, we get it. But now we're laughing *at* them, not *with* them. Still, what you see is what you get. It might be a bit tired and clichéd for bands to act rock 'n' roll in print, but in 1994, this was a refreshing change. The band realised they were being interviewed. They knew it would be out there but relentlessly continued insulting, arguing and refusing to step back. It was clear that they didn't care what you thought about them.

Apart from confirming laddish overconfidence was back, that interview did something far more profound: it established the soul, nature, character, rivalry and friction between the band's central characters. The band were already being set against each other. During the interview, Noel is angry at Liam for thinking it's rock 'n' roll to get thrown off a ferry. Noel calls him a football hooligan. By letting rip, they were keeping it real. They weren't faking it. There's a telling moment when Harris states – and again, this is before they've even released their debut single – that music fans were already viewing them in the same way as the Pistols and the Stones with their high-profile bad boy reputation. Harris also adds to the heated debate by suggesting The Who hated each other as well.

From the earliest interviews in the music press and on TV, Noel informed the world they would not be a flash in the pan, they would become the biggest band on the planet and play music the world would never grow tired of hearing. Yet even then, I still didn't buy into his level of ambition. Once I heard their debut album I started to think, this could happen. Most musicians think they can do the job of an A&R man and find the latest rock superstars. My problem was I *had* seen what became the biggest band in years. A band who believed they would become as big as The Beatles. But when I saw them, I didn't see it.

From the off, Oasis stood out as much for their attitude as they did their sound. The bands they were up against were introverted, snobbish and far too indie. This, on the other hand, was a band who would pray the shoegazers would look up so they could kick their heads in. This was the start of Sony's influence on the label. That brand of hedonism was cool again. McGee knew they could rock and party like Primal Scream, but they had something else too. When their music came out, they were far removed from the twee, quaint, idiosyncratic and indie origins of McGee's label. I still felt they were a band from the same lineage as The Stone Roses, Happy Mondays and Inspiral Carpets – and that they would remain at that level. Oasis, though, with a song like 'Live Forever', could become the next music business heavyweight, especially if America got on board.

Despite the complex love/hate relationship fuelled by frustration, animosity and that furious sibling rivalry central to the band's hot-tempered story, Liam and Noel remained nonchalant and untroubled. Nothing would stand in their way. That supreme confidence wasn't ill-founded; they firmly believed in their ability and weren't going to let anything knock them off course. Undoubtedly the friction between the brothers contributed an untold amount to any account of their history. Every band needs creative tension and an element of discord, but Oasis took theirs to an entirely unprecedented level. The madness and mayhem led to bitter feuds, mainly exacerbated by prodigious quantities of drink and drugs.

You would have the high-octane hedonism – well, it's rock 'n' roll, it would be rude not to – and the violence and paranoia. And, with Oasis, this was when the real drama kicked in: the bullying and aggression escalated, and suspicion started to eat away at everyone. Yet bands like this who become so fraught, when it looks like they're going to kill each other, are often the ones who somehow galvanise into professional musicians by showtime.

Oasis did this so many times, pulling off mesmerising shows, not great but exceptional benchmark performances. When it looked like they were on the precipice of the abyss, they managed to pull it back, compose themselves and deliver a stunning show.

They would also be guilty of going beyond the brink and, on many occasions blowing up, falling out and leaving millions of us wondering what might have been. But that is for the future; we don't know about the success and despair that lie ahead, how it came together and how it would blow up so many times, so publicly and so dramatically. When they get together, like it should be in the best dramas, it can be magnificent or chaotic but it's rarely boring and that's why we love them.

Any analysis of Liam and Noel's relationship with the press always comes back to the same premise. How much the streetwise scallies from Burnage were playing them, or how much were the tabloid hacks stitching them up? Knowing them like we do, we have to guess they were being themselves and those managing the PR planted a seed then left them to it, knowing their unfiltered comments would only help the publicity machine on its way. Whether by accident or design, most likely the latter, the floodgates opened and the press set their sights on the toxic relationship between Liam and Noel. I don't think the press ever truly grasped that the band honestly didn't give a fuck what anyone thought about them, so why worry? But the tone was set for the rest of their career.

In a diary entry around 2014, I noted the relationship had deteriorated and the brothers hadn't spoken for some time. However, I was then reliably informed that behind the scenes there had been a thaw, they do speak but aren't close. Their bust-ups tended to be dramatic, played out in public and the warring rivalry is something they try to manage in a reasonable, sustainable way. Life lived out in the public eye meant we'd see them take every available opportunity to slaughter each other across the media. The fights and the disagreements were real, I'm sure, but somewhere there would've been a professional decision to deliberately keep pushing and perpetuating the myth. They were two brothers with conflicting natures, fighting each other with the searing intensity, ferocity and ruthlessness of a drunk's chip-pan fire. One thing you have to admire is their honesty. They didn't make any attempts to dupe the public by pretending they were close. There were no attempts to show the public a united front in the face of a disagreement or argument. They played it out as it happened. No holds barred.

12

T in the Park

On 31 July 1994, Oasis headed for Hamilton, ten miles south-east of Glasgow, to play T in the Park. It's now part of rock folklore, holding its own as one of the band's best shows. It was. I was there. What isn't too well documented is how close Oasis came to missing the show. It has to be one of the most un-rock 'n' roll no-shows in history. Were they in jail after a drug bust? No. Did they drive a Rolls-Royce into a swimming pool? No. Did their private jet nosedive into a lake? No. None of these. The answer is that close to Carlisle, their van ceased to function: it became a dead van. The driver had filled it with the wrong fuel and it couldn't even be driven out of the forecourt. Thankfully, a friend of the band named Simon, also known as The Cat with the Hat, who I would later see introduce them at T in the Park, had brought loads of recreational pharmaceuticals to keep the band's spirits up.

They eventually made it to Hamilton and played a blinder of a set. Many words have been written about the band's T in the Park show in 1994 and I'm here to tell you, every single word is true. They had proved us all wrong by releasing two impressive singles, had a high-profile much talked about appearance on *The Word* under their belt, but it was the show at Hamilton that was fantastic, exceptional, stunning, glorious and outstanding.

They were full of confidence having returned from a brief visit to the USA. Noel modestly announced to those of us present in the Hamilton audience that they had played their best show to date at Wetlands in New York. Incidentally, on their return to London before heading to Scotland, they were booked into the infamous white-stucco Columbia hotel. There, they threw beer bottles out of the window and managed to hit a Mercedes belonging to the hotel manager, and thus Oasis entered the annals of rock 'n' roll miscreants, along with The Fall and The Mission, by being banned from the said establishment. No mean feat.

Since I last saw them, they'd signed to Creation, released 'Supersonic' and 'Shakermaker,' built up a substantial reputation in the music press and the hype around being the next saviours of rock 'n' roll was palpable as the release of *Definitely Maybe* beckoned. I still felt the music press's confidence was a bit misguided, especially the comparisons with The Beatles and the Sex Pistols and the band's aspirations to be mentioned in the same breath as the Stones and The Who. For me, Oasis were still possible candidates to take over from The Stone Roses and were, frankly, lucky to be viewed at that level; but then I saw them at Hamilton.

The tent was packed not only due to the excitement over the band but also because of a timely rain shower that saw hundreds run for cover. I had been there for a while. I was waiting close to the front, in the middle, there to see if Oasis had improved. I was watching, as if they were auditioning just for me. I was there to judge, to check their credentials. I saw the peculiar chap mentioned earlier, Simon, introduce them along the lines of being the greatest band in the world, while the band strolled onstage behind him and had to kick him off. This wasn't the same band I saw last May, was it? It couldn't be.

Oasis had the same mannerisms from the gig at King Tut's, physically they were the same shape and assumed the same positions on stage, but this version of the band had moved on from being over-rehearsed and nervous. They were relaxed, confident and happy.

I was impressed. The most noticeable development was their on-stage nonchalance. They had lost the anxiety. That may have been down to what Simon, that Cat with the Hat, had been doling out like sweets at a children's birthday party. Guigsy, Noel and Bonehead were stationary, but Liam was delighted to be there and uncharacteristically engaging with the crowd. From the opening chord, the band were supremely confident and had the T in the Park crowd – who were already always willing to be first to claim the band since they were 'found' and offered a deal (but not signed, please stop saying that) in Scotland by a Scotsman – eating out of the palms of their hands.

It's noticeable how many times the band played in Scotland over this period. They played at the Plaza in Glasgow on 2 December 1993 and returned eight days later, this time to the Cathouse supporting The Verve. In February, they played their show at the Sony Music Conference at Gleneagles in Perthshire to a room full of music executives. On 5, 6 and 7 April, they played three Scottish shows in Dundee, Edinburgh and Glasgow. At Dundee's Lucifer's Mill, Noel told the *Dundee Courier*'s Roddy Isles: 'We're the only working band in Manchester at the moment. We're not interested in recreating past glories, we're about now. Our record's the best thing that's been done in three years.' Seventy-four gig-goers showed up to see the band, paying £3 a ticket plus a 25p booking fee. They played Edinburgh's La Belle Angele (sadly destroyed in the Cowgate fire of 2002), then in Glasgow they played a show at the Tramway as part of Glasgow Sound City. On 12 and 13 June, they returned for two dates at Glasgow Cathouse. So between December and July, the T in the Park gig was their ninth Scottish show. They were playing other cities and building it up elsewhere too, but there was a keen Scottish focus.

Within seconds, the Hamilton crowd were up for it and you could sense something was happening; there was a powerful transformation. The band were in full cruise control, loud and impressive. They were also tighter musically and evidently enjoying themselves. It was one of those tipping points in the band's career. I've tried to analyse it but I think, ultimately, it was about timing and momentum; it was so palpable and obvious they were on the verge of breaking through. It's a well-worn cliché, but you needed to have been there. There was a positive energy, joyfulness and upbeat sense of exhilaration. And it was all intensified by a collective focus, everybody in the crowd and the band, we got it. We knew it was going to happen. The gig had an air of celebration. They were ready to take it on.

Until then I was scratching my head and wondering how a band that looked and sounded so average could get a record deal, but the Oasis set at T in the Park was about finally admitting how wrong I was. I was standing there smiling, buoyant, like everybody else in. They had done it. Oasis had made it. They were about to take off and were going to fly from here on in. I was proud of them. I was looking at the crowd. Loads of them were squealing at Liam; I mean, the others in the band were receiving plenty of adulation, but Liam was getting most of it. Truth is, to a man and woman, the crowd were going crazy.

When you detached yourself from the party and the

wondrous time going on around you, there was magic in the air. The band fed off the energy from the fans. The atmosphere and the interaction between the crowd and the band that afternoon was special. A few times throughout the gig I noticed Liam briefly look at Noel and, as both caught each other's smile, there was, dare I say it, an uncharacteristic look of modesty and bewilderment.

Underneath the machismo and the hard northern exterior, a few times in Hamilton in 1994 the band looked out at the crowd and seemed shocked and amazed: they must have realised this was going to be big. Stratospheric big. It was one of those moments, a connection: the crowd looked around at each other, then at the band, and they looked back and we knew. We all got it. This was it; every last person knew they were witnessing a significant moment. Was this take-off? Those moments don't happen much in life but when they do and you're around to witness them, you know it – and you make the most of it.

What makes it even more enjoyable is we now know how it turned out, the extraordinary highs and the bothersome lows, throughout their career. We also know that only a few hours before, they were stuck in Carlisle in an absurdly malfunctioning van, out of their face waiting on a lift. There's this spirit: we're going to make it to your town, where we'll fight your boys and shag your girls, and then move on and do it again. Oasis are getting into a van and playing in a town near you. It doesn't happen now. No iPhones or social media to share your plight. I can't imagine Coldplay's driver putting the wrong petrol in the van, the band getting wasted on powders, pills and joints, reaching a gig a few hours later and playing so well. And for that alone, they are probably the last great British rock 'n' roll band. Oasis dust themselves down, get up, get down and get on with the show.

Maybe there's something magical and poetic about the spirit of being young. That feeling of abandonment, of expression, of deciding to live life and realising it won't be this wonderful forever, so let's just enjoy ourselves. To have that freedom, to be carefree, on the road, out your face heading to play at the next venue and finding a van, any van, that will get you to the gig on time. I also remember, apart from Liam and Noel's eye contact and the smiles and the tightness, there was a brief moment on stage that day, a real, tangible visible point, when Noel put his foot on the accelerator and the Oasis monster truck boomed into turbo boost. In reality, it was only the effects pedal for his guitar, but he kicked it on and the party changed gear for the next thirty years.

All that, and their debut album wasn't even out yet.

This was the first T in the Park, and I remember Sharron, my girlfriend then, now my wife, driving over to Hamilton out of curiosity and we were able to drive right in. On our approach, we could hear the bands from miles away. We parked and I waved to a tech I knew, who beckoned us over and let us in. The first band we saw were Sharron's favourites, Pulp. Over the weekend, all these acts were playing on our doorstep: Teenage Fanclub, Primal Scream, Blur, Del Amitri, Manic Street Preachers, Grant Lee Buffalo and, of course, Oasis. On the Sunday we decided to go over again. I saw someone I knew doing security and he held back the fencing and invited us in like we were at a secret party. It's another example of how unique a time it was for music fans. Imagine walking up to a festival now and a friendly security guard letting you in.

Oasis will have played better and more important gigs than this one, but for those present who witnessed the show, it all made sense. It came into clear focus: there was no doubt Oasis were going to be serious players. T in the Park is when we knew the band were becoming unstoppable.

13

King Tut's 31.5.93 (Part 3)

As well as allegedly showing up unannounced and threatening to wreck the place, much is often made in many acclaimed books on the band of the alleged fact that Oasis didn't have any gear and how they didn't even have a mic stand. Poor Liam had to make do with singing with the mic in his hand. But there were mic stands, Liam had one, and King Tut's has its own in-house PA, monitors and on-stage set-up. Liam took the mic from the stand as if to say this is my instrument; I remember thinking he held the mic in the same confident manner as Ian Brown of the Stone Roses, swaying the flex to the beat. This was before he started his trademark pose with his hands behind his back, looking as if he was aggressively challenging the mic and maybe the audience to a fight.

When bands play King Tut's on multiple-band bills, the groups bring their own equipment. At the soundchecks, the best gear is usually selected from each of the bands and, unless they're a bit precious about their equipment, bands get together, muck in and share backline. The best drum kit is selected and drummers use their own snares and cymbals and maybe change to their preferred bass drum pedal. Most of the amps and equipment used that night belonged to Boyfriend, and I know them well enough to confirm they were generous with their equipment. (When we played a show together in

Bellshill I broke not one but two of their Vox AC30 amps and Stephen Jollie of the band returned with another one.) They also shortened their set to allow Oasis to play.

I knew the guitarist of 18 Wheeler, David Keenan, another Airdrie man and a familiar face from our local pub, the Staging Post. He always impressed with his MC5 haircut, superb chat and encyclopaedic knowledge of music, as well as his fondness for a Marshall stack. David had formed 18 Wheeler before leaving to form Telstar Ponies. It was no surprise, given his musical intellect and energy, that he went on to become a critic and then an author of some repute. So, I can confirm that between both bands, Oasis were well looked after regarding amps and gear.

While I'm upstairs, I see Alan McGee chatting to Oasis soundman Mark Coyle (who I always thought was a dead ringer for Johnny Vaughan). Coyle looks animated and is heatedly pointing and explaining what's going on. Meanwhile, DD explained to both Ross and me what was going on. Boyfriend had played shows with Afghan Whigs in Manchester and had met and got on with Sister Lovers. They were keen to come to play in Glasgow and Boyfriend had therefore invited them to play King Tut's in May.

Sister Lovers shared a rehearsal space with Oasis, and Debbie Turner (now Ellis) had said to them they were playing a gig at King Tut's and that they should jump up too. Mark Coyle was now working with Noel and Oasis. He was mates with Boyfriend's bass player Mark McAvoy and asked if it was OK if Oasis could drive up and squeeze on the bill. Boyfriend said yes, go for it. But then they forgot all about it.

When these significant moments in musical history occur, some detective work is required. I always wanted to know how Sister Lovers and Oasis shared the Boardwalk rehearsal rooms.

'It was Liam who asked us to share the practice room with them,' confirmed Debbie Ellis. 'They were already in there. I think they got the practice room when Noel joined. It seems like a bit of a Noel move to go to the Boardwalk as he knew everyone there.'

I asked when she first met Liam and Noel. 'I met Liam in the pub in 1990 but I knew Noel from going to gigs and the Haçienda but I didn't know Liam was his brother. My friend Lorraine and I worked in a pub in Cheadle Hulme, where I'm originally from and she really fancied Liam.' Debbie bursts into laughter. 'It's hilarious thinking about it now, I bought him a red rose, one of those plastic ones they sell in pubs for a quid. I went over to him with it and my boyfriend at the time had a trainer shop and was into cool trainers and Liam clocked the ones I was wearing. So we were all quite friendly and got on well.'

Both Coyle and McAvoy worked for Teenage Fanclub on tours of the United States, Europe and the UK and they had been roommates; Coyle had done front-of-house, that's the guy who controls the mix for the audience, and McAvoy had been Teenage Fanclub's guitar tech. So they knew each other well. This familiarity could be part of the breakdown in communications. Maybe the Marks were to blame! McAvoy had said to Coyle it was cool for Oasis to come up. And so this was why we have the fraught atmosphere with the angry mob from Manchester, who think they're supposed to be playing.

The way it was reported to me, it felt more like an oversight; it was on Sister Lovers for forgetting to remind Boyfriend that Oasis were coming up. This and the fact that the venue were a bit stubborn at first, as no one had spoken to them about a fourth band playing, thereby adding to the mix-up. I'm guessing Boyfriend were scratching their heads and thinking, it's true what they say, *no good deed goes unpunished*. However, for some weird reason, Boyfriend and Sister Lovers are perhaps responsible for the Oasis phenomenon.

Meanwhile, as Oasis and their mates were arguing and becoming ever more hostile, it was then that the venue's gig manager Ali Murdoch decided to call his boss in Edinburgh and see what he could do for them. Alan McGee was still talking to Coyle and both walked upstairs, to the dressing room to make sure there was no aggro. That's what DD told us on the night and this matches what McGee has subsequently said in interviews over the years. DD explained that Boyfriend and Sister Lovers both offered to play shorter sets to let Oasis play but the venue were a bit pissed off. Not so much at a band showing up unannounced, but their attitude. They made a stance, stood by it and demanded that the lads from Manchester get twenty minutes stage time.

The truth is maybe pitched between both camps: the calm King Tut's version of events and the aggro-filled rewrite later, cleverly adapted and adopted by Creation. I know it did get tense and didn't need to be. Equally, this was another moment that McGee would see Liam, the band and their mates and witness something in his manner and style he loved – and this was all before a note was sung. Though, as we've seen, at this point, McGee didn't know the cool guy in the middle of it all was the singer. He'd assumed he was the dealer.

So, to recap, Oasis showed up, but the venue didn't know they were coming. Then the Oasis camp made a stance. King Tut's have always remained consistent about their initial reticence on the night: it was about budget. Whoever is doing the sound is paid per band, so the fact Oasis had Coyle doing their sound perhaps helped their cause. Ultimately, a solution was reached, those involved were happy and history was made.

Oasis fans everywhere should be grateful to King Tut's, but also to the generosity of the other bands on the bill for letting them play a gig that would change their lives forever. Despite many later claiming to have been present, very few were there that night in King Tut's. Still, by 1996, Oasis were playing a gig at Loch Lomond in front of 80,000 people.

14

Promo, Football & Northern Soul

The promotion of *Definitely Maybe* was hampered by a meagre marketing budget, and reflected Sony's frustration towards Creation at the time. It got so tense that in June 1994, the label was nearly closed down. A compromise was reached, but Creation had to make some of their twenty-one staff redundant and lose at least half a dozen artists. Lists were made and the axe fell.

The financial restraints placed on Creation through the £2 million debt owed to Sony meant Tim Abbot had a meagre £60,000 to spend on one of the most eagerly anticipated albums in years. To put this in perspective, Oasis were up against *The Three Tenors in Concert 1994* and their marketing spend was £950,000, including a full TV campaign. (Their previous album had sold over 13 million.) Creation were forced to think creatively to compete with the Warner Classics-owned Teldec sales budget. Abbot had to apply a more imaginative strategy. The first three releases – 'Supersonic' (number 31), 'Shakermaker' (number 11) and 'Live Forever' (number 10) – were a statement of intent and a powerful introduction to the band.

Marcus Russell's idea to have the band constantly out on small tours across the UK, embracing the towns and cities but deliberately avoiding London, was reaping its reward. When sales figures came in for *Definitely Maybe* the provincial towns the band had played and kept returning to were buying the album in their droves.

Due to marketing budget restrictions and knowing the dance and rave scene loved listening to Oasis after a night of heavy clubbing, Abbot started advertising in the lads' mag market. The band and clubbers shared a love of hedonism, attitude and positivity. They proved the perfect listen while acclimatising to the drudgery of the 9 to 5 and preparing to face the boss on Monday morning. The band were a surprisingly fitting post-night-out soundtrack and made sense when played loud on the drive home. Abbot also advertised the album in DJ mags. In *Mixmag* the album famously received a fantastic five-star review. Noel was no stranger to rave culture and believed that if 'Live Forever' was a hit then the dance scene would embrace the euphoric exhilaration and the joyous elation behind the record. It was, undoubtedly, another clever move by Creation.

There was also the fashion tie-in. Abbot knew a huge swathe of the Oasis fan base were in the stands or terraces. They tuned into their football casual look. Abbot famously quipped that the band 'looked like a firm of hoolies on an away day'. So why not buy into that? The look had become widespread among football fans since the 1980s. Labels like Pringle, Ralph Lauren, Lyle & Scott, Lacoste, Sergio Tacchini, Ellesse, Fila, Lois jeans and cords with Clark Originals, Hush Puppies or Adidas Forest Hills. There was also a strong Fred Perry, Mod aspect to it. This style evolved at least in part through the rave and acid-house scene. Somewhere in that melting pot of partying, fashion and street cool is the look Oasis walked on stage with.

It was a marketing masterstroke. Not only were indie fans and the usual *NME*, *Melody Maker*, *Q* and *Select* pop fans getting what Oasis were about, but now the lads' mag market was targeted. Football and music had merged into an ad man's wet dream. This marked another creative evolution of a scene. Shows like Sky's *Soccer AM* became as important as appearances on *Top of the Pops* or *The Word*. It's interesting to note how this tied in with the band's attitude towards the Union Flag.

In April 1993, *Select* magazine did a 'Yanks Go Home' Special. Brett Anderson of Suede appeared on the cover with a Union Flag in the background. That edition featured bands like The Auteurs, Denim, Pulp and Saint Etienne, among others. *Select*, now defunct, was adept at covering Britpop, a term coined or at least dusted down and resurrected by Stuart Maconie. So it wasn't so much about revolution, but evolution, as bands moved towards taking visible pride in UK culture, music and art. The economy was finally improving by the latter part of 1993 and headed into 1994 with growing optimism.

Bands had to be careful when referring to and talking about Britpop; yes, it was cool to believe in Great Britain, but you couldn't be associated with the negative connotations of the Union Flag. Nationalism was frowned upon. It was always a gamble for any band adorning themselves in such Britishness or, more precisely, such Englishness. The perception was that it was indicative of right-wing – indeed, far-right – beliefs. And the significance of the Union Flag had been hijacked, and the flag of St George distorted by the neo-Nazi tendencies of some skinhead factions.

Oasis had an innate insight, a working-class bravado and confidence and were determined to reclaim the flag's posi-tivity. They maybe didn't have the intellect of some of their contemporaries, but Abbot shrewdly leveraged their belief and spirit in the concept of the flag. The same one adorned by gold-winning black Olympians. The flag The Beatles, the Rolling Stones and The Who stood under when they hit America in the 1960s. Oasis firmly, if at times naively, believed they could win back the flag from the bigots and racists. The artwork of their original demo had a distorted flag swirling down the toilet. It was a clumsy but heartfelt metaphor of a decaying, lost, directionless Great Britain, which was genuinely going down the tubes for many working-class towns and cities.

Creation and their management must have been worried. Here were a band whose mission statement was: we are going to behave like a band, and yes we are about sex and drugs and rock 'n' roll. Now they wanted to talk about winning back the Union Flag. This attitude felt out of step in the context of bands who embraced the underground indie scene and the network of influential labels and fanzines; they were arty, intellectual, a million miles away from the unthinking nationalism of flag-waving. For Oasis, though, it was a case of let's be happy to be alive, let's party, let's listen to some loud, joyous rock 'n' roll, take some E, fall in love every night, get loaded, get pissed . . . destroy.

Meanwhile back with Domingo, Pavarotti and Carreras, both Oasis and The Three Tenors were big football fans. While the Tenors loved the nuanced intricacies of the beautiful game, Oasis loved the speed, booze and away-day scraps. This was a band football supporters loved, so why not focus the marketing on this angle? The football demographic had opened up with the game at its 1990s peak. Suddenly, everyone loved football, aided and abetted by the fashion, the cash, the confidence and the drugs. Oasis wanted to be footballers and footballers wanted to be Oasis.

Any socioeconomic study of the band's popularity pointed

to cities passionate about music and football. Cities like Glasgow, Manchester, Liverpool, Sheffield, Newcastle, London, Rome, Paris, Madrid, Barcelona, Buenos Aires, São Paulo and Rio. Don't forget the timing. This was the post-Kurt Cobain era. Music fans wanted to enjoy and take pleasure from music again. Oasis brought that Happy Mondays, Stone Roses and Primal Scream party strut, but also had songs that sounded like The Kinks and The Who. There was an overlap of music and sensibility, which gave them a broad appeal. Indie kids felt it was OK to like them. They were on Creation after all.

Around this time, we had another development. In the mid-1990s, thanks to *Loaded* magazine, we had the advent of ladettes. Katie Puckrik flipped lad culture on its head when she coined the term. She was being funny, smart, ironic, sexy, opinionated, and celebrating feminism differently. It seemed a bit of fun then, but as the years passed, it proved more like a masterclass on Greek comedy from Aristophanes. The media took it on. Keeping it real. We had Zoe Ball, Sara Cox and Denise van Outen, amongst many others – all sharp and clever women who lived and loved life. Sisters were doing it for themselves and keeping up with the men, proving they could party just as hard. They wanted to get drunk and be loud and flip traditional gender roles on their head. And, of course, this suited Creation to a tee; there were always women at their gigs, but Oasis were, at least initially, regarded as more for the lads.

But what made them take off, and connect and become this unbelievable rock 'n' roll band? It could be Noel's songwriting. It could be Liam's at times plaintive and then sneering voice. There was another factor and that was definitely football. If you look at early or mid-career photos of Oasis they are dressed like football casuals. One of the biggest marketing strategies, which brought Oasis a broader popularity, was targeting the football audience. It was now football's turn to be the new rock 'n' roll. It was always deemed a bit uncool to be in a band, be lauded by the music press, but at the same time claim to support a football team. Before Oasis, the musical publications featured cool New York anti-jock art school bands. You quoted arthouse movies, the latest underground independent Brooklyn bands; the idea of rock 'n' roll cliché and boisterous, juvenile sexism was deeply uncool. They might have been up to all the fun stuff in the background but would never openly admit it. Now Oasis were going on about Man City's desperate need to sign a top international centre-half or a thirty-goal-a-season striker. They were claiming most bands were shite apart from them, and embracing the usual rock 'n' roll textbook of behaviour: drugs, girls and throwing TVs – and independent sensibility – from hotel windows.

Again, this peculiar, uncouth and vulgar outlook had to be put into context. In the music press, during interviews, indie acts were about subverting the cliché. The mess of rock 'n' roll excess was frowned upon; that's what airhead jock MTV hairspray bands did, and it was jaded, vacuous and worn out. True indie sensibility was the way forward now, not only in music but in books, film and art. Bands were more likely to leave a hotel room in better condition than they found it and the thought of throwing a TV out of a hotel window was a hideous, old-fashioned anomaly. For many of these bands, not being rock 'n' roll was the new rock 'n' roll. Now the worst excess was forgetting to place a coaster on the bedside table and leaving a ring on it from your hot Horlicks. Rock 'n' roll had become safe – far too serene and well-mannered. But Oasis interviews would always throw up some drama or a fight. Stories of their wildness would emerge in the tabloid press.

They gained even more prominence because they lived up to and embraced the clichéd spirit of rock 'n' roll.

There's long been a direct correlation between working-class towns and cities, football and music. Footballers are highly paid and popular; they are mostly working-class people living the dream, or at least they used to be. Just look at the 'El Beatle' lifestyle and superstar status of George Best in the late 1960s. In the 1970s, when football fans from the north took buses and trains down to away games in London there was one record store they loved to frequent, and it was called Soul City. The actual phrase 'Northern Soul' is credited to the journalist Dave Godin, who first publicly used it in his *Blues and Soul* column in June 1970. Godin explained to Chris Hunt in a 2002 interview with *Mojo* magazine that he came up with the term in 1968 to help staff in his Covent Garden record shop differentiate between the harder-edged, more backbeat-driven records and the less polished, smoother, Motown-influenced ones. Godin had noticed the away-day fans from the north preferred a distinct soul sound. 'I devised the name as a shorthand sales term. It was just to say, "If you've got customers from the north, don't waste time playing them records currently in the US black chart, just play them what they like: northern soul."' So, this is just one small example of how football and music are inextricably linked and part of our cultural history. Whether that's Luciano Pavarotti popularising 'Nessun Dorma' from Puccini's Turandot for the 1990 Italian World Cup to Handel's 'Zadok The Priest' for the UEFA Champions League anthem. From 'Sunshine On Leith' by the Proclaimers, 'You'll Never Walk Alone' by Gerry and the Pacemakers, to 'Seven Nation Army' by the White Stripes. There's a book or a podcast in the cultural connection between music and football.

You could imagine Tim Abbot sensing rock 'n' roll plus football anthems equals stadium rock. So, we have Abbot attempting to work miracles with a comparatively meagre marketing spend. He was incorporating dance magazines, emphasising the band's love of football, using their love of British bands from the 1960s and attempting to ease their new articulation of Britishness into a cool, branded campaign. The interviews with the fights, the attitude, the clothes, the look, the sound, it was all coming straight from the street. This swagger and confidence reflected their attitude and merged seamlessly into the whole Britpop phenomenon.

McGee, Russell and Abbot could be trying everything imaginable with their strategy and marketing plans, reaching for anything within their powers, but the most important element of the Oasis story wasn't as tangible or as easily pinned down. It can't be quantified but it's as essential in rock 'n' roll as it is in life: timing. When revisiting some intensive day-to-day analysis from the period (again, sorry, from King Tut's to Knebworth), it is apparent Ignition and Creation are perfectly operating the levers. It could be as simple as McGee's ambition to jump in and steal sales from a latent Stone Roses. You also get a sense from the minute the band emerged from the wings that momentum was building, that there was an urgency to capture the zeitgeist and throttle the public. More significantly, you see how expertly they were managed through the first two albums and the singles − if they'd dawdled around at any point, they would've missed this brief window to launch the band. It feels like they swaggered onto the scene at precisely the perfect moment for positive, upbeat, loud, British pop and rock. The country was ready for an album that sounded like *Definitely Maybe*.

15

Definitely Maybe, Review,
Impact & Aftermath

Definitely Maybe was released on Tuesday 30 August 1994. The day after a Bank Holiday Monday. (Their career thus far seems blessed by Holiday Mondays.) It's fitting that fans had to wait an extra day for an album that became as quintessentially British as a sunny Bank Holiday afternoon, a bacon buttie spiced up with HP Sauce and a Mod rally convoy of Vespas on the road to Brighton. It's a puzzling build-up, though; there's so much anticipation. There's an eagerness and, again, I'm concerned. Why? I realise I have a peculiar relationship with Oasis. I know them well, but they don't know me. It always goes back to that evening in King Tut's. I thought they were ordinary. They were loud. They were staggeringly average and – one of my least favourite adjectives, though I seem to use it a lot about them – workmanlike. The album did not immediately grab me. It was not a record that would transform into an epoch-making moment in popular culture, but over time it has evolved into one. And, honestly, I'm happier than anyone it turned out that way.

Most sections of the music press and the wider media have always been ridiculously snobbish in their attitude towards Oasis, which I always felt was unwarranted. Unlike other groups, they were rarely reviewed in an impartial, balanced way. From the start, most reviews or features about them referred to their working-class background, blethered on about how their songs were dumb and so were they. Their fans were louts who shopped in Top Man and lived in sprawling housing estates; some even walked around with devil dogs. It's clear their popularity triggered this disdain. The Oasis strategy and approach, and by that I mean what defined them, their sound, their attitude and their look, lacked subtlety, sure, but the songs and the spirit quickly attracted vast swathes of people to the cause.

Even today, in 2025, when you speak to people and ask what they think about the band, Oasis continue to split opinion. The response is either one of anger, scorn or sheer unadulterated joy. Those who just got it and loved the band and those who have never taken to them. In 1994, it was the same; many fans loved Oasis but loads did not get it. The music journalists always preferred Blur. They were the sharp, clever band and Oasis were the northern hooligans. Blur were cool, hip and read books; they had taste and a bit of savoir-faire. Oasis might not be as 'intellectual' as Blur, but they created songs that genuinely connected with millions of ordinary people. Songs that have kept *Definitely Maybe* in its rightful place as a generation-defining classic album.

By now, then, the press and media (at least those who are into the band) and the fans are buying into the rock 'n' roll attitude. They get the tough, northern, come-and-have-a-go positioning and the controversy of the gigs, intensified with drink, drugs and violence. Despite Creation and their management reining it in with a deliberate build up, the album is released and is eventually regarded as one of the most lauded debuts since the Sex Pistols unleashed *Never Mind The Bollocks* in 1977.

I always liked the idea that Marcus Russell was at Lord's on 4 September 1994 trying to watch the NatWest Trophy final when he heard the album had reached Number 1. (Worcestershire beat Warwickshire by eight wickets.) After the concerns of the original sessions with Dave Batchelor, then Noel's sessions with live sound engineer, Mark Coyle, through to Owen Morris's production and engineering, they finally got there. As we've seen, they managed to capture the essence of the band by transferring that live energy into a loud, vibrant record. There was no doubting Oasis had outstanding songs ready to let loose upon the world. What they needed were people who shared and understood their musical vision; Coyle and later Morris got the message. Make it sound big, make it sound forceful, make it sound live.

Here's the plan. Go and get your copy of *Definitely Maybe* right now. We're going to listen to the album as if it's our first time. I know it's unusual to listen to something cold but focus and listen as if you haven't heard or seen the album before. Listen with a fresh ear. Try to pick up on the references and influences. Look at the cover and the photo of Bonehead's Didsbury flat with its wooden floorboards and trio of high windows, the inflatable flamingo above the fire. Those pictures of their heroes: Rodney Marsh and Burt Bacharach. Even George Best is allowed in, despite playing for Man United (he transcends football rivalries, and Bonehead is a United fan, after all). The TV has a still of Eli Wallach and Antonio Casale from *The Good, the Bad and the Ugly*. The other side of the sleeve has *A Fistful of Dollars* actor Gian Maria Volonté. Your first introduction to any band is the album sleeve. Oasis know this and the image encapsulates the whole Oasis project.

It's meticulously planned, right down to all those influences and references on the cover, yet it's made to look random as if they're hanging around waiting on a taxi. (And, it has to be said, the pared-back, curated aesthetic with its plants and quiet moodiness feels contemporary too; it's Insta-worthy. And here's something else for the fanoraks: Liam's red wine is in fact, Ribena.)

Listening with a fresh ear to an album whose songs have become so popular is worth the effort. It's both the immediacy and energy of *Definitely Maybe* that grab you. The inevitable nostalgia and passage of time three decades on from its recording have added memories, yet the overall emotion is one that celebrates ordinary guys with a powerful sound that became an evocative soundtrack of the 1990s. It's direct and clear, and one of its unexpected qualities is the brilliance of its ordinariness. That's why it resonates. The clarity of the message. A prerequisite of a hit single and a classic song — apart from the immediate hook — is that you think you've heard it before. Something noticeable within the Oasis formula is that sense of familiarity. What's that melody? Noel Gallagher has a fine ear for taking a classic pop tune and turning it into his own. That doesn't mean he's stealing any more than Paul McCartney would have been with a Mozart melody swirling around his head, rearranging the notes and producing another hit. Noel is listening and if he loves an intricate or clever part in a song, a melody, a chord change, or even a line, he has the instinctive songwriting ability to work it out, take it in, spin it around in his head and bring it out sounding like an Oasis song.

'Rock 'n' Roll Star' is a fitting opener to the album and a song that in anyone else's hands would be considered arrogant self-aggrandisement. But for Oasis it's a clarion call. They spoke to so many people across the board. The posties, the teachers, accountants, lawyers, car mechanics, builders and electricians. More importantly, they spoke to those people who hated their jobs and lived for the weekend. Again, it's part of the connection. Oasis had this aura, and people believed in them. Their songs spoke directly to them. Oasis weren't living the dream; they were sharing it. On Noel's songwriting, Debbie Ellis believes his songs are unique because they are universal and there's a clarity. It's the simplicity that no one can quite figure out. 'I think they're brilliant. The thing is with Noel – and people could do studies on it – what he's got musically is so simplistic, but that's why he's got this massive appeal to everyone on the street, whether it's in this country or fucking Argentina. There's something in what he does that works. It's the same connection. And I don't know what he does. I can't put my finger on it. People just relate to him and the songs.'

'Rock 'n' Roll Star' has this intensity and confidence, a powerful energy, arrogance, excitement and conceit. It's a perfect start, a yardstick for what would eventually take hold with the album and their career. Oasis sing about escaping the everyday banality of the city. Their message is about daring to dream, it's a collective hope; they sing for ordinary people who can't believe they have found this band who speak for them, who play such loud, magnificent tunes and, better still, who know how to party. They set up the story. They are up there with the stars. It's not rocket science; it's loud, magnificent pop. This band doesn't do subtlety. They play. You listen. It sets the Oasis prototype, full of riffs, outstanding harmonies, loud vocals, a swirling yet controlled barrage and a killer chorus. I always felt the outro was a bit messy but, given that, a cracking start as Oasis gate-crash the party in true Mancunian style.

To some extent, 'Shakermaker' became overshadowed by the controversy around 'I'd Like To Teach The World To Sing'. The band had to pay $500,000 in damages after Coca-Cola sued for the song's similarity to 'I'd Like To Teach The World To Sing (In Perfect Harmony)', which featured in a Coke TV advert. Pesky Noel, when pushed on the damages, famously quipped: 'Now we only drink Pepsi.' It's a pity because the second single is a well-structured pop song from start to finish. It has a marvellous middle-eight, a fantastic chorus and a magic melody; a better outro than 'Rock 'n' Roll Star' and it's a phenomenal song.

There's plenty of lofty, academic criticism over its lyrical simplicity, but pop music is supposed to be about your life. Noel mentions the stuff that's strewn around him or talks about TV characters from when he was a kid – Mr Benn, for example, is a children's TV character from the early 1970s. Mr Soft was an advert for mints with the song sung by Cockney Rebel, and 'Mr. Clean' was a song by The Jam. We even have a fleeting mention of his favourite record shop, Sifters in Withington. Noel later explained Johnny Marr was pushing him to write and record some material in his home studio and Noel hadn't come up with anything. On the way to his house, the car stopped at traffic lights near Sifters Records and the line in the song came to him. It's pop music, it's disposable and it is near perfection. A Shaker Maker was a 1970s figure-making toy where you mixed water and powder into a mould and shook it and as if by magic . . . no, that was Mr Benn.

'Live Forever' is the song most people who have ever been involved in bands wished they could come close to writing. It's such a simple song and most artists wondered, why didn't I think of that? And if you didn't think like that, then you shouldn't be in a band. It's also reflective and well-structured and is arguably Noel Gallagher's finest moment. It was written in 1991 and was first played that night at Noel's flat to Liam, Guigsy and Bonehead when they wanted him to join the band.

Noel takes the standard *us versus them* slant, speaking directly to the fans, *we know and they're scared of us because we know*. It only got to number 10; unfortunately, it was up against 'Love Is All Around' by Wet Wet Wet, which was number 1 for fifteen painful weeks. They were dethroned for another four weeks by that epoch-making moment in pop history, Danish-born Italian Eurodance act Whigfield's 'Saturday Night'. I suppose fashion and style are temporary, but class is permanent. 'Live Forever' became a scene changer. If they hadn't done so by now, people were waking up to the band. 'Live Forever' is by far the stand-out track on the album. I still can't envisage the band I stood in front of in 1993 writing, performing and producing a song as exceptional as that. From the opening floor tom and ride cymbal to Liam's fantastic vocal to the romantic sentiment. It's an extraordinary collective effort.

On the subject of the intro and the drumming, and knowing what lay ahead for Tony McCarroll, it's a shame he wasn't given the chance to develop and improve. The drumming may not be Keith Moon or John Bonham, but it's undoubtedly part of the Oasis sound. Anyone close to the Oasis camp who is willing to talk will tell you the treatment of McCarroll was vicious. It says a lot for the drummer's doggedness that he prolonged his stay, especially with Noel so eager to jettison him from the band.

In any band, when the initial line-up changes, the group's sound alters. As soon as the drummer was changed, despite claims the band needed a more technical player, something of the spirit and the directness of the sound was lost. Like the best bands – I'm thinking here of Nirvana, the Sex Pistols and the Ramones – the cloud of anger hanging over the band and the fact it could explode at any time was an integral part of the appeal. I'm not alone in thinking McCarroll's drumming style suited the band. The band's producer Owen Morris agrees. Speaking to *Q* magazine in 2010, when discussing the recording of *Definitely Maybe*, Morris said: 'Tony's drumming was a big part of the Oasis sound to me, I loved Tony's drumming. It was simple, certainly, but his timing was immaculate and he hit the shit out of them. Tony's simple patterns allowed the space for Bonehead's strumming rhythm guitar playing to work. "Live Forever" is a wonderful song and will in time, be viewed and judged as their "Ticket To Ride".'

Again, it was the first casualty in the Oasis story, McCarroll, who is the star of 'Up In The Sky', playing nice and loose to Liam's fabulous vocal rendition. The riff is effortless; Neil Young meets REM's Peter Buck. The original song had backwards guitar and was more like a psychedelic tribute to The Beatles, but it wasn't in keeping with the sound of the rest of the album so they did it straight, as it were.

From the feedback at the beginning, 'Columbia' grabs you. It was released as a limited-edition promo and there's a brooding menace and edge throughout it. It's rarely focused upon, but I always think it's a key moment in 1990s pop history. You can hear they still have that Manchester scene dance influence but there's also a harsh electric edge and change towards what became Britpop. Dylan goes from folk to electric; on 'Columbia' Oasis switch from Happy Mondays/ Madchester to Britpop under our noses. Listen again. There are so many guitars going on but one particular line is so hypnotic it sounds like a disco soul vocal refrain. Noel has mentioned on many occasions that they were out of their faces when they recorded it, which might hint at the spirit of the Haçienda hanging over proceedings.

We have the debut single, 'Supersonic', released on 11 April 1994 which made it to the lofty heights of number 31 in the UK singles charts. This was recorded in the Pink Museum in Liverpool and the demo they recorded was of such superior quality that they used it. The song has a weird quality that gives it an unforgettable self-assurance. Technically, the beat is slightly slower than it should be yet it works and heightens the aggression. It kicks off with Tony McCarroll, then into Noel and Bonehead's Oasis wall of sound, full of reverb and heavy hooks. It's potent, it's funny, it's cool, and it is just what pop music should be. If Oasis could do a perfect bubblegum pop version of themselves then this was it. In case there are any Oasis fans left in the world who don't know it yet: Elsa was an overweight Rottweiler that kept on farting.

'Bring It On Down' sees Bonehead and Noel Gallagher head towards Rolling Stones territory with some fantastic axe interaction. Alan McGee wanted this to be the band's debut single. It was the first song they played at King Tut's. It's a soundscape of meshed feedback and rock 'n' roll, what's your problem with that? Amid the confusion and studio effects, like the trickery on Liam's voice, there lurks a song somewhere.

'Cigarettes & Alcohol' is bluesy in the way Led Zeppelin are bluesy. If Led Zep were inspired by Robert Johnson, Noel would have been inspired by T. Rex. Sometimes the simplest riffs are in front of you and it takes a skilled writer to realise that and make them their own. 'Cigarettes & Alcohol' was adopted by many as a hedonistic anthem for 1990s lad culture. The lyrics also contain a blatant reference to cocaine that the censors missed. If Led Zep dug the Delta blues, Oasis are there to dig the Burnage blues.

That 'Digsy's Dinner' finds its way onto this album tells you more about Noel's eye as a songwriter than anything else. Written about his hilarious mate, from the band Smaller, Digsy was a cousin of the guys from The Real People and found infamy when Noel picked up on his peculiarities. While jamming through a song, Noel played drums and Digsy shouted 'lasagne!' for most of the evening. Like the best writers, Noel took the minutiae and expanded it. The eye of an artist or a writer recognises inspiration is everywhere, the art is in the details. Not as accomplished or celebrated as some of the B-sides thus far but definitely up there in its magic and warmth. Listen out for Bonehead playing the piano, but only the white keys, fun and dollops of kitchen-sink northern humour. Yet again one the fans love, thanks to its quirkiness. In an *NME* interview in 2015, Alan McGee declared 'Digsy's Dinner' a piss-take at Blur, with Noel proving he could rattle out a 'Blur-like' song at the drop of a hat. When you listen knowing that it does make sense.

'Slide Away' is another live favourite, a cavernous, swirling anthem, well arranged with an outstanding solo and, like most of Noel's best songs to date, despite being written to share with thousands in a field somewhere like Knebworth, it is deeply personal and filled with imagery of walking off into the sunset. It's six minutes and thirty-three seconds of brilliance. It was written after Noel and Bonehead had a serious falling-out.

'Married With Children' closes one of the most successful debut albums in history in an upbeat style. A song that sounds like a Sunday afternoon jam in a bedroom. It's most memorable for a throwaway line by an ex-girlfriend who wasn't too keen on Noel's books, friends or the songs he was trying to write.

It also has a similar resonance to one of his favourite bands, The La's.

So there we have it, the main men, the brothers in arms, the siblings with the attitude and the eyebrows may have got the glory. But what about the others? Guigsy was always around if not playing on the album, then there for support and laughs. Tony appeared to be Noel's whipping boy and wasn't one for taking it from the boss. If you had to pick one guy every band needs it was Bonehead. A sounding board, adaptable, willing to graft, someone who understood the group dynamic. He was solid and dependable, like a holding midfielder who the fans love because they recognise and appreciate his efforts; he does the important but unglamorous groundwork to let the others shine. He deserves praise. (He also started it all with The Rain, bringing in Liam and encouraging him to bring in Noel.)

In 1995, while on tour in the US, Guigsy left the tour, ill from exhaustion. Replacement Scott McLeod was drafted in but quickly left. It was Bonehead who stepped in to play bass, including for their second appearance on *The Late Show with David Letterman* – a respectable performance of 'Morning Glory' though not as immense as their debut on the same show with 'Live Forever'.

Definitely Maybe has a distinct sound, one of a band playing live. It's a celebration, a compendium of the best bits of the last forty years of rock 'n' roll. Academics and experts endlessly over-analyse what made Oasis turn into such a phenomenon. The American essayist Susan Sontag, also known as 'The Dark Lady of American Letters', wrote *Against Interpretation* in which, to boil it down, she suggests critics spend so much time analysing art that they can't ever enjoy it. That is true in the case of Oasis. Stop working out what that riff is, or where those melodies come from, and enjoy the trip.

What needs to be stressed here is the timeframe and the way Oasis were perceived when *Definitely Maybe* came out. The album is lauded now but on release, despite the quality of the music they delivered, the critics were still unsure. For Oasis, though, it was the fans who were the real barometer and thankfully they got it, even if loads of music critics didn't. They criticised their music and lyrics, arguing they were too old-fashioned and formulaic, doing more for The New Seekers and T. Rex than they did for themselves. They refused to accept that pop music and especially guitar bands were the way forward, especially northern ones with an attitude whose songs were allegedly so derivative and the band not up to much. It was frowned upon when Noel argued back saying, yes, his songs were about three things: drinking, shagging and taking drugs. When we play Oasis now, they still have a collective resonance. Their work stands the test of time. Noel's songwriting elevated them to another league. One where they were mentioned in the upper echelons, with the best bands of all time, and the brilliant thing is, it's a place Noel undoubtedly believed he and the band deserved to be.

Oasis had this uncompromising attitude; they wanted to produce songs that sounded glorious on the radio, at a party and in a muddy field at a festival. They appealed to the millions who said *fuck this, let's go and get drunk*. It may not sound like the most nuanced of explanations, but music should be about the primal things. Enjoying yourself, living your life, some excitement, listening to The Dead Kennedys, the Ramones and the *Official Soundtrack to Bugsy Malone*, loud. It doesn't always have to be insular, about listening to Nick Drake in the dark, though given the correct frame of mind that's cool too. A broken heart can be mended in many ways. The tender way and the loud way. An Oasis audience is not there for subtle, artistic nuance. They want to scream. To bleed. The band connected with that. On *Definitely Maybe* many felt they were hopeful, optimistic. They weren't. Theirs was a world of defiance. A struggle. A sneering call to arms via the Gibson Les Paul.

I would say that, along with the first five songs on Nirvana's *Nevermind*, *Definitely Maybe* probably has the best opening to an album in the last thirty years. If only 'Supersonic' and 'Cigarettes & Alcohol' were tracks four and five they could've smashed it in sensational style. But don't listen to me. Remember, I thought they should have been locked up for murdering 'I Am The Walrus'.

From Elvis to Susan Boyle, two musical performers you've seldom heard together in a sentence, it's about one thing and that's selling to the masses. You have a hit when you open it up across the board, into the mainstream and the majority of people want to buy it. That's when you sell by the bucketload and make it big. Oasis were identifiable to so many people because they sounded like so many brilliant British bands. Journalist and musician John Robb perfectly encapsulated the spirit of Oasis: 'The key to Oasis is they are the sound of every great moment in British pop rolled into one. They're Slade, The Kinks, Bowie, Mott the Hoople, the melody of The Beatles, the power of The Pistols, Liam's sneer of John Lydon and the coolness of The Stone Roses.' It's probably the best description of the Oasis sound. And it captures how, ironically, Oasis sounded fresh and original because they were like so many groups. I also think they sound like T. Rex. Every time I hear 'Cigarettes & Alcohol' I hear that gritty, fat and lazy sound. It's also a British thing, to compare bands: artists always have to be influenced by someone else. If you flip this around, imagine you were American and a band came on stage and sounded like Neil Young, The Byrds, Jimi Hendrix, the Ramones, Big Star, Cheap Trick, Todd Rundgren and Nirvana. Though if that mythical band blagged their way onto the bill to play in front of fourteen people in a dingy club in Manhattan's Lower East Side, I'd no doubt think they were average too.

What Oasis did have was an in-built commercial radar to hit the sweet spot. They speak to so many people lyrically and musically because of the simplicity and directness of the words and music used to convey their message. It's only rock 'n' roll. There's no intellectual agenda, no cerebral manifesto, but what you do get is a song that resonates; like the best works of art, their music is simple and direct. Their songs are based on instinct, attitude and confrontation. They weren't trying to be musically clever; the melody was always familiar and obvious, but that's why we took to them. We don't need to work too hard when we hear them. It's that fleeting resemblance, that moment of hearing a song for the first time and thinking you've known it most of your life. In Oasis's case, you will have heard it before and that's part of the appeal. When you include the way the media homed in on the volatility, turmoil and excess you are now beginning to understand the Oasis phenomenon. When they were playing at their best and in the correct frame of mind, few could beat them.

Despite the flurry of detractors, loads of writers knew it was special. Keith Cameron of the *NME* wrote: 'Noel Gallagher is a pop craftsman in the classic tradition and a master of his trade. Of his generation, probably only Kurt Cobain wielded the manipulative power of melody better, and you can't imagine Noel having too many guilt pangs about whether or not "Live Forever" was just that little bit too perfect.'

At the time, the album was the fastest-selling debut in the UK and to date *Definitely Maybe* has sold well over 15 million copies. After their Reunion Tour was announced in August 2024, the Thirtieth Anniversary reissue of *Definitely Maybe* was straight in there at number 1.

16

'Live Forever', White Heat,
Wall of Sound

It was only a matter of weeks after the release of 'Live Forever' on 8 August 1994 and the release of *Definitely Maybe* a few weeks later that the game changed entirely. Up until then, Oasis were a presence in the music press; yet another cheeky northern band who liked a fight and a party, but we'd seen it before. They were mildly entertaining, gaining some notoriety, a band who playing a UK tour would fill venues of 350 to 600 people every night, then when the singles came out, tour around 1,000–1,500-capacity venues. It was as if we were on a plane and we'd taxied along the runway. We were awaiting clearance for take-off. Then, just as we were going along smoothly – BOOM! 'Live Forever' comes out. The gears changed. The band powered into the mainstream and we were going supersonic.

After the release of 'Live Forever', the dynamic and level of expectation changed. The band's profile shifted up a level. They had proved they were capable of being real contenders. When they toured, they would now be playing to 3,000 or 4,000 every night and soon it would be arenas. Their shows were the hottest-selling ticket in town. They had arrived. As well as catapulting the band to ever greater heights, 'Live Forever' convinced the non-believers they had both a skilled songwriter and a singer with a voice that matched their flawless, infinite ambition. And I remain convinced that as a song, it's up there with some of the best singles since 'Ticket To Ride', 'Waterloo Sunset', 'Pretty Vacant', 'How Soon Is Now?' or 'Smells Like Teen Spirit'.

'Live Forever' was the band's third single release and, as such, the chart position may have suffered as it came out immediately before *Definitely Maybe* and remarkably only peaked at number 10. It was the band's first single in America and did well there too. Released in 1995, it reached number 2 on *Billboard*'s Modern Rock Charts and number 10 on the Album Rock Charts. The cover immediately caught your eye, especially if you were a real Beatles aficionado. It depicted the home of John Lennon's Aunt Mimi, Menlove Avenue, Wooton. Read into that what you will. Is Noel saying that he and John Lennon are going to live forever and will always be so famous that their music will be revered throughout the ages? Perhaps. It might also be a nod to an undeniable and deeply felt musical heritage. Personally speaking, 'Live Forever' has a resonance and a thought-provoking vibrancy in my life because it was released in the months following Kurt Cobain's suicide; I will always associate 'Live Forever' with that time in 1994.

Around this time, I had something of an Oasis epiphany. As these occasions usually do, it happened accidentally. I wasn't looking for, or expecting, anything startling or historic other than a good night out with some cool music. Here's how it occurred. It's September 1994, Ross arrives to pick me up in his van – Ross, my pal, who was with me the night we saw Oasis at King Tut's. We are heading to the off-licence to return about a hundred empty bottles of Irn-Bru which have accumulated from rehearsals and buy a carry-out from the cash we receive in return. We then set off for Charlton Road in Bridge of Allan where Sharron shares this place with her friend Marion and two other PhD students. It's a big decaying house which hasn't been decorated since 1971 and has a quaintness and retro-style décor, particularly in the substantial kitchen, that then looked ridiculous but now would be 'must-have'.

The plan is to start a party, have a few drinks, head into Stirling Uni for an indie night, then head back home and finish the party. The house has these enormous and well-maintained vegetable patches full of potatoes, cabbages, lettuce, carrots, onions and rhubarb. At that time, I was a skint musician, who was by then nursing dreams of being a comedy writer and blossoming into a truly sad cliché. I'm that poor (and drunk), I'm thinking of going out during the night and digging up veg to take home. The garden leads downhill and backs onto private tennis courts behind a hedge. Such a posh area wouldn't miss a couple of cabbages, turnips and bags of beautiful big purple potatoes. In fact, they'd appreciate them going to a worthy home, surely?

We head from Charlton Road to check out Tackno, a popular indie night at Stirling University, to see if it lives up to its billing as the talk of the town. It was there it hit me. The core of what Oasis were truly about. It was powerful, raw, red hot, sweaty and sounded like a mixture of the UK garage punk of the 1960s and The Stooges. I had heard the songs that were hammering out loads of times now. But for some reason, it was that live sound, the venue's speakers, the loud guitars and vocals high up in the mix. The music reverberated around the room, ricocheting off every wall. It was like we'd been invited to a private party as the DJ (Trendy Wendy) played 'Live Forever', 'Rock 'n' Roll Star', 'Supersonic' and 'Cigarettes & Alcohol'. When you were in the white heat of this music, it was like taking a sledgehammer to a familiar reincarnation of Phil Spector's Wall of Sound. (I don't like being too muso, but there is a reason why they do sound so loud and intense. It's Owen Morris. He has this trick, the Brick Wall, where he turns everything up during recording until the dials are up to red. It's his version of the Wall of Sound – the Brick Wall of Sound.) The start of 'Supersonic' felt aptly named as the hall at Stirling Uni is shaped like an aircraft hangar. The indie club was bouncing, though to be honest, so were we.

The music was clear and sharp, exact and precise. I understood every nuanced beat, chord, sentiment and chime. I got it. I was there in it. I was sweating my socks off, but still I felt like the coolest punter in the venue. It was then I realised Oasis made music for people with a certain frame of mind and a distinct attitude to life. And that was one of: 'It's Friday night, let's fucking go for it.' I kept looking over, convinced the band were playing live in the corner. I thought it might just be me. Had I become a little *over* invested? Then when I looked at Ross, he had the same expression as well. We were both thinking and experiencing exactly the same: 'Fucking hell, this sounds – this is – mind-blowing.'

It was another Oasis moment, like the time at T in the Park when the band ramped it up a notch and this newly expressed intensity and power propelled them to greater heights. Something happened. It was as if somebody turned the dial and this amazingly powerful sound blasted out. It was like tuning in an old FM radio and listening as the sound went from a meandering interference to crystal clear. For vinyl lovers, maybe it was more like blowing a huge ball of fluff from a needle and hearing a record with an exquisite clarity. Perhaps it was because we were hearing their music while partying among hundreds of like-minded people who were going crazy for it. And it was so loud, it burned through, stinging and rattling, and the controlled cacophony started to make perfect sense. Then I wondered, is this what McGee heard? Was this the same sensation McGee had when he saw them at King Tut's? Maybe this is what made their story so illuminating, maybe it explains why they struck a deal off seemingly almost nothing. You could sense their attitude and spirit ooze from the speakers. It was as if Oasis were making this astonishing sound but with a dismissive indifference; they knew they absolutely had it going on and their confidence was soaring. Their music took on this buoyancy, a self-assuredness. And all this feeling, all this music was evoked by a circle of vinyl or a CD pumping out from the DJ's decks. I can't help saying it again: that night, you'd think we had walked into one of their gigs.

If, in the 1950s, producers made records for radio stations with basic rudimentary equipment that somehow made the music sound powerful through car radios and jukeboxes, in the 1990s, producers made rock 'n' roll music that sounded startling in clubs full of hundreds of students and two mature students who'd sneaked in. This is rock 'n' roll, my friends, and it has a pulse, it throbs and sweats; it lives among us. That night I realised Liam Gallagher was an exceptional rock 'n' roll vocalist. His voice fitted the music. Like Jerry Lee Lewis, Little Richard, Brian Wilson, John Lennon and Kurt Cobain.

Off on a musical and DJing tangential thought process, there's a Kenneth Anger film called *Scorpio Rising*. (I know I'm going off-topic but bear with me.) In 2002, the electronic rock group Death in Vegas released an album of the same name – with a title track featuring none other than Liam Gallagher. I happen to think one of Liam's best vocal performances is on that track, 'Scorpio Rising'. Maybe because he was singing to different songwriters, there's a change in his vocal emphasis. The song itself is a whirling loop based around the main riff and hook of Status Quo's splendid 'Pictures of Matchstick Men'; Francis Rossi receives a co-credit. I had a residency DJing for years, in a pub called the Mint, in Coatbridge. I loved it. Most of the time you were allowed to express yourself musically. I would play northern soul. I would play material off Kerb Darge's albums, on the BBE label. I would play punk and new wave and loads of 1960s garage. I was prone to playing loads of bubblegum pop too. I wouldn't be afraid to play the classics from Al Wilson's 'The Snake' to 'The KKK Took My Baby Away' by the Ramones. If I liked it, I played it. I would also try to play the room. One evening I played 'Scorpio Rising', the track featuring Liam Gallagher. I immediately sensed I split the room. While the more tasteful and cool punters happily listened, others weren't so happy. Then one less than favourable shaven-headed bodybuilding type angrily approached demanding I play something else. His critique was blunt: 'Fucking Oasis? What the fuck is that shite yer playing now?'

'Bongos on yer mum's arse, and she's loving it,' I replied. In my head. To myself. If you'd seen him you'd find my silent courage truly impressive. Trust me, even on the frontline, on the shop floor, the Oasis singer even guesting with another band still split the room.

17

Death in Vegas

The group's meteoric rise continues unabashed. Their debut album goes straight in at number 1, becoming up to that point, as we know, the fastest-selling debut album in the UK, ever. It's selling, the band are gigging and the world is waking up to Oasis. They are fast becoming the most talked about band in the world. In September, they play shows in Sweden, Dublin, Belfast, the Haçienda in Manchester, Hamburg and Amsterdam Arena, then they head off for a six-date tour of Japan. If the band were ever in doubt that they were rock stars, this trip confirmed their arrival among the big guns.

In Japan, they are welcomed like international superstars and, inevitably, they respond in time-honoured, rock-star style. They trash hotel swimming pools, bed loads of women, party twenty-four hours a day; they come close to becoming a mania. The fashion, the haircuts, the vibe and the attitude. The fans in Japan fell hook, line and sinker for what Oasis were about. 'It was like Beatlemania,' Johnny Hopkins, Creation's PR, said. 'Nobody really saw it coming. It just blew everyone's minds. They were chased everywhere, driven around in Popemobiles, given all these mad presents, hundreds of people waving and following them around.' As well as falling for their music, they were falling for Liam's look, image and attitude. All this attention and glory, but the band still didn't have a record out in Japan. Between 13 and 19 September, they played six shows; four in Tokyo and one each in Osaka and Nagoya. The trip was up there with the band's most hedonistic. Sex and drugs and sushi rolls. No sleep. Party central. Job done. Even the bass player, sporting black eyes, who doesn't usually speak to anyone, is arriving at airports and telling the press, 'I can't stand these groups who whine on about how tough life on the road is. We love it and we go for it.'

It's all going well, but as expected, pandemonium is never far off and wending its post-apocalyptic way towards Oasis and all who sail in it. After the high of Japan, the band headed to America and practically imploded. There's a production scale down, smaller gigs and a reality check. Marcus Russell has convinced them that the steady, moderated build-up has to be done in the US. Launching in respected venues, then returning to bigger and better shows for the next tour, slowly but surely winning over America.

There were many reasons why America seemed out of step with Oasis. It may have been the time taken to sort a deal with Epic and the label's buying into the band as a long-term project. It may have been geographical and logistical too, but most likely it was about taste. At the time, there was a fixation among American A&R staff that bands out of the UK should sound like Jesus Jones. To place the US career path of Oasis in perspective, the first American single was 'Live Forever' and only reached number 39 in the *Billboard* Hot 100. Their first Top 10 hit was 'Wonderwall' in late 1995. In the UK, that same song was the band's eighth single. Admittedly, the US charts are more album-based with the single used as a loss leader for promotion for the bigger purchase and as a way of inducing fans to buy the album.

Another crucial factor in the truculent relationship with

America was the band's reluctance to embrace how business is done on the other side of the Atlantic. When you include the band's mistrust towards anyone outside their circle and their disdain of anyone who was insincere or who 'didn't keep it real', then you can understand why they lost it so quickly when they landed in the epicentre of what to them must have seemed like planet bullshit. You also have to realise how much a band from Burnage were out of their comfort zone as they tried to operate with American music industry execs – and this might, naturally enough, have contributed to defensiveness and hostility on their part.

They were presented with an eclectic and divergent way of doing business. You had to play the game and play it their way. Noel understood from his experience with Inspiral Carpets that it was going to be exacting. Taking on America would require patience, tact and a more measured approach. It was so far removed from the record industry in the UK. You had to get onside with people and, even if you thought they were (to use the language of Noel and Liam) wankers and full of bullshit, you had to smile, shake hands and even sign an autograph for the kids of record company employees.

In November 2023, in conversation with photographer Jill Furmanovsky, ahead of her exhibition in London, Noel Gallagher opened up on why he felt Oasis never cracked America: 'They couldn't handle the fact that we didn't give a fuck about anything. I mean, I think that's the reason we've never really had a number 1 album in America – they wouldn't go the extra mile for us because we wouldn't go the extra mile for them.' He later revealed how Oasis could not fake it. 'That's why we've never been nominated for a Grammy – you've got to do all that stuff over there, you've got to kind of fake it a little bit and we just couldn't do it, which is why we'd always stall at number 2.'

It would take a radical change of mindset, especially for Liam. This was highlighted when he infamously instructed a record company boss to 'fuck off'. Far worse was to come. Again, it was Liam, trying to be smart, with comments that could have ruined their career in the US. While meeting MTV bosses, he insulted Kurt Cobain, suggesting he couldn't handle the fame. The guy's wife had been a close friend of the late Nirvana frontman. Noel later apologised in an interview for Liam's comments stating, 'I think he [Cobain] was a genius. I think we've lost the John Lennon of our generation.' In an interview in 1996, he also commented that the only writer he had respected in the past ten years was Nirvana's Kurt Cobain and, in keeping with Noel's modest outlook on rock 'n' roll, thought that he was the only other contemporary songwriter who could've written 'Wonderwall'. You can imagine Kurt writing that. It's effortless, plaintive and could easily sound like a Nirvana song.

Maybe it was immaturity, (or the drugs) but most likely it was Liam's reaction to a situation he hated being in, with people he didn't trust. He is in a world he isn't used to. He has his own set of rules. Don't apologise or back down, be straight, don't bullshit, don't grass, retaliate first. Then he's left in situations where he has to schmooze with wacky, strung-out record company people. These aren't guys working for a cool underground label like Sub Pop, Merge or Matador, who understand their British working-class attitude. These are key LA players in the music industry, record company execs and influential corporate people who could make calls and arrange to have the best promoters and agents handle you. The people who can get you the best record pluggers, who personally know producers on late-night TV shows and on MTV.

The band had to deal with people wearing a bespoke suit, handmade leather shoes and a watch that cost far more than a house or two on their street. The execs had a love of expensive sushi bars whereas Oasis would have loved to just find a chippie. It's perhaps too convenient and easy to say they couldn't adapt to the difference, and that they weren't used to the LA mindset. In the UK their notoriety and rock 'n' roll excesses weren't encouraged but they were tolerated because the people who understood the band knew they were capable of showing up and knocking it out the park when it came to performing live. In the US, their actions were skating close to seriously derailing the good work done thus far. They were upsetting some serious players who had seen it all before with bands brought low by their own bad attitude.

One of the reasons Liam liked and trusted both Marcus Russell and Alan McGee was because of their no-nonsense, straightforward approach. It was all old school, an honest handshake and your word. The band had proved how successful and popular they were in Britain. When they flew over to America after the Beatlemania-like energy of Japan, they were playing to people who didn't know them and who cared even less about them. Apart from the pocket of Oasis admirers already into the band, the venues they were playing were full of Pearl Jam and Soundgarden fans. Their first date after Japan was, ironically enough, in Seattle, where they played at a club called Moe's on 23 September.

They did OK but realised it wasn't going to be easy. It was a case of getting the head down and working hard. They were back to reality, playing the club circuit, and it felt like they were starting from scratch again. However, the same crowds of fans and influential people who had come to these gigs loved the band. That was the idea, again with the mantra on repeat, keep returning to the towns, play a bigger venue, spread the word, attract better reviews, get local airplay, and that way build momentum from show to show.

By now, Liam was becoming accustomed to receiving more respect. The towns and cities of Britain and Europe were treating the band like rock royalty; a visit from Oasis was like one from the Rolling Stones. There was excitement, the police were there, the papers, massed ranks of photographers; some anarchy, a decent amount of debauchery expected, disarray guaranteed. Such a promise was virtually printed at the bottom of an Oasis ticket. If it was too quiet, Creation's publicists were on the case, whipping up a media frenzy or at least encouraging something, anything, a minor skirmish or a run-in with the police, for the benefit of the papers. It was exciting, all part and parcel of the game, but here in America, they felt insignificant. Oasis were yet another noisy UK band who thought they were The Beatles. Some people loved them, of course, but not enough and not quickly enough for an impatient Liam. This was going to be a slog. They had a number 1 album in the UK, but in the US they were stuck in Hicksville playing to appreciative but undersized clubs.

After the gig at Moe's in Seattle, they played the Satyricon, Portland on the 24th then Bottom of the Hill in San Francisco on the 26th. They were booked to appear on a radio station, Live 105. The show's presenter thought it would be fun to book Blur too. Bad move. It wasn't fun. Liam was introduced and called Damon Albarn a wanker. This was the same show when someone rang in to ask if Noel had a penis extension and he said he didn't need one, he had one on drums. After a show at Malarkey's in Sacramento on 27 September, they had a day off on the 28th and travelled to LA. The bedlam and drinking continued there with an incident in the notorious Viper Room.

Come closing time, there had been an altercation with the club's bouncers. Oasis had been asked to drink up and move on, but didn't like this request so punches were thrown and a fight ensued. While staying at Bonehead's brother's, who lived close to the club, they set up their gear and Bonehead played 'Supersonic' about seventy times and half of the LAPD showed up and booked him.

The Irish blood was stirring, the party head was kicking in, and soon the anger and aggression followed; you could set your watch by it. Who was around to tell them to calm down? Who was there to keep them in check? The situation inevitably became more turbulent. As ever, when the plan was coming together, the band reached breaking point and cracked in spectacular fashion. As usual drink and drugs were to blame – at least in part. Noel prefers not to partake on the day of a show, opting to stay straight, and at this point he appears to be the only one who doesn't lose the plot. The others decided it was time to be rock 'n' roll. Anything to deal with the underwhelming reality of the club shows. Whatever the reason, you got the impression the tentative peace would dramatically dismantle.

Now in his sober, straight and more reflective days, Alan McGee has commented on the band's propensity to indulge. He claims that no one comes close to the drinking and drug-taking habits of Oasis. This is a man who has hung out and partied with Primal Scream and who later managed The Libertines, but still he claims Oasis were miles ahead in their consumption of everything and anything. In terms of keeping bands in check, controlling them and their careers, he has more than earned his money.

It wasn't just the ability to consume. What always impressed McGee was the band's ability to recover. It's not a badge of honour that's going to wow everyone, but you know you've arrived in the hedonism stakes when Alan McGee proclaims your greatness. However, when events took a turn for the worse and, let's be candid, with Oasis they often did, the undoing was always cinematic in scope.

For some inexplicable reason, on the afternoon of the band's most important gig to date, in front of key people at the legendary Whisky a Go Go on Sunset Strip, West Hollywood, their label, Epic, decide to throw a $50,000 party on the roof of the band's hotel. Meanwhile, ahead of the party and the show, the band were at Bonehead's brother's house, living it large, all, again, except Noel who at least had some idea of how important an industry moment this was for them. The drug of choice at the time was Tina, Krank, Tweak, Ice, crystal meth, aka methamphetamine; that is, conceivably the most addictive manmade stimulant. The quality was particularly superior, first-rate, outstanding. It was up there with Walter White aka Heisenberg from *Breaking Bad*. Then again, Walter's story is a fictional one; this was real.

So, what they were being offered is an extremely potent and highly addictive form of speed. No one was expecting them to stick to Mom's homemade lemonade, but crystal meth? Really, guys? We shouldn't at any level condone or encourage this kind of illicit activity, but it speaks volumes for either the luck or constitution of Liam that he was able to snort loads of the stuff in between songs from behind amps and the bass drum during the show. Most get hooked and get hooked badly. The rest of the band, apart from Noel, could shrug it off with a three-day extreme hangover and no doubt a dull, aching low. As I was saying, this was a hugely significant gig. A time to let Epic, who are owned by Sony, and their US label, see that Oasis were ready for the task. But this was a show which, I'm sure you can imagine, didn't pan out too well.

The Whisky a Go Go gig was a straight-up calamity. Noel must've looked around at the rest of the band, who are monumentally fucking up throughout each and every second of the show. The others hadn't slept for seventy-two hours, because they were bored and wanted to see how many days they could stay awake. Liam's singing is all over the place and Noel is struggling to harmonise with him. The crowd are egging them on to fight; Liam hits Noel on the head with his tambourine. Then the bass amp dies on the first song, a stage diver keeps hitting Liam, and he's getting angrier and angrier. *NME* photographer Kevin Cummins made it on stage, but he was also beginning to annoy Liam. For some reason, the band took to the stage with separate set lists. When they did start on time, they were playing the wrong songs. It was pandemonium from start to finish. Liam changes the words to songs and in one he calls Noel a wanker.

Loads of guests and VIPs are there at the gig. Ringo Starr had allegedly even turned up. It turns into another Oasis disaster zone. Crystal meth and booze aren't a creative combo. Well, not as far as I know; I haven't tried crystal meth, would never want to, so maybe I shouldn't judge. The band are oblivious to the fact that not only have the wheels come off but the juggernaut is now on its side, screeching and squealing across the highway, hurtling out of control doing 140 mph and about to cause no end of destruction as it impacts on the oncoming train carrying its cargo of gasoline and heading for the railroad crossing. Here we are again, living out part of the uncontrollable storyline of another Hollywood script in the life of Oasis.

Perhaps someone had forgotten to tell them that the drugs they were using weren't the same as the ones in Manchester. When they realised how crazy the crystal meth was, they were trying to come down off the meth by taking a couple of Es . . . and this was on top of an endless supply of Jack Daniel's. The drugs were too powerful and intoxicating – far too pure and intense compared to what they were used to. That was the problem with this show. The drugs did work. Liam recalled in the *Supersonic* documentary: 'I don't know who fucking got it but it was there and we all thought it was coke. We're doing big fucking lines of it and it just kept us up for fucking days. The band were not in the right place.'

And this was all against a backdrop in which the buzz about the band in the press and within the music industry had reached fever pitch. Their management were hyped and this high-profile show was the perfect launch. Then, as you might expect, there had to be the ever-present aggro between Liam and Noel. Those at the gig, people from their label, plus loads of important industry contacts who could make it happen in the States for the band, watched on in horror. The band not only disintegrated but looked as if they were burning out in front of them. Liam was wired. Marcus Russell was looking at the band and wondering: What the fuck now? When will this lot ever fucking learn? The gig ended in mayhem and confusion; to be blunt, they played like shit. Bonehead was jumping around taking photos on a disposable camera and laughing like a madman. Immediately after the gig, Russell, Noel and Liam headed straight to the dressing room, locked the door and locked themselves into an intense and bitter row. Oasis had fucked it up again. Had they monumentally screwed their career? Reports came in that Noel had been spotted forlorn and alone in Las Vegas.

18

Noel Leaves the Band & 'Whatever'

When Noel left the dressing room, the band was finished. He decided there and then he'd had enough. He took the tour float (a grand from the door money) from Maggie Mouzakitis, the band's trusted tour manager, and left. Shows in Austin, Dallas, Kansas and Missouri were cancelled. What did the Whisky a Go Go show tell us? This is Oasis. We know by now that when they have an opportunity to shine, the chances are they will monumentally fuck it up. Then again, maybe that's why so many millions would go on to love them. They are one of the few bands who mirror the trials and tribulations of real life. We see ourselves in both their outrageous fortune and their self-inflicted moments of disarray and disaster.

Noel had flown to San Francisco to stay with a friend. We do know, pop historians, that she was beautiful and had a particularly cool record collection. (In *Supersonic*, Noel said he couldn't remember the woman's name or face. She inspired him to write 'Talk Tonight'. Her name is Melissa Lim and she spoke to the *San Francisco Chronicle* saying she talked him out of breaking up the band.) The band didn't know where he had gone, not yet anyway. As far as they were concerned Noel had vanished. If they had been sober enough they'd be thinking about the west coast's magnetic pull. The writer heading off into the sunset, the heat, the drugs, the clichéd end of the road luring him in. The folklore of ashes spread under the lost soul's favourite desert tree. The body found too late, sunk into a running bath to softly and calmly drown. After booking into the nearest clichéd suicide hotel with its festering, decaying beauty; peyote and a litre of vodka for breakfast, some smack and Jack for lunch and an anecdote by dinner.

As the band were sobering up, someone realised that Noel's disappearance wasn't part of the story. He wasn't supposed to up and leave us here, was he? What was he up to? Was he planning to fuck off and die somewhere? Wait a minute. Where the fuck has he gone? These thoughts must've been running through their minds. When I read in the *NME* that Noel Gallagher had left the group and disappeared in LA, I thought the same. Though from afar, it fitted in with every pop fan's idea of Oasis. No one thought they would last. It was all too fragile and combustible, charged by an energy that looked set to implode. Noel was always going to be the one to split. It was always going to be that way. They had an unstoppable approach, an all-or-nothing attitude to drink and drugs (with that unparalleled recovery bonus), but they couldn't go on being so lucky. When you revisit their story and the scene of the crime, with hindsight it's miraculous that none of Oasis died of a drug overdose or choked to death on their vomit. Noel was 27 at the time, and I'm sure loads of people were thinking about but were too nervous to mention the prospect of him dying at that same fated age as Robert Johnson, Jimi Hendrix, Janis Joplin, Jim Morrison or Amy Winehouse.

The papers were full of drama and concern. There was a real apprehension hanging over the reports. Again, because of the location, the west coast of America, LA then to San Francisco, now the last report was placing him in and around Las Vegas, out in the desert. Noel's disappearance was a major story. The reports were dramatic and shocking. The music world was still coming to terms with the loss of Kurt Cobain. The wounds were raw, open. So there was an air of desperation and panic in the subtext of the reports of a famous rock star's disappearance. You kept hoping he needed a break from the peculiar dynamic of being on the road. Oasis weren't built to last, not creatively, but we all hoped that didn't mean a physical loss too. The Chief going AWOL on the road wasn't how I envisaged it unravelling. But that's how it was reported: Noel vanishes and no one knows where he is.

With each hour that passed without Noel reporting back or calling, the rest of the band must've believed their future hung in the balance. Had they taken it too far? It was always the same, the creative storm, the brittle friction. Power, remorse, forgiveness, then sin. The toxic cycle was reminiscent of a couple trapped in a violent co-dependency, both of them clinging to a pattern of bullying, manipulation and lies, both pushing it too far, then begging to try again, only to keep reoffending.

Noel hated being in the band. That was it, over. Fuck them and their lack of professionalism. He had steered them not only to a number 1 album but also the fastest-selling debut album ever. He now had everything he could dream of. He had the respect of his peers, the music industry, the fans and the press, but still his band couldn't care less and didn't have the professionalism to at least keep it straight for such an important gig. He couldn't understand this stupid disconnect between being a professional band with a job to do and the clichéd rock 'n' roll drunk and debauched band with an attitude. People had paid to see you play and you owed them a show. Liam's attitude, on the other hand, was always,

'Well, the kids should be grateful we've bothered to make the effort and even shown up here to play. They want to see us mad for it.' It wasn't always that simple and is hardly an original stance – it had happened countless times before them – but with Oasis, it almost became part of the attraction. What held them together was a tautness that could explode into a fight, could start a riot, and for many in attendance, that tension was worth the admission fee.

Calls were made to Creation, the situation explained and nerves were shattered. The band minus Noel would stay in LA until they found out what was happening. Then Noel rang Tim Abbot and asked him to tell Alan McGee and Marcus Russell he was sorry he'd let them all down but the band was over. Finished. Abbot was on a plane to LA within hours. Maggie the TM had asked the hotel manager for details of the outgoing phone calls from Noel's room and was finally able to trace him to that friend he'd had a fling with in San Francisco, a few more days passed and eventually Noel called Abbot and told him to fly out to San Francisco. Abbot did what he was told, and once there, after a few days, suggested they fly to Las Vegas so they could talk through the incident and maybe address Liam's behaviour. After three days of debauchery in the Luxor Hotel in Las Vegas, it was time to face the music.

Noel agreed to return to the fold. A session had been squeezed in between dates on the American tour to record B-sides. The studio was in Austin, Texas. Owen Morris had been booked for the session and bumped into Noel and Tim Abbot when he arrived at the airport in Austin. By the time they met up with the band at the hotel, it was hugs, kisses, love and peace all around, especially from the most worried band member of all, Liam. In my view, it was Tony McCarroll who should've been the most concerned. Noel had grown so fed up with Tony's playing that he played drums himself on one of the songs, 'Half A World Away'.

By the end of the year, Oasis had played 120 gigs, and the extra push into November and December finally got to them. Back in the UK, at a show in Glasgow's Barrowland, Liam lost his voice and walked off stage. I have been to hundreds of Barrowland gigs. The rules are simple. You deliver, the crowd respond. You don't take any audience for granted, especially not in Glasgow. As he left the stage, a mic was still live and their security guard Ian Robertson was heard saying that the bus was ready for a sharp exit. You don't do that either. As the anxiety mounted, Noel took over. He promised they'd come back and play the full show again (which they did, two weeks later). Noel continued playing, singing some songs. The night was saved, but the mood was sour and got uncomfortably close to escalating into a riot.

'Whatever' was the fifth single in ten months of a crazy year and each moment of that song's six minutes and twenty-seven seconds was important in many ways for the band. It was released between the first and second albums, creating a bridge between *Definitely Maybe* and *(What's The Story) Morning Glory?* The production shows maturity, meandering strings and a mid-era Beatles charm. The strings were played by the London Philharmonic featuring former ELO violinist Wilfred Gibson and were arranged by Nick Ingham and Noel. The shape is unusual; they chose an AB structure, moving away from the usual verse-chorus, meaning they opened with the chorus and the hook at the start of the song. The overall production and lush pop sound proved, despite the fallouts, that they were fast becoming the complete package, creating music that would confirm their place as major players in UK popular culture as well as in the charts.

'Whatever' was the type of song that kids, their parents and grandparents could and did sing along with. It reaches number 3, with only East 17 and Mariah Carey above them. Suddenly, it made everyone acknowledge, however reluctantly, that Oasis weren't merely bad boys from up north with a bit of a snarl but a band with a future, a major songwriting talent steering them and a debut album that had no intention of stopping selling.

'Whatever', though, was subject to a high-profile plagiarism case. It also gave rise to some seriously inaccurate reporting and exaggerated claims of legal power plays. Despite the sensational nature of the headlines, like most stories, when you look into them, the truth is somewhat more pedestrian.

The claims centre around part of the tune being stolen from 'How Sweet To Be An Idiot' by Neil Innes. That part was agreed upon. Neil Innes has subsequently explained that he didn't sue. However, he kept bumping into people who instructed him to listen to the Oasis song. He also received phone calls from friends telling him he had to listen to 'Whatever'. One of the phone calls was from The Scaffold's Mike McGear (McCartney). That led him to at least contact and speak to EMI Publishing Ltd, who owned the song, to let them know about it and they excitedly explained that their people were on it. The whole case was handled amicably and the resulting outcome meant a few bob for Innes, but hardly life-changing money. It was settled out of court with Innes receiving a songwriting credit, meaning a quarter of the song's royalty goes to EMI Publishing Ltd, where it's then divided fifty/fifty between them and Innes.

The start of 1995 saw the band try yet again to establish a foothold in America with another tour. They were getting there, slowly, through perseverance, a more committed attitude and loads of live dates. They realised how hard the job was going to be when they had sold 250,000 copies of *Definitely Maybe* yet barely managed to scrape into the Top 75 of the *Billboard* charts. The college charts, however, were far more positive. 'Live Forever' had been a hit on college radio and the signs were that the band were finally turning it around across the Atlantic.

As March 1995 beckoned, they headed to Wales to record 'Some Might Say', a song that would deliver their first UK number 1, and I was now taking some real – albeit slightly perverse – enjoyment from their success.

19

King Tut's 31.5.93 (Part 4)

Here in Glasgow, the legend has grown over the years about how spectacular Oasis were that night. They must've been: their performance would eventually earn them a lucrative recording contract and change their lives in a way that we couldn't come close to imagining. They were intriguing and tough to ignore, but all the same they were playing guitar-based rock 'n' roll when the music scene was all about baggy dance acts.

It was unusual for bands at this just-starting-out level and fourth on the bill to bring their own soundman, but I noticed Oasis had theirs with them. They were organised and evidently more than a mad crew of chancers, blagging their way onto the bill. I was standing in front of the mixing desk in the middle of the venue and, to my left, stood McGee. He was happy. He kept bouncing into me. But he was nice about it. I know he was drinking Jack and Coke because as he bumped into me, some of his drink splashed onto my biker jacket (you know the one), and I could smell it; I might even have had a taste. Eugene standing beside me to my right smiled as I gestured at the drink over my jacket.

At the time, we thought he was there to see Boyfriend and 18 Wheeler and had showed up on some Creation business to drop in and say hello to the troops while he was back home.

We didn't know about the link to Debbie Ellis's band, or at least I didn't, not then.

By the time Oasis played a few songs Alan McGee was transfixed. He'd gone from a leading light in the indie hierarchy to a slightly annoying but apologetic guy who was jumping around excitedly as each song seemed to be landing. Was that the magical 'connection' we keep speaking about? He was watching the band then pointing at them and chatting to someone who Eugene had told me earlier was his sister. As I watched McGee's dumbfounded reaction, I do remember trying to figure out what I was missing. Why was he so enthusiastic? The last thing I heard was anything fresh; they sounded like loads of bands I'd heard before. McGee told the *Guardian* in 2013, 'The first song was really good. Then the second was incredible. By the time they did this fantastic version of "I Am The Walrus", I'd decided I've got to sign this group, now.'

Alan McGee knew the soundman Mark Coyle from working with Teenage Fanclub. And, as the band were ending their set, he immediately went to him and asked who the band were and did they have a record deal or a manager. He was told that their name was Oasis, that they had no deal or manager, and Mark pointed out the main guy, who was Noel Gallagher. McGee was genuinely buzzing with excitement as he approached him.

This all took place about three feet from where we stood.

Later, when the venue was busier, I saw McGee again, this time upstairs, beside the mixing desk talking to Noel Gallagher, who appeared sober, friendly and, I remember thinking, he had a warm expressive smile in contrast to his grumpy on-stage persona. He was humouring McGee and still trying to hand him a demo. McGee again said he didn't need a demo; he'd seen the band and that was all the convincing he required. The guitarist kept insisting he should take a demo; I definitely heard him say that. This time McGee took it and shoved it in his jacket pocket. But again he repeated how he didn't need it as he'd loved the band live. As Alan McGee explains in *Creation Stories*: 'I said "Do you have a record deal? Do you want one? I wanna do it."' Eventually, they had twenty record companies offering them deals and at the last minute Mother Records, owned by U2, phoned and said: 'We'll offer double what McGee is offering.'

Musically, and this is based purely on first impression, their songs reminded me of bands like Northside, Mock Turtles and again that Manchester indie rock guitar sound, like The Stone Roses. There wasn't the same musical or lyrical intricacy, but there was a big full-on guitar sound. That was my immediate impression. It gets worse, though: I felt a bit sorry for them. I thought they had missed their chance. To me, far from being at the vanguard of the music scene, spearheading a fresh, contemporary sound, they felt eighteen months too late. One of the main reasons I stayed was because the venue was so quiet and it would've been noticeable if I had left. That would have been awkward, bad manners, a breach of basic gig etiquette. Manners aside, there was also the chance that one of the band or their pals would kick my head in.

I was also intrigued by what McGee saw in them. Why was this arbiter of taste so into them? I do remember at one point turning towards McGee and thinking, *you've lost it, big man*. What does he see in this band? It's bordering on impossible to convey how ordinary they were, yet I was shocked to see how crazy McGee appeared to be about them. His reaction and the way he spoke to Noel were more entertaining than their short set. They weren't crap or rubbish, but rather monumentally

OK. The guitarist and singer had the same intense eyebrows and had to be brothers. Could McGee already see the Jesus and Mary Chain in this four-song set? Would I have signed them? No. It was bordering on preposterous to think they'd even fit in as a Creation band. I remember they did 'Rock 'n' Roll Star.' I recall thinking, are they taking the piss here? OK, I get it. It's irony. They didn't look or sound like rock stars. Liam maybe, at a push, was a good frontman, looked the part of a football casual, with the feathered haircut and the pout, but they didn't show any signs of coming close to the international success they would find in the subsequent years.

They played 'Up In The Sky'. I remembered that because of the way the singer sang sky-skyyyyyyy and rhymed it with fly and I thought (a bit snippily, I know), here we go, Milton and Keats beware. That's what I noticed. I clearly remember how unremarkable the lyrics were. That was the first time I heard them, it's not until after their breakthrough that you hear the songs over and over and start to get into the music. You realise it's supposed to be simple and direct and grab you. What's more, Oasis looked tense, nervous and rigid. The singer was going for it and the guitarist was the boss, the rest took their cues from him. They didn't smile. The drummer and bass player, from memory, were far better than the way they were portrayed when the band took off. I also noticed, on the night, how lengthy each song was. Oasis weren't proponents of the three-minute, exquisitely contained pop song, even then. They only played four songs, but by the time they had finished playing an unwieldy and never-ending version of 'I Am The Walrus', I headed to the bar, was served and returned while Noel's guitar was left to create feedback, still blaring from an amp. I couldn't drag myself away from the unfolding drama of a drunk guy, in effect then scouting for Sony, offering a shaggy-browed Manchester lad wearing a terrible jumper a deal.

20

What's the Story . . . with the Drummer?

By spring 1995, Oasis had embarked on bigger dates, playing Southend, Paris and a memorable show at Sheffield with Ocean Colour Scene. The Verve were also on the bill but had to pull out owing to a member of the band being injured in a brawl in Paris. Pulp stepped in as a last-minute replacement to give the 10,000 crowd a day to remember. Oasis were welcomed like superstars and played a watertight show to a rapturous audience. They opened with 'Rock 'n' Roll Star' and didn't relent till they had fired through nineteen songs. Noel calmed down proceedings by playing his now familiar acoustic section. Here he introduced one song, which he claimed was so fresh that it still didn't have a title. It turned out to be 'Don't Look Back In Anger'. Those present claim it's another of those unforgettable Oasis gigs the band were capable of delivering. Their mum, Peggy, was there, so they were definitely on their best behaviour for her.

I appreciate the effort, ability and especially the dedication put in by over-elaborate drummers to learn rudiments. I do. However, bands are not about individuals, but the collective. They are about making music that connects. I like drummers and I love drumming, but it's my belief that we now have an over-dependence on technique garnered from millions of online drummers and their drum clinics, all worthy of parody. There are three essential factors required to be a decent drummer. Timing, playing with style, feel and soul, and serving the song. If you have those sorted you can always learn and improve.

I like the flourishes of Dave Grohl on Nirvana's break-through, *Nevermind*. He was about being dynamic and bringing a vibe of excitement but always with the song in mind. Like Mitch Mitchell and Ginger Baker, Dave was in a three-piece band and given more scope to elaborate with Bonhamesque triplets (named after the almighty John Henry Bonham of Led Zep). Drummers who served the song? Charlie Watts and Ringo Starr. Tommy then Marky Ramone are worthy of the same respect for playing eighth notes on the ride or hi-hat for those powerful Ramones songs: most drummers wilt after thirty seconds of playing those notes. I had no money for drums never mind lessons. Like many of my generation, it was the excitement of playing along to Charlie Watts, Ringo, Rat Scabies, Clem Burke, Larry Mullen, Pete de Freitas and Steve Jansen. Making noise with your mates; the end game wasn't about refining your paradiddles but maybe making a record and getting a girlfriend.

When I was copying Ginger Baker or Buddy Rich I didn't know I was copying a flam or a ruff or a five-stroke roll. When I tuned into Max Roach it was because I recognised the cat could play with soul. It's about taste. I was busy learning from records whereas theorists like my late drummer friend Ted McKenna were shocked and amazed that I didn't practise my rudiments. I copy records. While we're here, I don't think I've ever seen a better drummer than Charlie Smith, who years ago I saw playing on a YouTube clip with Charlie Parker and Dizzy Gillespie doing 'Hot House'. He had an extraordinary touch, especially with bebop, tremendous technique yet relaxed, clear, delicious intricacy and, most importantly, he served the song. What has this drum talk got to do with Oasis, you may ask. At the start of their career and until he left, Tony McCarroll served the song. He was part of the Oasis sound.

Despite an ongoing feud and constant criticism from Noel, Tony McCarroll's Oasis career was brought to a close after an alleged 'frenzied fight' with Liam in a Paris hotel. McCarroll later denied the fight ever took place and was invented to make his exit sound more dramatic and cool. He claims he was kicked out because he was the only one who stood up to Noel. Now the Chief had a tangible reason to sack the drummer. After Sheffield, he had played his last gig for the band. It had been festering away for some time and now the decision had been made: Oasis were changing the drummer who had been with them from the start. This was the first public sign of a harsher, ruthless business side to their behaviour around the band and its personnel. Noel never liked McCarroll and the feeling was mutual. He took every opportunity to belittle him. He didn't think McCarroll was competent enough and felt he would struggle with the material they were due to start recording for *(What's The Story) Morning Glory?* In 1999, speaking after his settlement, and discussing his dismissal, McCarroll told the *Guardian*: 'I don't have a bad thing to say about Noel Gallagher. He's an a******* though. We were in it together. I worked my b*****ks off to set up the group. I was a member of a super-group one day and unemployed the next. I was trying to work out how.'

This is rock 'n' roll; no two days are the same. Life is a list of scenarios and issues and the pace is relentless. The drummer is gone. If you get into a 'fight' with the singer and his big brother wants you out, it's never going to end well. McCarroll missed out on a *Top of the Pops* appearance when 'Some Might Say' became Oasis's first number 1 single in the UK on 30 April 1995. I felt that was a shame, but then again I wasn't there in the middle of it and trying to deal with the situation.

Oasis certainly were accomplished with Alan White, but I felt they'd lost that looseness and that garage feel, which was a significant part of the initial Oasis sound. McCarroll's drumming style was perhaps a bit limited but it fitted with the loud, strident yet simple rock 'n' roll sound. His style of drumming was also very effective live, but McCarroll perhaps made himself an easy target by not working on his playing.

Surprisingly, when they were The Rain, at the start of the band, he was viewed as one of the better musicians, but while the others worked and developed, he appeared to have peaked. Noel and their manager Marcus Russell felt he at least deserved to be part of the group's initial flush of success. The songs Noel had written and arranged for the subsequent albums involved a more intricate drumming style. Tony's playing, a shuffle and a floor tom four-four garage punk beat, was no longer felt to be sophisticated enough for the next phase of the band's career.

One of the Oasis camp, producer Owen Morris, was keen for McCarroll to take drum lessons sensing he had the ability if he worked on his weaknesses and improved his technique, but that takes time, dedication, discipline and practice. Around this time, former drummer with The Bible and session man Dave Larcombe was brought in to work with McCarroll. He recognised his weaknesses and gave him routines and exercises to help, but Tony didn't do them. And so Russell was left with the job of telling him he was out. That's show business, I guess. Now Oasis were closing a chapter and moving on to the next.

Noel had already heard his new drummer play. He was walking past a session for Swedish singer-songwriter, Idha

(Andy Bell's then-wife). He loved what he heard; he didn't speak to him but kept the drummer's name in mind. As it turned out, that drummer, Alan White, would add something fresh to the Oasis camp, some Cockney cheek. To the Oasis people, anyone from London – north, south, east or west, it didn't matter – was a Cockney. He could play a bit, being a soul fan, loving Motown and James Brown but also The Who. It didn't go unnoticed that he was the brother of arguably one of the most respected players in the country at the time, Paul Weller's drummer, Steve White.

Alan White had been drummer in the short-lived but highly fancied Starclub, who'd signed with Island Records before they were unexpectedly dropped. The fact his brother drummed for Weller was enough for Noel. If White could handle the banter from the notoriously tight-knit band and crew, the inner sanctum of Oasis, then the 23-year-old had the job. Noel met him at Café Delancey in Camden and over a beer gave him a CD with the next single on it, telling him to learn it as tomorrow he'd be playing it on *Top of the Pops*. Within weeks 'Some Might Say' was number 1.

Days later, Noel had White rehearsing songs for the upcoming recording of *(What's The Story) Morning Glory?* White was able to handle Liam's demands: he kept testing his drumming ability up against his favourite Beatles or Stones songs. White was also collectively accepted as he could handle the Cockney slagging and, better still, he was more than capable of hitting back when it started. They liked the fact he could play anything from soul to punk to The Beatles, The Kinks and The Who. Noel enlightened anyone who'd listen with his view that Alan White was the new Keith Moon. He wasn't. But he was in. The *Top of the Pops* appearance was his first outing with the band as they performed 'Some Might

Say'. The first of many traumatic experiences in White's Oasis career. At times he'd be wondering if there was a safety belt or emergency parachute attached to his drum stool.

Now we're in sunny Monmouth, south Wales, and the band meet to start recording at Rockfield Studios. They are recording and working through songs for *(What's The Story) Morning Glory?* Alan White's presence is improving the vibe, he can play and the band are running through Noel's songs quickly and so far it's going well. They work as they always do, getting the drums, bass and guitars down live with Liam and Noel doing the vocals and guitar overdubs later. They have already nailed 'Roll With It' and 'Hello', and Noel plays both 'Wonderwall' and 'Don't Look Back In Anger' to Liam and asks him to pick one. Noel will sing the other. Liam chooses 'Wonderwall'. When they move on to 'Champagne Supernova' some of the previous Oasis antagonism rears its ugly, resentful head. Liam's voice is suffering due to his drinking. The boredom of hanging around at the studios meant he was taking off to the pub and drinking heavily. Noel had recorded the music to 'Don't Look Back In Anger' and was going in to record his vocals while Liam, who was out of sorts and listless, made the short country walk to the local, the Three Horseshoes.

After one memorable drinking session, Liam invited half the pub back to the studio. The crowd included Oasis fans who were aware the band were recording there, some punters from the pub looking for a party and some random members of a band. Noel comes in, sees these kids messing about with his guitars and tells them to fuck off. Liam goes off on one at Noel's attitude and display of bad manners towards his guests. A fight breaks out, Bonehead receives a few punches, and Liam goes berserk, starting a riot and wrecking the place. Liam attacks Noel and almost kills him. Noel gets away, then comes back at Liam and starts beating his crazed brother up with Guigsy's cricket bat.

Alan White was the nearest driver Noel could find. They fled off into the night. White and Noel escaped as Liam chased their car throwing anything he could get his hands on at them. They didn't stop till they'd done the 127 miles back to London. Liam was taken back to Wigan from Wales by Brian Cannon (who designed the Oasis albums and single sleeves), who was also present. The following day, while Guigsy tried to fix the place up (the owners still have the door that had to be replaced, which is held in the same memorabilia high esteem as the piano used on Queen's 'Bohemian Rhapsody'), there was a phone call from Marcus Russell to the rest of the band. It was time to pack up and go home, Noel had quit the band. He couldn't deal with the violence and the aggro and Liam's crazed outbursts. It was over . . . yet again.

*

After a few weeks of soul searching, Noel came back, much like he did the first time he left after the Whisky a Go Go gig and fled to San Francisco. His kid brother was crazy and full of anger but he was still his kid brother and he could sing. He'd created a monster but it was up to him to control him and deal with it. The band slowly started to reconvene at Rockfield and Noel came back into the fold. Liam apologised again and Noel got on with it. Work resumed on *(What's The Story) Morning Glory?* The album, full of ballads, mature string arrangements and about seven hit singles, was finally recorded. The last part of the plan involved Noel, and his fast-becoming second lieutenant, Owen Morris, retreating to Orinoco Studios in south London to begin mixing the album.

If Maggie Mouzakitis and Tim Abbot were pivotal in saving the band in Las Vegas, then it was Noel's partner, Meg

Mathews, who convinced him to get back to work. They had a break in Guernsey, then Jersey, and with time to think and reflect she convinced him to go back to the band. He was the boss of this chaotic, unrestrained force of nature; they needed him and he needed them. Many infamous bands are driven by the same fragility and volatile friction. The Ramones, The MC5 and The Stooges. They are the sum of many unstable but essential parts, which can be beautifully creative but also viciously disturbed and destructive.

With a warm-up show at Bath Pavilion, Alan White's second gig with the band was headlining the twenty-fifth anniversary of Glastonbury. The show itself, which should've been a benchmark gig, is best described as perfunctory. The expectant crowd at a festival is the wrong place to play so many unfamiliar songs. If they had stuck to the hits, despite the wind-affected sound, they would have blown those present away. What could have been an away victory turned out to be a respectful nil–nil; a clean sheet but one that offered a chance to fight another day. The Glastonbury concert is remembered more for Liam inviting Robbie Williams on stage, an act which freed him from the shackles of Take That, than it was for the band's appearance. They were off to festivals in Denmark, Italy, France and Switzerland, but would redeem themselves on UK soil on 14 and 15 July by playing two legendary gigs in Scotland at Irvine.

21

Blur: What's Their Story?

Up until the mid-1990s, Britpop was a relatively unimportant alternative scene made up of independent bands. Most of the bands in this subgenre reacted to US groups – in particular, grunge – by looking back and championing 1960s and 1970s bands. By 1992, groups like Suede and Blur juxtaposed their sound by deliberately being more British. Suede, in particular, were embraced by the music press and became the UK music scene's glam antidote to grunge.

Meanwhile, the animosity between Blur and Oasis was brewing up nicely. Everything was heading towards that significant moment, in August 1995, when Britpop was propelled into overdrive. The music world went crazy. The news reached every home in the country when Blur decided to bring the release of their single forward to deliberately clash with Oasis in what would turn out to be a bitter race to reach number 1 in the UK singles charts.

The Britpop battle between Oasis and Blur might have remained within the confines of the music press and pop fans had the mainstream newspapers not picked up the story. Once the tabloids framed it as a class war, they captured the public's imagination and the dynamic dramatically changed. The 'war' between Oasis and Blur had become about Oasis, the mouthy working-class northerners, winding up Blur, the posh middle-class arty southerners. It was deliberately pivoted and framed as a class thing. Blur were not without blame, though; they knew full well how to wind up Oasis. They were also more calculated about playing the game. The late boss of Food, Andy Ross, met Damon Albarn and suggested they stop pussyfooting around. If they were going to have a head-to-head and ignite the story, they should bring forward the release of 'Country House' to the same day, stand back and let the fun and games begin. 'Damon and I were sitting outside the Freemasons Arms, near the old EMI building, having this chat, and I said, "Look, if we go the week after, we're number 2. If we go the same week, we have a chance of maybe number 1." So we looked at each other, Damon seemed up for it, and we thought, "Well, let's go head-to-head, go for broke." We perceived that we were picking up the gauntlet that they'd cast down.'

By 1995, Blur had a substantial amount of music industry experience to draw upon and that's exactly what they did in the Battle of Britpop. Let's recap here, just in case you were living on another planet at the time or you are a young person who is wondering what chat about two ancient bands releasing two mediocre songs on the same day is about.

It's 1995, and Blur and Oasis are constantly slagging each other off at every chance they get in interviews, in print, on TV and radio. The bad-mouthing reached a crescendo, capturing the imagination of music fans, the general public and the media when both released a single on the same day. It shook the music scene out of its slumbers. The front cover of the *NME* of 12 August 1995 led with Blur versus Oasis mocked up like a vintage boxing poster and emblazoned with the 'British Heavyweight Championship' as Oasis released 'Roll With It' and Blur 'Country House' on the same day. Instead of boxers, we had Damon Albarn taking on Liam Gallagher. It was a massive, thrilling story and it morphed into a division of north and south as much as it was a race of two pop rivals to reach number 1.

On two premeditated incidents, Blur hoped Oasis would bite, and they did. First, by deliberately bringing the release of 'Country House' forward to coincide with the release of 'Roll With It'. The second incident occurred when Oasis were scheduled to play a short British tour and Blur waited for the Oasis dates to be revealed before announcing that they would play the same night in Bournemouth. There was also talk of transferring a Blur logo onto the Bournemouth Centre to provoke Oasis even further. Blur's actions were tantamount to inviting every hooligan down to Bournemouth for a full-scale riot, a side of arty, middle-class Blur that's rarely highlighted.

In Paul Mathur's charming Oasis tome *Take Me There: Oasis – The Story*, he goes into full detail about this scenario, but there's a telling quote from Noel at the time which highlights his concern for the fans as well as his disdain for the way Blur are behaving. 'I hate Blur but I know we've got fans who like them and if they bought tickets for our show that night, they wouldn't have been able to see them. Blur were just trying to do something to piss us off and they didn't even care about their own fans. That says a lot about them.' It was always implied that Oasis were instigating the rivalry; clearly, the truth is that Blur were equally bad.

Blur were well established in the music industry in comparison to Oasis, having started in 1989 and they'd already had their nose bloodied many times. By 1994, Blur's story and survival garnered respect due to their remarkable determination and unwavering self-belief. For music fans, Blur were enjoyable, catchy and spirited, but they were complicated to pin down. They were too poppy to be alternative. They looked and sounded more like a major-label pop act than an independent band. And, if they were jumping on so many bandwagons, when would we ever hear their real voice? Blur had a special knack for assimilating and absorbing the times. They always wrote brilliant-sounding songs. They flipped in and out of scenes, the shoegazing of 'She's So High' and the indie-dance crossover of Inspiral Carpets, Charlatans and Happy Mondays on the hit single 'There's No Other Way'. By the time this was a hit single, peaking at number 8 on 27 April 1991, the short-lived shoegazing scene had become passé.

On *Leisure*, their debut album, released in August 1991 (just as Nirvana debuted at the Reading Festival, stealing the show in an afternoon slot between Silverfish and Chapterhouse), we have the sound of a band still finding themselves musically. We know that by the time we get to 'Bang' that the third single is forced and the band have since admitted writing it quickly to keep the record company happy because of the financial pressures they were under. Then Blur sounded more like their contemporaries who were enjoying a decent amount of success with guitar-edged pop underpinned by a more dancefloor-friendly drum beat. Paradoxically, when Blur were changing direction, it was with their fourth release, 'Popscene', that we finally get closer to the band's vision. This song is the truest and most accurate representation of the band. It's indie, alternative, but it's also clever, witty and has that characteristic Englishness we would later hear on *Modern Life Is Rubbish*; it feels more in keeping with the musical and lyrical direction taken on that album. It failed in the charts, only getting to number 32, leaving the band wondering what they needed to do. Thankfully, they stuck to their guns and despite being under dreadful pressure from their label, pressed on. 'Popscene' was a notable tune and is considered by cultural commentator John Harris as a defining moment in this version of Britpop.

Something that has always gone in the band's favour and saw them through this period of their career was the velocity, power and energy of their live shows. Those who saw Blur at this time could see, despite record company difficulties or the lack of follow-up singles, that they were a fantastic live band, far rockier and louder than their records, energised by Graham Coxon's post-punk guitar spectacularly driving the band.

Blur came out of their first few years in the music industry battered and beaten, but their debut album peaked at number 7 and spawned a Top 10 hit. Blur had flirted with their sound and songs before truly announcing themselves as a fully formed alternative rock and pop band with *Parklife* in 1994.

Unlike Damon Albarn, I liked *Leisure* but adored 1993's *Modern Life Is Rubbish*. It's an album laced with the spirit of The Kinks, The Beatles and XTC. *Modern Life Is Rubbish* was viewed by the critics as the output of a band desperate for another drastic musical reinvention. Out with the baggy; in with 1960s guitar pop hooks. I loved it and to this day it's my favourite Blur album (though *The Ballad of Darren*, their unexpected modern classic from July 2023, comes close).

Modern Life Is Rubbish was deemed by many as too 'English'. At the height of grunge (it was recorded between October 1991 and March 1993), they deliberately made an album that was the antithesis of the genre. Already under pressure from their record company due to the lukewarm reception and sales of 1991's *Leisure*, the band were expected to make an album that would take the Yanks on at their own game. The label wanted to re-record the songs with Nirvana producer, Butch Vig. 'Popscene' was originally the first single from *Modern Life is Rubbish* but was pulled from the album when it was poorly received and that turn of events forced the band to change direction. There were plenty of teething problems and setbacks too. The sessions by original producer XTC's Andy Partridge were scrapped. I'm not entirely sure why. He sounded like the perfect producer for Blur. Over the years, some of the sessions he worked on have been released. You can hear the XTC sound and influence on songs like 'Coping', 'Sunday Sleep' and 'Seven Days'. They had more energy; they were alive, with heavier drums and bass. Through the trials and tribulations, the band held firm and should be given far more credit than they are for going with their instinct.

*

Beset by creative and financial problems after going into debt to the tune of over £60,000, to earn some money back, their American label, SBK, put Blur out on the road in 1992. They were on a lucrative, if soulless 44-date US tour at the peak of grunge, a move that virtually killed off the band and left them frustrated, angry and, on some occasions, at each other's throats. So if you're a homesick, frustrated and angry English pop band playing shows to Pearl Jam fans in lumberjack shirts and ripped jeans, what do you do? You listen to The Kinks on a cassette for most of the tour. You write songs about England, about village greens, cricket matches, steam trains, bank holidays and endless cups of tea. You broaden that sound and vision with bands like The Jam and The Small Faces and you start to see where they are heading. Blur were close to being dropped by Food Records. The band were still squabbling, playing shows drunk, including a high-profile gig on the same bill as Suede, their nemesis, who as you would expect, played a blinder. The band found themselves at a creative and personal low.

With such a blatant disregard for American music of the time, Blur had drawn a line. In going up against the post-Nirvana corporate rock bands they reaffirmed this desire to fortify their Britishness. Their music and fashion hinted at a change too. Suddenly, it was cool to be in the Mod scene. Their look had evolved into Dr. Martens, Fred Perry and Lonsdale.

Scenes are cyclical and ever-evolving, but something was clicking into place. There was a deliberate move towards writing about the culture and lifestyle of the day, mirroring the way The Kinks wrote songs in the 1960s. Crucially, while Blur were finding themselves and refocusing, it was Suede who stole the limelight.

Blur were adjusting, fine-tuning. There was less of that English eccentricity and a more full-on pop band for *Parklife*. It was Blur who kick-started the soundtrack of this period. They embraced the famous British bands of the 1960s, the Mod look, and they would sound like The Yardbirds and The Pretty Things. As Blur found their unique sensibility, they inadvertently or even ironically were paving the way and creating a musical environment that would allow a band like Oasis to achieve a breakthrough. So, whatever your opinion of Blur and the later Blur/Oasis joust, this is a band that didn't have it easy. A band who perhaps found themselves reluctantly making albums the record company thought people would like instead of one they wanted to make.

By the time they delivered *Parklife*, Blur were astute at reflecting the culture of mass consumerism, fame and greed. Up until the imminent release of *The Great Escape* in 1995, Blur had been through a steep learning curve, musically, creatively and financially. So now when they look back at the reviews for their first album – the *NME* said 'Blur are merely the present of rock 'n' roll' – they can laugh and ask, innocently enough, 'So where's your country house and how big is your farm, mate?'

Blur have endured many setbacks and, by the time they're shaping up to take on Oasis, they are wholly aware of what they're doing. You could go as far as to say it was a calculated plan to get a reaction, and Oasis didn't let them down. The spat generated a remarkable amount of publicity and changed the rule book by bringing Britpop into every house, onto every news channel and upping the intensity of the game for Creation, Food EMI and the music industry as a whole. In his eminently readable book, *A Bit of a Blur*, bass player Alex James accurately sums up Britpop by comparing it to the art scene at the time. 'Britpop was never a scene. It was a lot of not-very-brilliant bands copying two or three good ones, and the good bands never really saw eye to eye. The burgeoning art explosion was exactly the opposite. The artists were unified as a group and they relied on each other but they didn't plagiarise each other.'

As for Oasis, they weren't faking it. Time hasn't diminished Liam's deep-rooted suspicion and disdain. It's hilarious how he's still so easily riled by the mere mention of Blur. So, if he's still angry so many years on, you can imagine what it was like at the time. I have always viewed the spat with a healthy dollop of cynicism. To this day I suspect something was happening behind the scenes, but I could never get a definitive take on proceedings. But then, in the *NME* in 2019, everyone involved couldn't wait to speak out. I'm not saying we were being duped. It's true that Liam didn't like Blur, but I've always felt the whole thing was too well orchestrated, too neat.

The Blur versus Oasis feud was such classic tabloid material that I'm still convinced there must have been wheels within wheels, calls made, late-night meetings done. But it seems there were no clandestine meetings in Camden's the Good Mixer between Noel and Damon, laughing as they added millions to their bank accounts overnight. I've had a few conversations over the years with people close to Alan McGee and around Creation. There were no meetings. It was real. 'We were gonna go the week after them I believe,' Alan McGee told the *NME* in 2019, 'and they were going the week before us. It might have been the other way around, I can't remember. Damon moved it, so we went head-to-head. Damon made it a big battle.'

Initially, McGee and Ross, the label bosses, would have distanced themselves from this sort of battle and rearranged dates around releases for maximum impact. Andy Ross told the same *NME* piece in 2019: 'The perceived way of things seems to be that the whole thing was rigged and arranged between the two bands, but we'd spent at least six months trying to prevent this from arising.' Ross sounded irked. 'The plan, if there was a plan, was that Oasis would have a number 1 then we would, or vice-versa, and they wouldn't clash. Our lines of communication were pretty rock solid. But then, for some unexpected reason from our point of view, they brought forward their single by something like six weeks, weeks and weeks ahead of schedule. That threw us into complete confusion. All of a sudden, they're going to put their record out before ours.'

The start of the conflict could've been Liam's reaction to Damon Albarn at an Oasis party to celebrate 'Some Might Say' reaching number 1. 'When Oasis got to number 1 with "Some Might Say", I went to their celebration party, y'know, just to say, "Well done," said Albarn. And Liam came over and, like he is, he goes, "Number fookin' 1!", right in my face. So I thought, OK we'll see . . .' Albarn never mentioned that Liam had been rude to his then-girlfriend, Elastica singer, Justine Frischmann.

The general public was unaware of several contributory factors at the time. For most pop fans, the Britpop battle to reach number 1 didn't seem like a fair fight. Blur were a much bigger band with the full weight and heft of EMI's considerable marketing department behind them. According to Alan McGee: 'Blur had the might of EMI, they won the battle because they were giving away an extra CD format, I think both CDs were 99p. So you get extra tracks for 99p. And that's why they beat us, they had three formats, we had two.' McGee continues, relaxed to be speaking about it in 2019, 'They had the EMI marketing machine behind them whereas we had about twenty guys giving out cards saying, "We'll give you some Oasis tracks." There was a barcode issue, but that was a week before, so I don't think the barcodes got in the way.'

Andy Ross, meanwhile, was frank about the excuses coming from Creation. 'The EMI sales force was two blokes from Leicester called Roger and John – they were really, really good at getting stuff racked in stores. We can't be disingenuous about "tiny Creation versus major label". Oasis were signed to Sony, not Creation. So it wasn't a lopsided fight – they had the same level of resources, or firepower, as we did. It was fairly even. It was like a nuclear arms race. You could have up to four formats at that particular time. It was all neck-and-neck, but our fourth format outsold theirs by twenty to one.'

Johnny Hopkins (the Oasis press officer) believed it was all Blur's making. 'There was talk of should we move it away from the Blur date. But that was the date we had already fixed and publicised, and we had all our bits in place,' Hopkins told the *NME* in 2019. He went on: 'If they want to move their date, that's their prerogative. But we'll stick to ours.' He also believed that the actual name and branding of Britpop was too insignificant; he was keen to distance Oasis from anything to do with it. However, it was Ignition, Oasis's management, and not Alan McGee or Creation, who decided to run with it and try to take Blur on. I'm sure McGee to this day is happy they did. Taking the bait from Blur gave Oasis game-changing national exposure. Their album sold 21 million worldwide, so something worked – and worked impressively well. It was a challenge Oasis couldn't step back from. But once they had used the race to number 1 to get a major foothold and sell millions, most involved found the term and any inference to Britpop tiresome.

Blur were posh, stuck-up and privileged. Allegedly. In fact, they weren't. Well, perhaps compared to Oasis. They weren't that posh or stuck-up; it was more that they were the product of creative, musical and wealthier parents: more encouraging than posh. Albarn's mother was a theatrical set designer, his dad briefly managed The Soft Machine and was Head of Art and Design at Colchester Institute. Coxon's dad was a clarinet player and band leader in the British army. Rowntree's mum was a viola player and his dad a sound engineer at the BBC. James's father was a sales director. Albarn, Coxon and James were at Goldsmiths, University of London, where their ambitions would've been more likely to have been encouraged. Noel and Liam's mum was a dinner lady. Blur and Oasis were two diverse bands, with dissimilar influences and tastes, thrown up against each other because the media and the record industry loved the idea of casting them as rivals in a class war. What was there to lose?

Whether it truly was a golden age of British music is up for debate. Was it up there with The Beatles and the Stones competing against one another in the 1960s? The music wasn't as accomplished. Also, The Beatles and the Stones press officers would be in constant contact; they would be coordinating releases so as not to take away from each other's sales. If they couldn't work it out, Keith Richards would phone John Lennon and they'd agree to hold back if the other was ready to go. They understood it was business and as such they were better off working together than going up against each other. The ongoing slanging match between the posh southerners and the cheeky former shoplifters from up north continued.

Oasis and Blur briefly shone a light on the British music industry and the media in general picked up on it. By the time it reached fever pitch, they were erroneously hyping it into the 1990s equivalent of The Beatles versus the Stones. It became moderately entertaining. Suddenly the charts became exciting, a chart war, this high-profile campaign to reach number 1 and hold your own there. Two of the biggest bands of the day slogging it out to be the biggest selling act that week. I was watching on as a music fan who wanted to write comedy or do journalism, and I was fascinated by how the press and media handled it. It was back to the days of Margaret Thatcher and the north/south divide. It was class warfare.

Oasis called Blur 'The Chas 'n' Dave of Pop' and Blur called Oasis 'Quoasis'. Funny, playground stuff. Blur beat Oasis to number 1, selling 274,000 copies to Oasis's 216,000. Food cleverly released 'Country House' on various formats, a single and two CDs with added bonus tracks, knowing fans would want to buy everything. They also had a better, more imaginative video, directed by Young British Artist and Goldsmiths alumnus, Damien Hirst. It was McGee as ever at the height of the battle who reeled it in: 'We are now in a golden era of British pop music. These are two groups who formed on the indie circuit, who have grown popular through playing lots and lots of gigs in the country and who have crossed over to the public at large. And they're duking it out to see who is the biggest.'

22

Morning Glory v. *The Great Escape*

There was an erroneous assumption in the reporting of the Britpop battle between Oasis and Blur that fans liked either one or the other. Those involved in the music industry, from those in bands, record company staff, promoters, distributors, even down to the shop assistants on the frontline in the record shop, knew the real story. They were banking on the same fans buying both albums. Budget and marketing spend are a boring, economic part of the equation, but the reality is that they are probably the most important part. The chief cost of any film, album or book lies in its advertising and promotion. Letting people know about your product is a major expense. So it was a positive for both bands and the record companies to perpetuate the rivalry. The more hyped up into an enormous news story, the more people would know about it, and the more albums both Blur and Oasis would sell. Win. Win. It was that most valued of all commodities: free publicity.

The slanging match between the two bands gave the music business the biggest kick in the balls since punk. By the time their fight was on the BBC's *Six O'Clock News* and ITV's *News at Ten* the rules of engagement had changed. Let them chunder on with their clumsy comparisons to The Beatles and the Rolling Stones fighting it out at their peak in the 1960s. Every second it was highlighted in print, on TV or radio, thousands more of *(What's The Story) Morning Glory?* and *The Great Escape* flew out of the shops.

I recall two key things about the albums. There was a three-week gap between them. Blur released *The Great Escape* on 11 September 1995. *(What's The Story) Morning Glory?* wasn't released until 2 October 1995. My friend Tom had bought the latest Oasis album *(What's The Story) Morning Glory?* and brought it along with the Blur album to listen to. I had an adequate sound system (and tea and coffee skills) and he had a respectable record collection. We were both genuinely excited as we listened simultaneously to both CDs on two machines track by track. We were in a band together and we were music fans, that meant we were allowed to judge. On the first listen, Oasis, through immediacy and impact, wiped the floor with Blur.

The Great Escape is fifty-six minutes and fifty-six seconds in length. It's produced by Stephen Street. The cover depicts the tanned shins and pointed toes of someone flawlessly diving from a speedboat into a beautiful deep blue ocean. *(What's The Story) Morning Glory?* is fifty minutes and fifty seconds in length, and it was produced by Owen Morris and Noel Gallagher. The cover is an image taken by photographer Michael Spencer Jones, and shows DJ Sean Rowley and sleeve designer Brian Cannon (Noel was supposed to do it but called off 'sick') pass each other on Berwick Street in Soho, at 5 a.m. It's the dawning of a new day. It looks more vibrant and has something of the man in the street about it. Two slightly smudged strangers – where are they coming from? A rave? A party? They also look like they might turn on each other and start a fight. It has a freshness, is more alive, it already has an energy and vitality to it. Both covers are photographic, but this feels less pristine, less stylised. More real.

What did come across was how these were two entirely different bands. When Blur hit the mark on *The Great Escape* they get it spot on. Stephen Street's production of 'It Could Be You' and 'The Universal' are beautifully structured and lush sounding. Blur tend to shine infrequently; it's Oasis who are more consistent throughout.

We were both into Blur, especially their second album, *Modern Life Is Rubbish*, but were left shaking our heads as Oasis bulldozed Blur song for song. 'Hello', 'Roll With It', then 'Wonderwall' and 'Don't Look Back In Anger' are up against 'Stereotypes', 'Country House', 'Best Days' and 'Charmless Man'. It has to be contextualised, of course, as Blur were not releasing poor or sub-standard songs. It was just the songs Oasis had written for *(What's The Story) Morning Glory?* were markedly better; the songs, the melodies, the arrangements and the production sounded miles ahead of anything their rivals had done. We both agreed that *The Great Escape*, being a Blur album, was more of a grower: it might have more longevity.

I always thought it was a serious miscalculation for Blur to take on Oasis. At the time Blur were far more popular, having found commercial success with *Parklife*. They were the major player when they entered the fight with Oasis. (Initial UK sales for *Definitely Maybe* were around 600,000 whereas *Parklife* sold over 1.5 million.) It's funny how this changed as Oasis seamlessly grabbed the limelight and the dominant position as both bands went up against each other album to album. Maybe it was misguided confidence brought on by winning the battle for number 1 with 'Country House'. Blur won the battle of the singles, but Oasis won the war with the albums.

What was fantastic as a pop fan was the sheer quality of music the two bands were producing. To give both bands credit, they released music which treated the fans with a bit of respect. Blur had set the agenda but Oasis were whipping them in the album sales. If Blur had released *The Great Escape* a year earlier, in October 1994, it would've sold a lot more. Though it's also interesting to note that, from the time, the reviews for Blur were far better than those for Oasis. Blur's album was critically acclaimed. The *NME* gave it 9/10 and one of the best reviews for an album I've ever read. *Melody Maker* gave them 12/10 and *Q* gave it perfect marks.

At times, music has to be instinctive and less knowing. If you were reviewing from an objective sense as a piece of art, then *The Great Escape* is clever, but how clever is 'Louis Louis' or 'Tutti Frutti' and how majestic are they as songs? Sometimes it's about animal instinct; frankly, you need to know when to fuck, not make love. I would say, having heard more of their work, I was a fan of Blur's music and their Kinks, Small Faces, XTC quaint English poppy take on the world. Like millions of others, I also liked both bands. When it came to listening track by track, like a taste test on a crap TV cooking show, it was about the reaction, the immediacy, the actual moment and the initial impact of each song.

Compared to his sound and input in the first three albums, it was noticeable that Blur's Graham Coxon wasn't in the mood. Nowhere near his subsequent solo projects. On *The Great Escape*, neither his heart nor his head were in it. This is an album about Damon Albarn's demons. His obsessive attention to detail, stories about despair, neurosis and people dreaming about winning the lottery. It also, if we are being over-critical, has songs that are too eclectic and sound too suburban in their narratives that tell of the struggles of modern life. We needed to hear songs that were more direct. If there were a few more songs like 'Charmless Man', 'The Universal' and 'Country House', it would've been a better album, but then again it wouldn't be Blur if they released twelve pop singles. They always incorporated songs which were less accessible at first; they were masters of those excellent album tracks that took a while to grow on you.

What immediately strikes you on *(What's The Story) Morning Glory?* is the unshakeable confidence of a band who know their time has come and you can sense they are driving it on. Instead of being grateful and apologising for that, they do what bands with attitude should do and remain unrepentant, unforgiving and go for it full throttle. Like the band itself, the album is confident, authoritative, loud and batters the rafters like a full-force gale. You also notice a development in the structure and arrangement; it's now close to Burt Bacharach-esque and has that Lennon and McCartney vibe with stylish strings; it's full of ballads and huge, soaring choruses.

Given the enormous sales and the commercial success of *(What's The Story) Morning Glory?* it's hard to believe how mediocre and lukewarm the reviews were in the music press at the time of its release. As the years have passed, it's been accepted as a hugely significant British album, but again there was a consensus that it wasn't a patch on their debut or even analogous to *The Great Escape*. This could be down to critics being so desperate to get to hear it that they were also too quick to judge and knock it; I get the sense that, no matter how magnificent it was, they refused to be complimentary.

Definitely Maybe was the sound of a band with sneering ambition, daring to dream. A grandiose tale of two brothers and their gang who believed, who wanted to escape the torturous tedium of their dull, dreary existence. It was about a band inspired by The Stone Roses to use music as a way out. Their upbeat positive songs reflected that. *(What's The Story) Morning Glory?* is the sound of a band who know they've arrived. It opens with 'Hello', a curious doffing of the cap to a bygone age of British rock, to dark winter nights watching *Top of the Pops*. Keen listeners will also hear the opening of 'Wonderwall' for the first fifteen seconds. I'm not convinced it was the best opener but it sets up the rest of the album well. 'Roll With It' hits you bang on the head like a perfectly weighted crossed ball to the back post, met with surety by Liam, in sterling fashion. His voice has more depth, and his singing is purposeful and direct. 'Roll With It', like many of the songs on *(What's The Story) Morning Glory?*, connects with that sense of the common man and has a glorious footballing terrace-anthem feel about it.

The dynamic changes for track three, the superb 'Don't Look Back In Anger'; Noel sang this one, with a melancholic, soulful and reflective vocal. A song which is impeccably and seamlessly structured and flawlessly delivered. Noel's song-writing was developing a more sophisticated touch. One of the 'Don't Look Back In Anger' lyrics was the result of a 'mondegreen' (when a phrase or a lyric is misheard, for example, 'Sue Lawley' for The Police's 'So Lonely'). Noel had written the song in France and had a French word or phrase jammed in to fill the bars of the song while he was working and developing it. Liam thought he was talking about a girl named Sally and asked who he was singing about; Noel loved his brother's childlike misunderstanding and used it.

Opening with a piano that is redolent in tone and melody of John Lennon's 'Imagine', the song kicks in with a loose drum fill and quickly reaches out with a sentiment that could melt even the most cynical of hearts. It's an epic paean for Noel Gallagher and an epic paean in the arse for John Lennon if he happened upon it somewhere in the ether.

We then move on to the underrated and much glossed-over

'Hey Now!' The song is seldom, if ever, played live. It always reminds me, with the loose drumming and Bonehead's rhythm guitar work accentuating the wall of sound, of Neil Young through the verses and The Beatles meets Teenage Fanclub pop choruses. It deserves more credit. Ironically, it needs some loud, hard and straight Tony McCarroll drumming. Perhaps it feels more like a song from *Definitely Maybe* in sound, structure and looseness, which means it could be viewed as not sophisticated enough, and maybe a little bit too long.

We then move on to 'Untitled' aka 'The Swamp Song (Excerpt 1)' with its swirling Beatles guitar and Paul Weller on harmonica. The familiar chords of the first single from the album, 'Some Might Say' (which had been out since 30 April that year), meander through. It's funny but it sounds like an Oasis tribute band doing a cover of an Oasis song. It's the same structure and shape but with Alan White's more disciplined drumming; the effect is that they sound like they should, only better. Both Gallagher brothers are confident, with a well-delivered vocal from Liam and Noel's stadium-rocking licks; a definite number 1 single if ever I heard one.

'Cast No Shadow' is another archetypal Noel Gallagher tune. It's a classic because you think you've heard it before and it sounds familiar, but it's not. The best songwriters always make you think you have caught a glimpse of a song somewhere before. The harmonies are stunning, the sentiment heartfelt; it's an astounding, epic ballad. It was the last song written for the album and came to Noel while on the train back to the studio. It's about his friend Richard Ashcroft of The Verve.

'She's Electric' splits the crowd. Straightforward 1960s pop, check out the familiar ending; is it The Beatles' 'With A Little Help From My Friends'? Or is it a disposable throwaway filler track from a band that finds this all so effortless? Liam doesn't like singing it live. It's pop music and it's witty. It's this album's equivalent of 'Digsy's Dinner'. The album's title track opens with a muddy mix of a helicopter, a radio tuning in, some white noise, then Noel's characteristic wailing guitar for 'Morning Glory'.

'Champagne Supernova' is over seven minutes long and is a fitting climax and ending to the album; an anthemic song tailor-made for arenas and stadiums. Interestingly, it wasn't released as a single here (it's probably three minutes too long), but an edited radio single was released in the USA, Canada, Australia, New Zealand and France. It found its biggest success as a radio single in the States. It became their second number 1 single on the Modern Rock Tracks chart and eventually peaked at number 20 on the *Billboard* charts. It's a firm live favourite and is always played at shows.

If *Definitely Maybe* showed that Oasis were an indie band who were crossing over into the UK mainstream, then *(What's The Story) Morning Glory?* propelled them into a major worldwide rock act. The songs were better, there was a real maturity, more sweeping ballads, with a tighter rhythm section and Liam's singing was far better both in terms of richness and technique.

Awaiting the follow-up to *Definitely Maybe*, for fans at least, was always going to be nerve-wracking. Would it be possible to ever release anything as scintillating as that debut? The longer the music press had to wait, the more the scales were tipping towards it being deemed a critical failure. Again, it's worth repeating that original reviews for the album were less than favourable. It looked like no matter what Oasis released, the reception would be begrudging. I loved it. If you got the music that Oasis loved and played, then you understood it. Blur were doing The Kinks and Oasis, well, they were doing

The Kinks but also The Beatles, The Who, T. Rex, the Sex Pistols and The Stone Roses.

While growing up, I was always obsessed with pop music and pop culture; I saw a direct line from 'Telstar' by The Tornados, through to 'Smells Like Teen Spirit' by Nirvana. They stood out because they sounded unusual. It was about music for the people, it was music of the time. Whether it was a song about a satellite or an anthem intrinsically about boredom and apathy, they were both part of a history that wove its way from Elvis to The Beatles, the Sex Pistols to Oasis. From bubblegum pop and the garage punk of the 1960s to new wave bands and everything in between. I understood that Oasis had released two albums that guaranteed their place among the artists who would always be listened to and revisited by future generations. Thankfully, even those who didn't like it originally have been won over by *(What's The Story) Morning Glory?*, which is now viewed as a seminal moment in musical history.

Some reviews were still disrespectful but there were many fine ones. I remember one particular *Rolling Stone* review by Jon Wiederhorn, which embraced the band's love of The Beatles while remaining sympathetic to the tension within the band. It also ended brilliantly . . . 'Yesterday, Noel Gallagher's troubles may have seemed so far away, but today Oasis are grappling with success and fear in a way that gives their glorious pop a potency. If Oasis can avoid falling prey to the kind of brotherly shove that eventually destroyed the Kinks artistically, the future looks bright indeed.'

23

King Tut's 31.5.93 (Part 5)

When McGee started the Creation label he wanted indie guitar bands, on limited edition singles, with colourful artwork. He wanted bands like The Television Personalities, quirky, real, independent artists. You could maybe see Oasis on a label like Beggars Banquet or Go Discs, the home of The La's, a band Noel loved and respected, and you could maybe see them developing to that level and selling enough to have a few good years in the music scene, but then moving on to something else. I saw nothing of any promise in their performance. For me, they weren't anywhere near ready, not yet and even if they were, Creation wasn't the right label. Again, I didn't know then that Creation were bankrolled by Sony and that bands were going to have to be more conventional and, to be blunt, sell.

I was comparing Oasis to The Pastels or The Jasmine Minks. And to put this in perspective, it's as McGee explained in an interview in the *Guardian*: 'In September 1992, I got fed up with selling 200,000 records in England and 18,000 in Germany. I got tired of selling only 3,000 copies of *Bandwagonesque* there. It's about distribution. If you're signed to some shit fuckin' indie, no matter what it does for your credibility, it does nothing to promote your group. Sony help us get worldwide distribution. At the moment, we're still getting some crap sales, but the potential is there. I've sold

Sony 49 per cent, which makes them feel good, but I'm very loyal to our bands. I've got their best interests at heart.'

But at the time, I didn't know the game had changed as had the type of band McGee was now looking for. And Oasis didn't come across as the correct fit. Why is McGee going for this kind of group that millions of ordinary people would like? Am I missing something here? Evidently, I was.

It's OK to revel in the glory of hindsight, of course it is. McGee hit the jackpot with Oasis and suddenly every bad bet was forgotten about. What has to be underlined and stressed at this exact point in proceedings is how monumentally lucky or monumentally skilled Alan McGee was. One of the rumours – and it was a strong one – going around the city was that he had to be showing off and felt like signing a band that night. For the buzz, for the bragging rights. That's grossly unfair and inaccurate, but it was one of the stories doing the rounds. Here's how it happened and it involves most of the previous elements of luck and bravado, but it also includes the crucial bit: talent-spotting.

When the evening became tense earlier, McGee had seen Liam downstairs at the bar, hanging around the pool table (the mysterious pool table!). He thought Liam was the cool leader of the pack, the tall one he'd already seen prowling around the venue. He didn't know the guy with the Adidas tracksuit top was the singer. When he saw him come on stage, he must have thought, if he can sing, this could be on. If he had a couple of passable songs, then he would sign them. To him, they were even better than he had hoped. So that could explain his excitement. McGee suggested that Liam looked the type who would be in the middle of it and, what's more, he looked as if he'd be able to handle and enjoy being there. The rest of the band and their pals looked like they were part of a gang.

They had that Stone Roses look, the clothes, the hair, and a debauched wasted elegance as if they were part of the club scene. He could see there was another element too, the football, the lads' mag culture, then with those to hand you could start to broaden the popularity and the market considerably.

The aggression that was noticeable downstairs was also obvious when Liam and Noel took to the stage. Liam had this antagonistic posture and biting singing style. Nothing was said and there was little eye contact between the two brothers. The band took their cues from Noel. It's funny how first impressions stick and while the Oasis story might have been about the music, the hit singles and the success they garnered, it was also about the monumental fuckups and the destruction between the warring brothers. So at least I called one thing perfectly that night. As the years passed, Liam (especially) and Noel (occasionally) proved they were prone to the odd fight. McGee's experienced eye would have already calculated the importance of the band's profile around that look and edge. If he could transfer and channel this on-stage hostility, he realised it would mean an unlimited supply of free press and publicity. The odd high-octane fight on stage wouldn't do anyone any harm. To him, the balance of disorder, intrigue and fascination was exactly what was needed. They played what he thought were three exceptional songs and that sprawling cover of 'I Am The Walrus' – which happens to be one of McGee's favourite songs. Research confirmed they usually finished their set with the song, going off stage one by one and leaving a guitar on a stand, blaring out feedback. It was, when push came to shove, one of their strongest songs.

McGee may have sensed audiences would relate and empathise with the guys on stage. With a bit of luck, a suitable, patient and sympathetic producer could capture and unleash this live sound, and then they might even have the songs to be a commercially viable proposition. But no one will ever tell me that it was planned out. Yes, McGee had a hunch and a killer intuition, but for it to transform into such a success for Oasis, was unbelievable. It involved a substantial amount of perspicacity, yes, but most importantly, loads of luck.

This would have all been easier if I lied and said, yeah, yeah, I saw it straight away, you could tell they'd be superstars and have countless hit records, be surrounded by the beautiful people, they'd hang out with Kate Moss, marry Patsy Kensit and be playing Knebworth in a few years. Again I'd defy even the best A&R man to see something so sparkling in the future for the band that played that night. At this point, anyone suggesting they'd get close to that kind of success would be laughed out of the venue. The lasting image of their physical presence at King Tut's, which went on to become their on-stage style, was that they didn't move much.

By the time they were putting together enough cash to hire a van (with their friends following in a Mercedes mini coach) and drive to Glasgow on 31 May 1993, to play at King Tut's, Noel felt they were finally ready. But even he couldn't have imagined that the set was tight enough to blow away a certain record company boss, who was actively searching for a band who would turn around his fortunes. Someone with an eye for bands with a set full of timeless tunes that people in the street would sing along to at weddings, birthdays, post-football celebrations, Friday night parties . . . Everywhere. Again, I missed that.

24

Macca & Woolworths

As if to accentuate the slings and arrows of outrageous fortune, it's the end of 1995, Noel is hanging out with Paul McCartney and chatting to him about his band. I'm talking with a girl in the Job Centre I know from school who is calling to arrange my interview for a Christmas job in Woolworths. Noel is now exceptionally rich and famous. He's everywhere. On magazines, always in the papers, on radio and TV. He's talking about his latest pal, Paul McCartney. McCartney is talking about Noel. He likes Noel's style, his clothes and especially his hair. Macca thinks Noel's hair and fashion are similar to The Beatles.

I've now forced myself to meet the manager at Woolworths in Airdrie, about a job at the record counter; it's coming up to Christmas and I need the cash. I'm fed up being skint and figured it was time to earn some money and at least try to ensure I could be more generous with my Christmas gifts. I'd played in bands since I was 14 and I'd spent the following fifteen years attempting to make my mark in music.

I was in my late twenties and had at last started thinking about what I wanted to do. I wanted to write, maybe try journalism. I liked comedy and had started writing jokes and sketches for TV and radio. I also realised my dream of signing a recording deal had passed me by. I had my tail between my legs as I convinced the manager of Woolworths that she should give me the job for twenty-four days from 1 December to Christmas Eve. I was the man for the job, I told her; I had previous record shop experience. I used to work in Our Price, remember that? Our Price, in Cumbernauld, so I understood what it was like to be underpaid, overworked, dealing with stock, customers and music.

The manager is a nice woman, with blond curly hair, business-like, but friendly. The staff are lovely, welcoming another stupid guy into Airdrie's music central, which is behind the counter of Woolworths. I look like a giant. It might sound as if I thought the job was beneath me, but I genuinely didn't think that. I found it a bit of a culture shock but I needed the money and was prepared to fit in and earn my way. I'm a bit embarrassed about it, but it's always stayed with me. Most didn't notice, but a few, especially those involved in bands and people I would see around, at gigs or in the pub, would do a double-take. There was a lot of schadenfreude. A few years previously, I was making records and playing shows with Mudhoney, Hole, Nirvana and The Screaming Trees. But now I wasn't. But I had finally found my rightful place in the music industry, behind the record counter of Woolworths, selling Oasis.

Walking to work on cold winter mornings in the dark helped make my mind up. If I was going to try this writing malarkey, I had to do it properly. If I wanted to write, I'd need to put the same work and effort that I'd put into music over the years. I felt purged, my mind free. I know, I hear you. Why is he still rabbiting on about Woolworths?

By the end of 1995, Oasis are making tremendous, unrelenting inroads. Guigsy has come back into the fold, they are playing to 20,000 at Earls Court, then heading for the west coast to play shows in the States. They had just released

(What's The Story) Morning Glory? On release in October 1995, it stayed at number 1 on the album charts for ten weeks. On 22 December they recorded five songs for *The White Room* New Year Special, which would go out on New Year's Eve. Three of these, 'Don't Look Back In Anger', 'Wonderwall' and 'Roll With It', were shown on 31 December with 'Round Are Way' and 'Some Might Say' shown at a later date on 27 January 1996.

I'm serving the public in Airdrie crap music, crap films, crap computer games and, bizarrely for the music counter, twenty and thirty pounds' worth of the latest must-have: lottery tickets. It's a serious reality check. I want to suggest they consider the probability and work out the odds of winning.

Worlds briefly collide, as a famous comedy actor who worked with people I know and whom I would later write for on the show *Naked Radio*, comes in. She's called Elaine C. Smith and she was shopping at Woolworths in Airdrie. I remember among her Christmas shopping she bought a Montgomery Clift movie. I consider striking up a writer/actor conversation, but the queues are meandering through half the shop and I'm too shy to endure more embarrassment.

The manager asks if I'd fancy coming in at 4 a.m. to super-vise the shop's Christmas delivery. It arrives in a battered, ancient van and I realise it's just one guy, with no security. I'm wondering, OK, if I were a robber with a heart of gold, I could easily steal this truck from you. The only thing I need to do is jump into your van and I can be like Airdrie's Robin Hood . . . if only I could drive. I realise I've been asked in case anyone does decide to rob the van, which was admittedly an easier job than the queue and stress of the shop floor on Christmas Eve, but I'm there in case the scene turns a bit Tarantino-esque. I'm there to help my lovely colleague in the event of an armed robbery. Thankfully, she knows what she's doing. It's 9 a.m.

and I've been up since three in the morning and I'm on £3 an hour. Around this time, Creation are having a Christmas party and Noel receives a £60,000 chocolate-brown Rolls-Royce, a gift from his grateful publisher, Sony Music. It's OK, there's a reason for this vivid memory.

As you know by now, I've watched on since I saw them in King Tut's nineteen months previously and Alan McGee eventually signed them. My Christmas job in Woolworths remains so clear in my mind because of the surreal nature of the music scene at the time. Like many people, my life and memories are guided by music in the charts, or at least they used to be. You eventually drift off into a land of Radio 4, then Radio 3 and the music in the charts doesn't connect with you in any way at all. In 1995, I was busy convincing colleagues we needed to order more of The Mike Flowers Pops' version of 'Wonderwall', which reached number 2, in December 1995. Not only were Oasis popular, they now had kitsch cabaret covers of their songs. It gets even more bizarre. The shop's biggest selling single, which sadly kept The Beatles' 'Free As A Bird' off number 1, was Michael Jackson's 'Earth Song'.

In the album charts, *(What's The Story) Morning Glory?* had sold by the truckload. That's not hyperbole, I know, because I was helping to empty the truck. The Beatles had *Anthology*, which was also selling well, but as this was Christmas and since gifts were being bought for so many mums, grannies and aunties at this time of year, Oasis and The Beatles were held off the album number 1 spot by the singing squaddies, Robson & Jerome. (Remember them? My apologies if you'd wiped them from your mind.) Hilarious. This huge focus and razor-sharp industry talk of Britpop and the media all engrossed in this battle between Oasis and Blur, and what happens but Robson & Jerome swoop in to take the top spot. (While mums, grannies and aunties swoon.) I remember looking around and staff and customers were nonchalantly chatting about Oasis in the same breath as The Beatles and Michael Jackson. Best of all, they didn't sound out of place in the various conversations.

It's odd explaining how I felt watching Oasis succeed. I'm not in the slightest bit jealous or bitter, I'm proud of what they have achieved as if I'm part of it. Then I realise I *am* part of it. That's what their music is about: inclusion. We are part of their story; we don't know where it can lead or what's ahead of us. It's our arc, our path, our soundtrack. The best songs do that and the best songwriters have that uncanny ability to reach in and get you. I always got through shifts by playing The Beatles' *Anthology* and *(What's The Story) Morning Glory?* by Oasis.

Whenever I played Oasis, even on the shop's poor music system, the shopfloor came alive. Liam's singing is loud and the sound is clear. The music cuts through. Again, you could be forgiven for thinking the band were playing live behind the counter. The people in the shop suddenly have a spring in their step. Everything becomes instinctively choreographed. Shoppers are moving to the music, singing and walking to the beat.

Each time I play the album, I have a bundle of around thirty copies beside me under the counter. There's always the same reaction. 'Hello' comes on and there's a buzz. That continues when the band kicks into 'Roll With It'. Then there's the reason for the Woolworths anecdote: 'Wonderwall' comes on and loads of customers, a wide demographic, keep asking me who it is. It's not only the more youthful customers but across the board, from 14 to 75 years old, mostly older people who you might consider wouldn't be too into pop music, come up and ask the same thing.

'Who's that, son? That's a magic song . . .'

They kept asking it all throughout my time there.

'Is that The Beatles, son? That's lovely . . .'

It's clear for many reasons that Oasis wouldn't be their normal purchase. 'Wonderwall' was released as a single way back in October. They have probably heard it on the radio or TV, but when they hear it in the shop, it reconnects. When I play it, I'm busy serving, but still I grab a copy of an album and hand it to them. They queue up and another one is sold. You can set your watch by it. Here comes track three, 'Wonderwall'. Here we go. During the song's four minutes and eighteen seconds, I could sell eight or nine copies.

'Excuse me,' comes the shout, 'who's that yer playing, mate? Is that from that Beatles *Anthology*?'

'No, sir, it's Oasis. A song called "Wonderwall".'

'Is that Oasis? Do you have the single? It's smashing.'

'We might have a copy of the single but it was released back in October. You'd be better off buying the album for a few quid more. There are four hits on it and loads of cracking songs. I'd love it as a stocking filler.' And they trust me. And they go ahead and buy it. It's not like I'm hoodwinking them or on commission. Price is what you pay; value is what you get. In hindsight, it was the easiest sale; most times you were doing customers a favour.

So there I am, spreading the word in a working-class town in North Lanarkshire. Imagine that rolled out across every record shop and retail outlet in every town and city in the world and you'd get close to seeing why the album sold so well. I'd like to think I played a tiny part, but the truth is, it was down to one thing, the quality of the songs and the band's uncanny knack for writing surefire hits that connected with a broad cross-section of people. As I sold their second album it often flashed through my mind that I wouldn't have given them a record deal and I'd smile ruefully to myself, a smile which helped keep me sane and kept the Christmas shopper lunatics at bay.

'What are you smiling at?' the lovely assistant who knows what she's doing with the killer smile of her own would ask.

'Nothing,' I'd say, 'and you wouldn't believe me if I told you. Who's first, please?'

25

Sibling Rivalry, Made in
Manchester & Breaking America

Initially, a major part of the Oasis DNA was their erratic, fiery and intense interviews. It was always the same: dry, lightning-quick, instinctive and honest. At first, I used to think it was staged. They couldn't mean half of what they were saying, could they? Maybe they were drunk, speeding out their nuts or high and that made them less guarded. Part of the interest in the band, especially with Liam, was that he was a character, a bit of a lad, a thief, a hooligan, a fighter, maybe not the brightest but he had street smarts, he wasn't an academic. Liam would come out with tirades, whereas Noel had a better internal editor. His comments were usually more guarded, but he had his moments too.

Liam's attitude and behaviour attracted the music press and when the band crashed headlong into an unbelievable level of fame and widespread popularity, the tabloids couldn't get enough of them. This was another part of the fascination with Oasis, the charisma and the magnetism, that element of danger. Their appeal, the talented songwriter who had those songs that connected with millions of ordinary people, the people who keep the country moving. The bus drivers, the sparkies and the brickies, the nurses, cleaners and call centre workers. The papers saw the good-looking confident singer, with his football casual vibe who sang better than the guy from The Stone Roses. They saw a band that chimed with and reached football fans, Mods, indie kids and students. They spoke to them all and they loved them.

But why did everybody buy into it? Well, apart from the stirring pop songs, one of the key elements to their popularity was the gravitational pull of the relationship between Liam and Noel. One which could explode at any time and fall apart in front of you. There was always that nervousness when watching them perform live. Why are we so intrigued by the sight of legendary stuntmen on motorbikes flying over buses? It's because there's a chance they might make a clown of themselves and crash. Why do we watch people walking on high wires between skyscrapers? Because they might fall. (Well, at least that's part of the reason.) It's the same with Oasis. Many have the perverse hope at the back of their mind that it might go wrong and descend into an all-out fight.

Despite the arguing, bickering, violence and fights, Oasis were a powerful and entertaining rock 'n' roll band. What's not to love about two feuding brothers? It's a central theme of so many dramas and part of the unique unpredictability of the band. Liam's mad-for-it, game-for-a-fight attitude could be down to his upbringing, to alcohol, drugs, but I'd hazard a guess that some of it comes from an inability to express himself in the way Noel was able to with his songwriting.

Everywhere you look, ask around, or read, in the articles or interviews even from those closest to them, it's always the same description. Liam is nuts. Liam is funny. Liam is mad for it! Liam is venomous. Liam is crazy. Liam is the best frontman in rock 'n' roll. Liam is a bully. I find him amusing. Here's a random list of quotes attributed to the singer:

'There's Elvis and me. I couldn't say which of the two is best.'

'Americans want grungy people, stabbing themselves in the head on-stage. They get a bright bunch like us, with deodorant on, they don't get it.'

'She can't even chew gum and walk in a straight line, let alone write a book.' (On Victoria Beckham's aspirations to become an author.)

'I suppose I do get sad, but not for too long. I just look in the mirror and go, "What a f**king good-looking f**k you are." And then I brighten up.'

Those closest to him say he is complex. They say he has some kind of multiple personality disorder. Liam thinks he's John Lennon. Liam doesn't know who he is. How are we expected to know who he is if Liam doesn't?

Well, what about Noel? Noel is arrogant. Noel is kind. Noel is a genius. Noel is a big-headed fuck. Noel is a control freak. Noel is obsessive. Noel is a perfectionist. Noel is shy and self-conscious. The only certain thing, whatever your opinion on the personality traits of the two brothers, is that Liam is a magnificent lead singer and Noel a distinguished guitarist and songwriter. And together they are a creative force of nature.

*

Oasis could only be a Manchester band. They are so clearly part of the same musical tradition that goes from Joy Division to The Smiths, from New Order to James, from The Happy Mondays to The Stone Roses. They are also part of the DNA of the northwest of England. One of protest, of radical thought and deed. They are part of that Manchester tradition, the same city that on 16 August 1819 saw a cavalry charge with sabres on 80,000 people, killing fifteen and injuring hundreds more who were gathering to protest against the Corn Laws. The same city that in 1856 would build Manchester Free Trade Hall. The same city that engineered the Manchester Ship Canal, turning a landlocked city into a port, allowing ocean-going cargo ships to sail to the centre of the city. A city with a population who demanded to be listened to. The same Manchester that, at the Free Trade Hall, heckled Bob Dylan in May 1966, shouting out 'Judas' because he'd dared to go electric. Then who hosted one of the most influential gigs of all time: the Sex Pistols at Manchester's Lesser Free Trade Hall in June 1976. A gig that's now witnessed as a seminal moment in the emergence of the British punk movement. In keeping with Oasis at King Tut's, hundreds claimed to be there too. However, just over forty people were present, each paying 50p for a ticket.

Add the historic spirit of Manchester's DNA, the beauty and poetic turbulence of first- and second-generation Irishness and you have an irresistible cocktail ready to explode at any moment. How vital is this feuding pandemonium? The Gallagher brothers will argue and punch and fight and criticise and fall out yet in a crisis they are as one. Will hate each other, and come close to killing each other, but if anyone else does it, there's trouble cos they're family. So throw that into the insanity and you have an intoxicating and hazardous mix. One where the attitude is to party hard, laugh hard and for most of the time work hard. As much as that crazy spirit and force could be so destructive, it was also what defined the band.

They've hooked into the hooligan and football casual aspect with their fashion, but their management must've felt like a frustrated football manager dealing with errant football geniuses like George Best or Paul Gascoigne. That kind of mentality which can't be controlled or have its wings clipped, because if it is, the natural genius and energy and all-out approach is stifled. That resistance and refusal to conform, the manic, crazy, restless spirit of Liam, that destructive force that gave the newspapers so much to write about. Football and Manchester and being mercurial? Best and Marsh, Cantona and the short-lived City career of Noel's hero, the outrageous mad bad boy, Mario Balotelli. Stylish, eye-catching, irresistible players who exist on another plane, who are wonderfully entertaining but flawed often beyond measure.

Those fights at gigs, on ferries, the shows that were stopped, cancelled or descended into mayhem because Liam lost his voice, usually down to boredom that resulted in too much drinking. The tabloid red tops also understood how to flick his switch. From the first news stories before they released a single it was never going to last. It was too erratic, violent and unruly, yet they did stay together, much longer than expected.

After the success of the first two albums in the UK and Europe, breaking America was always the next logical step for the band. The question of Oasis cracking America is, however, as we've seen, a thorny issue. It's still assumed Oasis failed to make hay when the sun shone in the USA. Timing and striking while the iron is hot is everything in music. Eventually, much later on in their career when they were a bit more grown up, they did finally make serious inroads, but the band and America seemed destined to be at odds with each other, thanks to stubbornness, bad luck and the familiar story of self-inflicted hedonistic damage. America and Oasis took far too much time to fall in love with each other.

The trouble with Oasis and America in 1995 was mainly down to ego. They were now a gigantic draw in the UK, big in Europe, Japan and Australia, yet conquering the States continually dogged them. It wasn't as if America didn't know about the band. It was always willing to accept UK bands who were happening and take them to their hearts. It's more that the band were not prepared to scale down and play club gigs and deal with starting from scratch again. Even though it was an approach that had yielded success for many bands like The Police and U2. It could have been the sheer magnitude of conquering America that seemed daunting, impossible, when they felt they were doing well everywhere else.

I remember documentaries about the Rolling Stones touring America and for years they were popular on both the east coast and the west coast, but the reception was lukewarm in between. The only way to earn your stripes in America is to go there and gig. You must commit to bursts of at least thirty or forty dates, at least twice a year. To play from the beginning of your career and after each album is out, come back and hopefully play bigger and better venues. Oasis finally yielded and did as they were asked. Their manager Marcus Russell stuck with the tried and trusted template, and later in their career it came good. It was about developing a reputation as a live band and returning and gathering momentum. Yet at their peak and arguably at their most potent, Oasis failed to make the expected impact on America.

While on the subject of U2, as we briefly were, their label Mother made a serious bid to sign Oasis. You can't imagine Oasis on any other label than Creation, but there was a determined attempt made to lure them. Mother was part of Polygram, whose A&R man, Richard Brown, was keen to sign Oasis. His boss Malcolm Dunbar had loved the demo and was keen to snap them up, famously offering double what McGee had offered. There was also serious interest from Andy McDonald of Go! Discs who was into the band. So, until Oasis finally signed their contract it was feasible that they could have gone to U2's label or the home of The La's and Paul Weller. Fate plays its hand and there are so many threads and what-if moments in the Oasis story. In the end, Oasis signed a worldwide deal with Sony, who licensed the band to Creation for the UK while Sony-owned Epic dealt with the US.

It wasn't as if the band didn't have chances and massive opportunities to grab America earlier in their career. The record company and management must've been going crazy. Apart from blowing the Whisky a Go Go gig, another high-profile controversy occurred in August 1996 which encapsulates the problem. Like so many of the previous high-profile implosions, this one is played out as the band prepares for an appearance on MTV's *Unplugged* show. Leading up to the show, Liam showed up for five minutes, sang a bit, complained about his voice and disappeared. Bear in mind here that MTV *Unplugged* is a much sought-after and career-changing gig. It's an enormous opportunity to showcase your songs to America and worldwide. The band were locked away in full production rehearsals for the MTV show for the two weeks leading up to it. During this time, Liam's appearances were sporadic at best. The others were hoping he was saving his voice for the main recording and would deliver on the day.

Then, on the day of the show, he turned up shit-faced before they were due to go on. Noel asks if he can sing, then asks him to try, but he can't, he's dreadful, and it's decided that Noel will sing as Liam's too drunk and can't do it. Then, to add insult to injury, the cameras spot him in the director's gantry and he's smoking, drinking and heckling Noel and the band. It's uncomfortable to watch. Another major blow to their chances of cracking America. Is it rock 'n' roll? Is it selfishness? Or is it the DNA of Oasis?

The weekend before the band officially split in 2009 following the gig at the Rock en Seine festival in Paris on 28 August, they had to cancel playing the V Festival in Chelmsford with Liam reportedly suffering from viral laryngitis. From then on, the mudslinging really started between the two brothers. Amid the bitter feuds, there's a significantly forceful quote from 2011, in an interview with the *New York Times* in which Noel explains why he thinks the band didn't make it as big in America. 'As I'm getting on the plane he's getting off cos his wife called saying: "We need to buy a house." What they were doing for the previous three months is anybody's guess. Probably picking gnats off each other's hair like monkeys. The first gig was in a 16,000-seat arena, and the singer's not turned up? That killed us stone dead in America. This is rock 'n' roll. Would Johnny Rotten have gotten a house on the eve of an American Tour? Keith Richards? John Lennon? You either want it or you don't and I blame him for us never becoming as big in America as we were in England.'

It still exasperates Noel that they couldn't take it to that next stage in the US when they should've done, at their peak around late 1995 into 1996. The real focus was always on America. Those behind the group had heard the songs. They were listening to music they believed would set the band up to easily crack it in the States. There was a genuine sense that momentum was picking up. Another element of the strategy was playing three or four band bills with radio station-linked tours; this meant they were playing the game while gaining loads of radio play.

For Creation, until now, the most successful band in the States with regards to sales were Teenage Fanclub. They had reached around 200,000 with *Bandwagonesque*. Expectations were high for Primal Scream's album *Give Out But Don't Give Up*. The band headed to Ardent Studios in Memphis to work with legendary producer Tom Dowd. Sony had become impatient with the recording bill hitting £350,000 and still no sign of a hit. They wanted rock 'n' roll and got country soul. McGee was nervous too, and The Black Crowes producer George Drakoulias, along with Jim Dickinson, George Clinton and Kenney Jones, was brought in to beef out the sound and make it more 'American radio friendly'. The original work was considered lost until Andrew Innes came across the tapes in his basement and *Give Out But Don't Give Up: The Original Memphis Recordings* were released to critical acclaim in 2018.

By now, Oasis had become a global success. Their *Dig Out Your Soul* tour, between August 2008 and August 2009, played arena and stadium shows. A hundred and nineteen concerts across North America, South America, Europe, Asia and Africa. Hitting this level and maintaining it is tough. These sorts of tours when you're strategically taking on a continent take a lot of energy, skill and a tremendous amount of luck. Devotees of the band often ask what if? What if they could remain cool when it came to those defining moments, when they virtually had true greatness in their grasp, when they needed to take that leap and leave their mark, but then something happened. Generally, it always came back to two things. One, Noel's professionalism annoying Liam and two, Liam's lack of discipline irritating Noel.

Their seventh and final studio album *Dig Out Your Soul* got to number 5 on the *Billboard* charts in 2008. The reason behind the upsurge in Oasis popularity (they also sold 20,000 downloads and charted at number 2 on the *Billboard* digital sales chart) was attributed to the success of British bands like Coldplay. Also, the band's profile was much higher than usual after Noel was attacked on stage at the V Festival in Toronto on 7 September. The attack was more a drunken shove, and if it hadn't been so painful for Noel who fell awkwardly, it would be comedic. Liam's reaction to the 'attacker', wanting to take the guy on, was hilarious, as three security guards are dragging him off stage. Noel broke three ribs; they had to cancel five gigs and he needed eight months to recover. Drunk people shouldn't be allowed to fuck about on stage unless they're in the band.

As the band got bigger in the UK and Europe, they became more relaxed about worrying whether America had truly taken them to their hearts. Enthusiasm and support in the US had been loyal from the initial success of *Definitely Maybe* in the college charts. They did have success there, mostly down to having toured across America nine times. By the time Andy Bell and Gem Archer joined they were a commercial success in the States. It's undeniable that, across their career, Oasis had hugely significant moments with America, successes other bands would love to have enjoyed.

Whether it was a sought-after slot on MTV *Unplugged* or arena dates booked and ready to go, or the shocking implosions before key gigs like the one at Whisky a Go Go, there was always something unpredictable and unstable hanging over the world which Liam and Noel frequented. Something that could randomly snap and flare up without warning.

In the spring of 2013, I watched the Denzel Washington and Robert Zemeckis movie, *Flight*. I won't waste the film for anyone who hasn't seen it, but the first twenty minutes of that movie accurately sum up Oasis and their career. It's disorderly, full of terrifying moments of heroism, with a few casualties. It's mostly all down to drink and drugs, but you can't take your eyes off the action unravelling in front of you.

26

Irish Blood, English Heart

It's what legendary Mancunian, and child of an Irish Catholic immigrant family, Morrissey, would describe as the Irish blood and English heart. That which courses through your body and determines what you're made of, the lineage from which you descend. Morrissey was being poetic and metaphorical. He was drawing parallels with the creative and political struggle of being an Englishman of Irish descent. The late George Byrne, the legendary Irish music journalist and radio pundit, once said, 'Oasis are the greatest Irish band ever . . . after The Smiths.' The Irish have the words. The poetry. Byrne was always loquacious, spiky and funny.

For our purposes, to take a serious overview of the band's career thus far, it would be remiss to disregard the Irish blood coursing through their veins. The distinct Irishness and the effect and impact this heritage would have on them, their music and their attitude. It's a compelling part of their story. For some reason, it stoked the fragile instability. You have to incorporate their Irishness into the narrative, that lineage of poetry, wine and song, passing down through the generations. As much as it can be intoxicating, it can also be unstable, changing from one extreme to the other, detonating at any given time, driven with passion and a dark, troubled soul. As we've seen, the brothers will argue, fight and criticise yet in a crisis are as one.

It's a gripping mix. It has brought both success and excess. It's the will, drive and stubbornness to make it, to get out of the housing estate and that entrenched mental attitude to enjoy everything life throws at you. To maybe enjoy it too much, but to always have an attitude that wants to live for today. No one knows where the next meal, piece of luck or money will come from. Who cares about tomorrow? As much as that wildness of spirit could be a destructive force, it was also what defined them as a band . . . and it came from Ireland.

We automatically associate Oasis with Manchester and the scene coming out of England, yet the band (the original line-up) are Irish, from Levenshulme, and for the Greater Manchester area, that's not unremarkable. Millions of Irish have been part of a continual movement and migration to the major industrial cities of the UK for centuries, particularly Glasgow, Liverpool, Birmingham and Manchester. The band's Irish upbringing was key to their music and success. '*Definitely Maybe* was the sound of five second-generation Irish Catholics coming out of a council estate,' Noel famously said. The question is, has the band's second-generation Irishness played a part in their career? I believe it has.

An area at Oxford Road Station, near the Salisbury pub on Wakefield Street, was once called 'Little Ireland'. It was also one of the poorest slums in the city. It was so wretched it made the pages of German philosopher Friedrich Engels's 1845 book *The Condition of the Working Class in England.* 'The cottages are old, dirty, and of the smallest sort,' wrote Engels, 'the streets uneven, fallen into ruts and in part without drains or pavement; masses of refuse, offal and sickening filth lie among standing pools in all directions; the atmosphere is poisoned by the effluvia from these, and laden and darkened by the smoke of a dozen tall factory chimneys.'

The city has always had a huge Irish community. One in five Mancunians can claim Irish blood. Many left Ireland and headed to Manchester because of the Great Irish Famine (1845–1852). Thanks to the Industrial Revolution, thousands emigrated from Ireland to Lancashire where there was plenty of work available. More than a third of those building the city's canals were Irish.

Margaret 'Peggy' Sweeney came from Charlestown in County Mayo, one of eleven children. She moved to Manchester in 1961, aged 18. It almost sounds like a folk song. She met Tommy, from County Meath, north Dublin, one of six children, who arrived in Manchester, aged 17. They married in 1965. The first of three sons, Paul Anthony Gallagher, was followed by Noel Thomas David Gallagher on 29 May 1967. Paul and Noel were joined by a brother William John Paul Gallagher, on 21 September 1972. The family later moved to Burnage after Liam was born. In 1984 Peggy left her husband, taking the boys to live in a nearby council house where she still resides.

On the subject of his Irishness, Noel explained, 'I clearly remember my mam saying to me and my two brothers when we were growing up: *You're only English because you were born here.* With a mother from County Mayo and a father from County Meath, there's not a drop of English blood in me. I recently had a child with my Scottish girlfriend and there's no English blood in him at all. I feel as Irish as the next person.' He's not wrong, of course, but there's a uniquely romanticised, poetic element to the claim to be 'Irish', even if only in distant part. Americans especially love it, and, understandably, it offers a feeling of connection and heritage, which is irresistible in a nation of immigrants. From Gene Kelly to James Cagney, from Jim Morrison to Kurt Cobain. From John F. Kennedy to Barack

Obama (who, on a visit to Moneygall, brilliantly quipped to his eighth cousin that they shared the same 'Irish' ears).

In movies or fiction, the Irish have often been badly, some would say comically, portrayed. It's generally a mix of discord, of being unable to cope, and then they usually descend into cliché. It's either the dewy-eyed Hollywood version of John Wayne and Scarlett O'Hara in *The Quiet Man* or the stereotypical alcoholic redhead cop or fireman with gambling issues and a serious drink (aka tumbler of whisky) problem. The ubiquitous unsung detective who heroically saves 1,800 school kids from a terrorist blowing up their school but a deep childhood trauma means he's afraid of sleeping in the dark. The Irish, it seems, nearly always have remnants of their heritage, some kind of trauma linked back to poverty.

Oasis fed off their Irishness. They channelled the attitude and aggression and it made them want 'it' more. 'From my point of view, you have to try that bit harder with the Irish thing or if you're Scottish,' said Liam, 'you've got to dig deep because everything revolves around England. The others had everything on a plate.' Maybe that was the main driver, they wanted it more, maybe even needed it more.

We know Peggy Gallagher is Irish but few know that the other band members had Irish parents too. This is seldom mentioned in the broader Oasis conversation but could explain why their fans were so loyal. The music chimed, and the songs connected. The Oasis canon is linked to the rousing songs of revolution, a call to arms. The songs Noel heard when growing up either in the house or down the Irish Centre would've been uplifting, full of love, pain, heartache, remorse; they were fist-pumping songs. That's why his songs are as at home played on an acoustic guitar in a folk music jam in a small pub in Galway in front of three men and a dog as they are to 125,000 at Knebworth. 'Wonderwall', 'Live Forever', 'Don't Look Back In Anger' and 'Slide Away' are transferable from plaintive acoustic ballads to stadium anthems. In songs like 'Cigarettes & Alcohol' and 'Supersonic,' we have a different call to arms; this time, it's about working-class disenchantment, rallying the troops and dreaming of escape. Bonehead agrees: 'We were five lads off the street. I get asked that a lot; "what is it about Manchester that brings out such great music?" and my answer is the same, Celtic blood. It has to be that. It's the only explanation. Working-class people from strong Irish backgrounds making music. My mother was from the west of Ireland in Mayo. A town called Swinford, it's literally a few miles from Noel and Liam's grandparents.'

When this English heart and Irish blood combine and Noel's writing, that flash of genius, sparks the flame, that's when we have an intoxicating mix. One that makes Oasis mercurial and unpredictable and can give us wonderful live performances and self-destructive gigs and hissy fits in front of thousands. Drama in spades. From the gigs at the Tivoli Theatre to Liam's strops at the Point, to Slane Castle, to the knockout gigs at Cork (three days after Knebworth) and the landmark gig at Slane, again, in 2009. From the start, Ireland embraced the band and treated them as their own.

At one point, Oasis had seven singles in the Irish Top 40 and when *(What's The Story) Morning Glory?* came out, *Definitely Maybe* returned to number 1. Not least because of Noel's countless appearances on *The Late Late Show* (their mum's favourite), the whole country adored them and took them to their hearts.

27

King Tut's 31.5.93 (Part 6)

(One night in May:
14 people, a million tales)

As someone who had previously managed two brothers from East Kilbride who were a force of nature, McGee must have been attracted to the sibling rivalry. Those two were, of course, Jim and William Reid of the Jesus and Mary Chain. It's something that has, over time, proved to be an essential element of the Oasis appeal, one which McGee spotted. Apart from the lack of brotherly love, there's also that provocative confidence and pent-up, non-apologetic attitude. You're lucky we're here for you tonight. We're a rock 'n' roll band and we're here, so you better fucking shut up and listen. McGee's roster of bands at Creation was packed full of groups who nervously plugged in and hoped to win the respect of those present with a shyness that was at times criminally vulgar.

Oasis, like the Jesus and Mary Chain, said no way, this is what we've got, it's loud, we like it, let's fucking go. It was thunderous, sweaty and dramatic, and there wasn't an introverted original Creation act to be found anywhere near them. So always remember I was two feet from Alan McGee when he saw it and I didn't. Perhaps the Creation boss understood how brothers' voices have unique harmonies.

The others, you know, the invisible hordes, the hundreds of thousands who've lied (or maybe it's more of a wish-fulfilment fantasy, if I'm being kind) about being there, who squeezed in to witness this momentous pop moment, they are surprisingly lavish in their praise. Quick to add to the hyperbole. That's the difference. I cast a cold, sober eye on the proceedings. My take is real, and I know it is. As I've said earlier, Oasis were over-rehearsed and not relaxed enough on stage. I'd go as far as to say they were pedestrian, safe, not bad but nowhere near the level assumed by those who'd stayed at home or gone to a different pub.

This night in May 1993 has the ring of a movie to it. How could McGee stand there and see something in this band? I was like Decca's Dick Rowe with The Beatles. 'Sorry, Mr McGee, guitar groups are on the way out!' (Dick Rowe did sign the Rolling Stones, Them, The Zombies and The Small Faces but is unfairly remembered as the man who didn't like a particularly ropey Beatles audition tape. It wasn't him who made the decision either but Mike Smith, one of his assistants. Apart from a fantastic vocal on 'Money' from Lennon, if you heard the tape you'd agree with Decca's decision. The same people who love this anecdote are generally the ones who think Ringo's a crap drummer because that fits with the narrative. No one in The Beatles thought Ringo was a poor drummer. They loved his playing. Few served the song with a rock 'n' roll shuffle better than Richard Starkey. Equally, each of the Beatles over time (except Ringo) have openly stated that Dick Rowe or Decca were correct to pass based on that demo.)

For the others that night, I have to say that Boyfriend, despite being overshadowed by pop history, played a blistering, loud set. Much tighter than usual, they were on their game.

DD was powerful on drums, and driving the band on; clearly they had been working hard. Sister Lovers were enjoyable: they had one song I remembered which I thought was great. I asked Debbie about it: 'I think it's a song called "Brazil" because Liam liked that one. He asked if that was a cover or our own song.'

Ironically, again, to show you what I know about music, they were the ones I would've thought were the more natural Creation band. By that I mean they were the band you could see on the front of the *NME* as that kind of indie Creation signing. 18 Wheeler were tight and played well and were on longer. I got the sense that they maybe were the least reluctant to give up any of their allotted time, sensing that their boss was in the crowd checking them out. Quite right too.

There was an occasion when Alan McGee and Oasis nearly crossed paths some months before. He was visiting Debbie at the rehearsal room both Oasis and Sister Lovers shared at the Boardwalk in Manchester and he noticed the incongruous Union Flag painted on the wall. He assumed the band shared the rehearsal space with a far-right punk band. She explained they were called Oasis and may have mischievously agreed, suggesting to McGee that they were racist and fascist and a right bad lot. Debbie tells me that Noel and Alan McGee had met before in 1989 at the Reading Festival. Unsurprisingly, neither of them can remember it. She also explains that when Alan saw the Union Flag painted on the wall, he was sitting on Tony's drum stool in the Boardwalk. So they had been that close.

I couldn't resist asking what it was like watching your old mates make it in such a crazy way. To have seen the band we saw at King Tut's go supersonic and become massive stars. Debbie is generous and pragmatic. 'I actually live in Burnage now (laughing), which adds symmetry to it all. I think you know what, good for them because they're decent people. It's just like what you're saying. It's like a dream come true. The other thing is if you're in a band, you're doing your thing. If I was in a lad band and sharing a room with Oasis and that had happened, I'd maybe have been a little bit jealous. But I was in a girl band with a lad on drums, and we were doing our thing. It was never what I wanted, so there never was an "Oh, I wish it was me". I wasn't anywhere remotely near what they were doing musically.'

So maybe it was easier because they had different sensibilities and musical tastes, and you didn't have much in common? 'Yeah. Maybe. What I remember from back in the day, and this is a different take on it. It was harder even then for women to be taken seriously. And we were there sharing a room with them and they are lads you know, they were just looking at us and thinking, what are they about?'

So, in summation, I would suggest the way it played out was down to a bit of everything. McGee hadn't seen or heard them before and showed up to surprise his friend, Oasis fancied an away trip to Glasgow and Boyfriend and Sister Lovers forgot to tell anyone at the venue. As an eyewitness, I have to highlight a few key things. I saw McGee go crazy about this band. I saw an incredulous look on Noel Gallagher's face when he offered them a deal. When I said to those around me I thought McGee had offered the band who played first a deal, I was laughed at. That's how it happened. I was there.

Despite going on to achieve so much success, Oasis didn't forget Boyfriend. Even on the night they played King Tut's, Mark Coyle and Noel gave DD a demo which he still treasures and for a while he preferred some of the songs on it to the production on *Definitely Maybe*. Whenever Oasis played in town they always looked after Boyfriend and invited them to their gigs and after-show parties. On one occasion, Liam found the time to meet DD and have a quick pint with him while his security guard looked on. He was also sorted out for VIP tickets for the Sunday show at Loch Lomond. With due respect to DD, you get the impression that Liam and Noel and the rest of the band will treat thousands of people like that everywhere they go.

I was interested in the last time Debbie spoke to any of the brothers. 'I last spoke to Liam at a Stones Roses gig in Warrington. He was nice, and funny, just the same Liam. He asked if I was still in a band before having to be ushered away with his security, then he turns round and smiles and shouts: "Debbie! The cheque's in the post."'

Despite Ticketmaster's 'dynamic pricing' for the 2024 dates, Oasis strike me as the type of band who would remember the people who helped and looked after them on the way up. Better still, I bet they also remember those who crossed them on their journey, one which, for now at least, is nowhere near finished.

28

Rashomon Ruffians

Once the dust settled and it became apparent the rumours were true, Alan McGee *had* offered Oasis a deal, one which a few months later they officially accepted, the evening of 31 May 1993 took on even greater significance. It immediately entered into the clichéd pantheon of legendary nights out. To the handful of music-loving fans who sauntered upstairs to see a support band, to those who were present, this was another Monday in Glasgow. You would think it would be straightforward. Gig happens, people go, people like or don't like it, people then go home. However, with this particular gig, something weird started to happen. Now, over three decades later, when you ask around, the story has become increasingly more confused and even a little bewildering.

Around this dust-settling time, I noticed a baffling development in the story. When I looked at the individual accounts of the evening I couldn't make sense of it. While researching and asking around, I received so many contradictory versions of what took place. When I checked if my facts corroborated with what others thought happened on the same evening, in the same venue, on the same night, at the same gig, everyone had a conflicting take on the evening and how it panned out.

I wanted a definitive take on what happened, but it was

impossible to pin one down. I needed clear-cut, unmistakable, conclusive facts and evidence which would match my diary, but finding these proved troublesome. Some are lucid and happy to share, others who were there can hardly remember it. Some have lied about being there. It's such a huge story and something people want to be part of. It's also feels vague and random. Also, can anyone prove you weren't there? I'm not being disparaging or judgemental, it's what we said from the start; on a big story like this, people want to be a part of it. That's fine, it's human nature.

We need clarification, there can be no ambiguity. Sometimes you have to say, sorry, I know it's a bit unfair as it's your treasured take on the evening, but Oasis didn't do a version of 'Magical Mystery Tour' and 'Hello Goodbye' and nor did they do a Kinks cover. I'm sorry, I'm going to have to leave out the notion that it's the best gig you've ever been to and it took place in a blistering, sweating, cramped King Tut's. The venue was notably quiet, verging on empty. When Oasis started, the place was so empty that the sound echoed and rattled and boomed for the first minute or two until it was brought under control. Someone said that it was the first gig they'd ever been to when a band so low down on the bill had been asked back on for an encore. I was at the bar at the stairs for a drink at the end of 'I Am The Walrus' when Noel's guitar was left to feedback. I could still hear his guitar. There was no encore. I know this encore story wasn't true.

But then, something peculiar happened while I was standing at the bar. The same quiet venue I vacated, as if by magic, became filled to the brim: no one could move, it was jam-packed. Someone started a stage invasion and tried to steal the band's guitars. Then there were the reports of the police being called after a riot broke out downstairs when it kicked off because someone touched Liam's hair. The Manchester casuals flipped. Crazy on speed, they overturned the pool table and then wrecked the bar. I heard tales, too, of the band physically muscling themselves onto the stage to play, while their friends prevented King Tut's staff from stopping them. Amusing to imagine, but none of them have the merit of being true.

For clarity, I tried to speak to as many people as I could track down who were involved on the night. I felt a duty, no matter how ridiculous, to rule out the stories that I believed didn't happen. I followed up on most of the reports which at least sounded feasible. After a while, you could tell those who were making it up. I felt the people included were a respectable cross-section, who I can mostly remember being there. I've spoken to a few who aren't mentioned in my diary. That doesn't mean they weren't there. Only that I didn't mention them being there. I've done my best to listen to each person's story and to record it as accurately as possible. It was awkward nailing a quote from people claiming to be there when your instinct is telling you their only reference to Manchester from that evening was from being at home watching *Coronation Street*.

I didn't have a choice other than to stick with my version of events. I was there. I had a clear head; I was there to see a support band before my mate's band came on. I asked everyone the same question: 'Do you have any memories of the night?' Maybe my question was too loose. Perhaps it wasn't tight or precise enough. The answers were interesting. I felt that for clarity, I had to include what most people had recounted. Their version of events is their version of events.

The responses have provided us with some kind of *Rashomon* Effect. (The term is taken from Kurosawa's *Rashomon*, an enthralling Japanese psychological thriller, released in 1950, which explores the nature of truth and justice and is arguably one of the most influential films ever made. The plot centres around four differing accounts of the same event by witnesses, suspects and victims.) In our story, there was no real crime, though Alan McGee's red Gucci loafers were criminal: part Cardinal, part intense German architect. Noel Gallagher's jumper was criminal too. For some reason that stuck with me. So I asked those who were there if they could give me as much information as they could remember . . . Here they are, in their own words.

Derek McKee, (aka DD) drummer, headline band, Boyfriend

Boyfriend had toured with Sub Pop band The Afghan Whigs in September 1992 and met up with Sister Lovers at the Boardwalk, in Manchester. They asked to support us on a future Glasgow gig, so we invited them up for our gig on the last night of the old Mayfest on 31 May 1993 at King Tut's. We were joint headlining with 18 Wheeler. We were going on last, as our album *Hairy Banjo* was out and theirs wasn't. Mark Coyle [early Oasis producer and soundman] contacted us after he found out about the Sister Lovers arrangement, asking if he could bring Oasis up to play which we agreed to. He was a pal of Mark McAvoy [Teenage Fanclub's guitar tech and Boyfriend's bass player]. Boyfriend didn't see it as a problem having a fourth band on the bill, but we didn't tell the promoter and they were being difficult about it. There were rumours of veiled threats of violence but I don't remember that. Boyfriend and Sister Lovers offered to cut their sets to allow Oasis to play for fifteen to twenty minutes. And, well, they played and the rest is history.

There were only a handful of people watching, I do remember they were loud! I enjoyed the tunes, I thought the guitar player was excellent and I loved their cover of 'I Am The Walrus', which is a personal fav. It was Boyfriend's backline they used. Tony McCarroll asked to borrow my cymbals, I kindly consented as I'm a nice guy. You'll know from being a drummer yourself that usually, asking something like that is considered a major *No! No!* He loved my kit and cymbals and after they signed their Creation deal, I noticed that he had gone out and bought the exact same set up as mine!

I had a chat with Noel and Mark Coyle after the set, Mark gave me a copy of their demo, a cassette which I still have. I loved the tunes and played that cassette to death! Funnily enough, when their first album came out, it took me a while to get into it. I thought initially it was over-produced!

Back to the night in question and what I remember. They ate at McDonald's; I sent them round towards Sauchiehall Street direction. They travelled up in one of those Mercedes coaches, bigger than a mini bus but smaller than a small coach. They had major attitude but were polite and friendly with the Boyfriend boys through our Mark Coyle connection. Whenever Oasis were in town, they looked us up and we met up, got into their gigs and they invited us to after-show parties. Last time I met them was when they played Loch Lomond. I had a quick pint with Liam (and his bouncer) in town, he sorted me out with VIP tickets for the Sunday.

Eugene Kelly, The Vaselines

I can't remember a thing.

Susan McGee, sister of Alan McGee

I honestly don't remember much. I do remember thinking Liam was like Paul Weller but it was their eyebrows. Noel was like Parker, from *Thunderbirds*.

Paul Cardow, promoter

I have to say I thought they were interesting and Liam looked amazing, really different from everyone else there. I do remember Susan [McGee] telling me after that night [Alan] McGee was going to sign them. I just thought they were unusual and looked distinctive and kept in touch with them and did end up working with them since. [On the low crowd turnout] I always remembered it as busier than that but maybe it wasn't, I remember asking the venue for more names on the guest list but as sales weren't good they gave us some two for ones, at least I think it was that night.

Ross Clark, bassist, friend of the author

You know, when I saw DD post the bill on Facebook recently, of the King Tut's door, it came to mind that I was there with you but to be honest I don't remember them playing or the gig. I recall seeing them later with The Verve at the Cathouse and exchanging a few words with Noel afterwards. He wasn't that impressed with Liam's performance that night . . . Was that the same week or later . . .? I had sort of thought I must have been there but it could be one of those things like the Sex Pistols first gig . . . I have plausible deniability! Most of the early 1990s are a bit hazy to say the least . . . There are photos of me in places I have no recollection of being . . . I do remember thinking how that night they were sort of baggy at one of the gigs, shell suits, Burberry floppy hat types. Not Noel as much but certainly some of the others. Did McGee jump on the stage or something after their set? That vaguely rings a bell but I might have heard it somewhere. I do remember that girl from the Staging Post (our local pub in Airdrie) who used to follow them everywhere. She always claimed that one of the songs was about her but that was later on of course.

Murray Webster, King Tut's sound engineer

King Tut's shook the club tour world when it opened and is still there, longer than the Marquee and other legendary London clubs. Stuart Clumpas [King Tut's original owner] did it properly and gave me the money to put the best gear in there, he fed the bands, gave them beer, a decent place to sleep, and a decent payment and combined with a Glasgow audience changed the whole club tour perspective.

King Tut's was much-admired. Bands love to play there. The sound was part of it, and therefore me too! Have you forgotten how much shit we had to work with when we did toilet tours? King Tut's was legendary, nearly every band couldn't believe that such a sound system was in such a club, why do you think so many showcases happened there?

With regards to Oasis, yes I was there and I mixed, what you probably don't know or remember was that they were not booked for the evening, they turned up because someone who didn't have the right said they could play as third band as far as I remember, there was a lot of discussion if they could go on stage, while they played directly after the doors opened, but were allowed to go onstage because of Alan McGee, hence only fourteen people; they were not announced and were onstage forty-five minutes before the normal support slot. It was a showcase for Alan McGee. Strangely enough when I met them, I was technical director and promoter's rep in Germany across four tours, they didn't remember me . . . They didn't remember much about the night. Still I was there, and the decision if they went onstage was mine because it meant extra unpaid work. I thought to myself, WTF, they've come a long way on a promise. Not sure if that's exactly how it happened but that's what I remember. I did five shows a week back then in Tut's, it was just another one.

Debbie Ellis (née Turner), Sister Lovers

In a phone interview Debbie confirmed that everyone shortened their sets to allow some time for Oasis.

We said we're not playing if they're not playing. Then Boyfriend and 18 Wheeler said the same. So there was solidarity with the bands.

As for the threats and violence:

There was a story of them (the Oasis friends) smashing up the gaff, and I don't think it was that; I think it was just there were twelve of them, and we don't want to piss off twelve people, so let them on, what difference does it make? At the same time, I'd heard Alan and a few of the guys from the bands were up trying to talk to the promoter, calming it down. In the end, I think it was a case of look they've come all this way. Just let them play.

I've always wondered what made Debbie ask Oasis to come up to play King Tut's that day in the Boardwalk practice room. This is a crucial bit, pop kids. Our inciting incident. The moment when fate started its dance.

That's why I said in the *Supersonic* film that I was showing off about having a gig in Glasgow, as it was a massive step to get out of Manchester. The furthest you'd get was playing upstairs at the Boardwalk venue. To be playing somewhere else was a big thing. Fuck knows why I said you should come up and play too. I can't believe how gobby I was back in the day. I think it was Noel giving me a dirty look while putting his guitar away.

This was the source. The crucial part of our story. You gave them this break, and it changed their lives, I said.

I know, so from asking Noel [to come up and play in Glasgow] and then Alan doing that [randomly showing up to annoy her on her first gig], it all came together on that night. That's so weird. Crazy isn't it? It was fate, totally cosmic.

Eugene Kelly, The Vaselines, December 2024

I still can't remember a thing.

*

You get the idea. It ranges from someone having a Rolling Stones-like epiphany, this band, full of unbridled arrogance and potency to a wondrously captivating show, to a mostly forgettable, workmanlike Monday night out in Glasgow. People's memories of events are varied to say the least. It's not for me to say who is right or wrong, but the memories create an interesting side effect from the night itself. This is the same event seen from many points of view, from people who were there. Some quotes from those who weren't there are hilarious. Such was the desperation for many a hipster to have been there, that even up to a few years ago, one chap who will remain nameless raved most assuredly about the night Oasis played King Tut's. It had to be one of the greatest, most memorable gigs he'd ever attended and the quality of the cover of The Beatles' 'Hello Goodbye' was unforgettable. One particular story he included was that he couldn't believe his eyes when he saw an excited Alan McGee do a one-man stage invasion. I heard that from about three unrelated, random sources. The lie told often enough becomes the truth. I didn't have the heart to tell him he was a psychopathic liar, so instead I said I was there and missed that.

29

And in the End . . . Legacy

By 1996, it felt like the end of the first act for Oasis. Where could they go from here? How could they match the career-defining first two albums? To reach that promised land of rock deity they had to release a killer third album and lay down their legacy. They had already played iconic gigs at Maine Road and Knebworth. A few years ago, they were struggling to get gigs and as likely to have ended up in jail as becoming rock stars. At this time in their career, despite the high-profile fallouts, arguments, flare-ups and fights, they are rarely off the front pages and are outselling their contemporaries. This being Oasis, it's not enough to outsell them. They are engulfing, eclipsing and destroying them. When Oasis are playing and hitting the mark, part of the thrill is the tangible connection between the fans and the band. Oasis on form can change gears and kick it off in their live shows. Their songs have a directness, a sense of coming together – they want you to be part of the party. The band were selling and performing and probably one of the best bands in the world.

Don't forget that the overriding consensus throughout Oasis's fifteen-year career was that it wouldn't last. But with *Definitely Maybe*, *(What's The Story) Morning Glory?*, *Be Here Now*, *Standing On The Shoulder of Giants*, *Heathen Chemistry*, *Don't Believe The Truth* and *Dig Out Your Soul*, eight – yes, eight – number 1 albums later, they are still selling. This is a band as famous for their explosive notoriety as their music. In case there are any doubts that it wouldn't last, Oasis had twenty-three Top 10 singles, including eight which reached number 1: 'Some Might Say', 'Don't Look Back In Anger', 'D'You Know What I Mean?', 'All Around The World', 'Go Let It Out', 'The Hindu Times', 'Lyla' and 'The Importance Of Being Idle'. Their hit single ratio is even more astounding because of the era they were a part of. The nature of the pop fan has changed. Now, you can download the album and buy concert tickets for the tour without leaving home. Due to the huge range of choices and availability, it's more challenging for bands to make it in the modern era than the 1960s and 1970s. Despite these radical changes and, as much as the consumer side may have changed, the rules are the same for bands at sixteen as they have always been. You form a group, rehearse, demo, gig, get contacts, get out there, play live, work on the craft of songwriting, keep on going, create a buzz, get to know A&R people, secure better gigs, support bigger bands, record better demos, make it happen. It's still the same principle, and, at the heart of it, you need to have the songs and then get out there and play them – and then you need a bit of luck.

By the summer of 1997, as the world waits for *Be Here Now*, Creation looks barely recognisable. It's an accurate assertion to say that the key people still involved felt that Creation, the label they knew and loved, was dead. There was still a label but it was Sony. There were too many ambitious corporate record industry new-bloods cutting their teeth at the label before climbing up the slippery pole. They are no longer the cheeky indie kid on the block; they have an owner who is invited in to lead think tanks with the Cabinet Secretary for Culture, Media and Sport, Chris Smith. That's right, McGee is part of a six-man Creative Industries Task Force brought in to help target funding for the arts.

Creation were raking it in and their profile was spectacular. On the downside, due to being so seriously leveraged, with everything placed on one stock, they were vulnerable if Oasis didn't keep delivering. It wasn't clever business practice to be so dependent on the one band. Ironically, Creation could have done with a few bands like Blur, Pulp or Suede on their roster to help spread the risk; as it was, the label was always only one bad album away from calamitous problems. Suede would maybe have been the best suited for a label like Creation, but they famously made it clear they wanted to remain outsiders and stay independent. They thought Creation was a club and they didn't want to be members. They signed with Saul Galpern's label, Nude Records, remaining independent in the UK and were able to stay quiet about being backed by Sony elsewhere in the world.

Oasis made it impossible for other bands to come through. Heavy Stereo were thought to be the band with the sound, look and songs that could make a serious breakthrough. They were caught up in a vacuum created by Oasis's enormous success and suffered terribly from a backlash. The radio pluggers, the music press and many key music industry players were turning against Creation. When Oasis hit big, everything changed for the label that had once had the kudos and dedicated following of the indie underground. How could you still have any credibility if you were so much a part of the establishment you were hanging out with Tony Blair at 10 Downing Street? McGee had been a long-time Labour supporter and party donor and now he and Oasis were invited into the heart of the British establishment. Again, McGee never fully believed in the 'indie thing'. And for prime ministers, it was always smart to be seen hanging out with the popular bands of the day. Harold Wilson did it in the 1960s with The Beatles, now Blair was doing it with Oasis.

With Oasis, Blair realised how many young people weren't voting and saw it as a chance to get down with the hottest ticket in music at the time. He was, for what it's worth, a fan of their music, and admitted to listening to their albums in the car. There would be plenty of political mileage in getting down with two of the leading lights of what was spun by the government as a whole Cool Britannia movement, while showing voters that you have your finger on the cultural pulse or at least that week's latest musical bandwagon.

Alan McGee and Noel Gallagher were into the concept of New Labour and had much in common with Blair: they played in bands and loved football (although they weren't into taking the country into an illegal war). The band's timing was perfect. Everything aligned at an exact point. There was a unique consumer, one who loved *Loaded* magazine, couldn't get enough of football, was into 'mad for it' music, a fan of fashion, all buoyed by some kind of relentless positivity. And this chimed with that initial early promise and optimism of the New Labour political backdrop.

It feels anecdotal now, but it's important to recognise the cultural significance of 'Cool Britannia' and the 10 Downing Street story. It was a landmark moment. There was a connection. A tangible feeling of optimism seeing Alan McGee, Noel Gallagher and the leading lights of the creative arts in the heart of power.

The optics were clear; having witnessed McGee's influence on youth culture, he was invited to spearhead a media campaign ahead of the election. The New Deal changed legislation and allowed musicians three years of development funding instead of taking on jobs to survive. After Labour's 1997 win, Oasis and McGee were there, riding high on the positivity of Cool Britannia as Blair sought out the label boss and band of the moment's approval. McGee's donation to New Labour of £50,000 for the privilege no doubt helped. Speaking years later, Alan McGee described New Labour as 'Orwellian' and criticised the New Deal, commenting that it stifled creativity.

In reality Cool Britannia remained London-centric and laddish, coke-fuelled and white, with a lack of diversity. It was more Euro 96 and Gazza, Chris Evans and Britpop. It was *Four Weddings and a Funeral* – and a brief regional doff of the cap to *Trainspotting*. It was fashion designer Alexander McQueen, and the Young British Artists, Damien Hirst and Tracey Emin. It was Suede's Brett Anderson on the cover of *Select* in the Union Jack telling the Yanks to go home. Many artists did not like the term 'Cool Britannia'. Speaking in *VICE* Magazine in 2021, Lush's Miki Berenyi stated: 'It's a bit meaningless. It's PR – something that really suited politicians. It was *Vanity Fair* that came up with it, so it was an outsider's view.' Andy Bell, who later joined Oasis, described Cool Britannia as 'a weird imperialist neediness'.

The *Select* cover still irks many artists. Here's Luke Haines of The Auteurs who wrote the best-selling Britpop memoir *Bad Vibes: Britpop and My Part in Its Downfall*: 'With that *Select* cover, none of the bands knew they were going to smear the Union Jack all over it. It was moronic. If you're going to put a Union Jack on the cover of a magazine under the headline "Yanks Go Home", then you are a fucking cretin. Maybe all that had a subliminal effect. All those teenagers who bought *Select* became middle-aged in 2016 and voted for Brexit. Was *Select* magazine responsible for Brexit? Probably.'

Let's leave Cool Britannia to Miki Berenyi who sums up

the feeling amongst most bands mentioned in that April 1993 edition of *Select*: 'People were moving the goalposts to suit their own success. That whole anti-American, Yanks go home thing – a lot of those bands weren't really successful in America. It felt a bit sour grapes, like, "We don't want to be big in America because it's shit, we're big in Britain." Then suddenly they get a bit big in America and it's like, "We've conquered it. Fuck off."'

In one unedifying anecdote, McGee talks about arriving at 10 Downing Street and being whisked away and briefed by security staff. He was expecting a stern lecture on making sure Noel behaved, with no arguments, swearing, drugs or fighting. Instead, he was left in charge of Mick Hucknall and instructed to keep the infamous 'playboy' away from women.

*

It turned out that Oasis had, despite the wheels spectacularly coming off with the two main players on so many occasions, a considerable lifespan, but history will always highlight *Definitely Maybe* and *(What's The Story) Morning Glory?* and the spats with Blur. Music was big then, in those heady late-1990s days, and these bands, Blur, Oasis, Suede and Pulp, had made it so. Album sales in 1996 reached over one billion.

The band's journey has been part of that larger-than-life tale of a spectacular music scene in the 1990s and beyond. Oasis were all about taking a 1960s-style pop formula with a majestically sweeping chorus and a hook that has everyone who hears it whistling it – from, it seems, the terraces at Maine Road to the PM in his chauffeured Jag. Blur had astonishing songs too and proved over the years that they could deliver hook and structure with the best of them.

During the Britpop years and especially with *The Great Escape* Blur chose sophistication and self-indulgence. But perhaps it wasn't the time to be elegant and rueful. On their 1997 album, *Blur*, they whitewashed anything Oasis could do on *Be Here Now* and with *13*, released in 1999, proved with songs like 'Beetlebum' and 'Song 2' that they had re-evaluated their earlier criticism of that American garage grunge sound.

As the 2012 Olympics closed in London, Blur played to a huge crowd at Hyde Park. Blur, who are still around, playing shows, celebrated twenty-one years together at that stage (despite being beset by fallouts over the band's direction and image). Graham Coxon left while recording *Think Tank* in 2002 and the band took a break in 2003, before getting back together in 2009, the same year Oasis officially announced their split after the gig at the Festival in Paris. In 2015 they released the critically acclaimed album *The Magic Whip*. In May 2023, Blur announced European and South American dates, including two nights at Wembley Stadium to promote their ninth studio album, which became the critically acclaimed *The Ballad of Darren* (the Darren of the title is their lifelong bodyguard, Darren 'Smoggy' Evans), with its singles 'The Narcissist', 'St. Charles Square' and 'Barbaric'. Produced by James Ford at Studio 13, the cover features a desolate yet oddly comforting image by photographer Martin Parr of a solitary man swimming in Gourock's outdoor pool with a grey-green mass of banked clouds and sea rippling beyond. It's tempting to see the stark blue of the lido as a visual link to the glossy Mediterranean of *The Great Escape* (or the indoor pool of *Leisure* perhaps). Blur, and crucially the original line-up, were still able to come together, record a critically acclaimed album and play groundbreaking live shows.

Surely, if nothing else, seeing their 1990s adversaries back in the spotlight and playing to sold-out audiences from Barcelona to Buenos Aires must make Noel and Liam at least think of picking up the phone? In January 2014, Oasis devotees were convinced there was going to be a reunion. There were a few promising strands in the various lines and stories emanating from both camps. Liam was in the midst of a costly divorce settlement. And strong reports were surfacing that they'd been offered millions to reform. There were also newspaper reports claiming the brothers had kissed and made up at a family wedding in Ireland. Before long, the internet was going into overload, buzzing with talk of dates across the summer to celebrate the twentieth anniversary of *Definitely Maybe* with some major European tour date announcements.

This tied in with an impeccable source (aren't they always?) telling me that Oasis planned to play *Definitely Maybe* in its entirety, possibly at Glastonbury. Both had tentatively pencilled it around solo projects, I was informed. This window closed and then there was talk in 2016 of a reunion to mark twenty-five years since the band first formed.

But any excitement was short-lived, cut down to size when Noel announced it wouldn't be happening. What would be happening was a remastered version of *Definitely Maybe* and loads of goodies like rare and unreleased recordings. *(What's The Story) Morning Glory?* and *Be Here Now* would follow later in the year and be released as part of the Chasing the Sun series on Big Brother Records.

Definitely Maybe would be available in a variety of formats, including a digital download of the original album, a three-disc Special Edition version (including the rare recordings and demos), a 12-inch vinyl LP featuring the bonus CD content as a free download, and a Deluxe Box Set which features the LP and the CDs. They also announced a reissue of 'Supersonic' as a 12-inch vinyl on Record Store Day on 19 April 2014. It's difficult not to see this as another money-making fleecing of the fans with content they already had. But they weren't getting back together. Maybe they would for the twenty-fifth anniversary of the band?

In October 2015 we had news which probably excited Oasis fans the most. It felt like, this time, something was happening. There was serious talk of the band getting back together. It almost hit fever pitch. The newspapers knew something and kept leaking the odd quote from one of the brothers. Unbelievable money was being offered. There's only so long they can go on without signing up to play together again. Surely.

Definitely Maybe, their debut album, has subsequently been placed in the pantheon of all-time great albums. To think this 'nervous, tense group, who sounded like The Stone Roses doing covers of Mott the Hoople and Slade' could achieve so much. It's testament to at least two things: Alan McGee's eye for talent and potential, without a doubt, and something I keep repeating, especially for anyone forming a band, that you should never be afraid to dream. Believe in it, work hard, try harder and who knows, there's always a chance.

*

In a poll conducted by HMV, the *Guardian*, *Channel 4* and *Classic FM*, Oasis and *Definitely Maybe* finished fourteenth in 1997 in a vote for the greatest album of the Millennium. In Channel 4's own greatest album poll they finished at number 6. In 2005, *Q* readers placed the album at number 5 in their poll of the greatest albums ever, with the *NME* naming it the greatest album of all time. Then, in a 2008 poll by *Q* and *HMV*, *Definitely Maybe* found itself in first place on a list of the greatest British albums of all time.

Sometimes we need to put these votes into perspective. The nature of how the polls are done tells you more about the age, tastes and people who vote in them than the artists themselves. In other words, there may be albums included that are popular at the time, as opposed to those classic albums that are generally perceived and accepted as innovative or groundbreaking. However, as debuts go, *Definitely Maybe* was an astonishing album. Like most of the best-ever albums, it continues to improve with age. In common with so many of the top albums regularly mentioned in these polls, there's an enduring quality that hasn't diminished as the years pass.

The legendary rock critic Lester Bangs described The Velvet Underground's *White Light/White Heat* as 'rock 'n' roll's ultimate expression of nihilism and destruction'. While heading towards that goal, Alan McGee may have thought he'd come close with the Jesus and Mary Chain and Primal Scream but it was Oasis who would deliver the nihilism and destruction in a convoy marked excess and annihilation. The Velvet Underground always treated rock as art. They were artists doing a rock performance. The band who had most inspired Alan McGee were a million miles from the band who played in front of him on that night in King Tut's. McGee's decision was based on instinct, on an expert hunch. This band had a presence, edge and menace, and the timing would be perfect. McGee knew that with Liam at the helm and Noel's songs Oasis would whip up a storm.

Critics are split; still, most think Oasis are derivative and unoriginal. But even that mindset is unoriginal. Rock 'n' roll, as each generation steals from the previous one, has been unoriginal since March 1951 when Sam Phillips recorded 'Rocket 88' by Jackie Brenston and his Delta Cats (who were Ike Turner and his backing band The Kings of Rhythm).

For over seventy years it's been reinventing itself and, more accurately, recycling itself from The Beatles with Little

Richard, Buddy Holly and Chuck Berry, to the Rolling Stones with Muddy Waters. From The Kingsmen's 'Louis Louis' to The Kinks' 'You Really Got Me' to The Stooges' 'No Fun', they are all ripping off and tweaking and changing as they add their own methods, techniques and variations of a theme. It's been done before; everyone knows that. It's how you develop your take on it that matters. What these bands and others like the Sex Pistols, the Ramones and Oasis have is a nerve and attitude that transcends their ability. That confidence is a fundamental element in the make-up of any top rock 'n' roll (loosely speaking) band. Musical virtuosity is vital too, but the spirit of being (or at least seeming to be) primitive and keeping it simple, pared back, loud and exciting shouldn't be underestimated.

If you're a romantic about the concept of rock 'n' roll music, then few moments could beat being 14 years old in the 1950s and hearing Elvis Presley for the first time. Being 14 in the 1960s and hearing The Beatles for the first time then a few weeks later hearing the Rolling Stones. Once you get over the fact that everything else is more or less downhill and a disappointment after that, if something moves you then grab it and run.

The more astute pop fan will say the first two Oasis albums were outstanding, and the soundtrack of 1994 to 1996. Their place in the annals of British rock is assured and guaranteed. A few blemishes arise when they are judged in the context of *Be Here Now* and their arrogance and conceit after they became millionaires. Britpop is now a washed-out memory, a discarded, faded Polaroid in an envelope with some dog-eared postcards in the bottom drawer. *Be Here Now* had been badly received. *The Masterplan*, a compilation of B-sides released in 1998, was warmly received. Noel Gallagher commented that there were songs on *The Masterplan* that were better than some of the material on *Be Here Now.* An unusual admission of an error of judgement from The Chief.

So, the first two Oasis albums are unarguably classics, but by the third, they had started to dip. If you look back at the progression of The Beatles, on the other hand, their records got better and better. By the much anticipated third album *Be Here Now*, which was released amid a backdrop of bitter quarrels and fallouts, the reviews didn't live up to the preposterous scrutiny and media attention it received. By the time of its release, *Be Here Now* had been overhyped. The songs, though, are far better than the reviews from the time suggest. I'd argue that most of those were governed more by resentment and petty jealousies than by actual attempts to listen to and judge the music on its own terms. Considering the weight of expectation and the pressure on Noel to deliver anything that could match *Definitely Maybe* and *(What's The Story) Morning Glory?* some of the songs are fabulous. 'Stand By Me' and 'All Around The World' are terrific pop songs.

The album is viewed as the moment it all got too big, released amid paranoia and secrecy over fears of bootleggers and bad reviews. It's now mostly regarded as a coke-fuelled folly. It was also the Oasis CD you could always pick up cheap in Oxfam. Despite being preceded by the number 1 single 'D'You Know What I Mean?' as was becoming the way with Oasis, the critics were saying it was derivative, over-produced and the songs were too lengthy, but the fans bought it and bought it fast. *Be Here Now* sold over 350,000 units on its first day of release and, in selling over 696,000 by the end of the week, became the fastest-selling album in British history. In America, there was a more tepid response, despite debuting at number 2 on the *Billboard* charts, it sold only

152,000 in the first week, far less than the expected sales of 400,000. I remember my only complaint about the album at the time was the lack of bass. I couldn't hear any bass. I like bass.

During the recording of *Standing On The Shoulder Of Giants*, their fourth album, more changes were afoot. Bonehead and Guigsy left, stating they wanted to spend more time with their families. Despite the timing, their departures were played down and their decisions treated with a bit of respect as they were founding members. Both sides, in public at least, were agreeable to the plan. Bonehead and Guigsy perhaps sensed that the days of fun and partying had gone and it was now a lot more serious and grown up. Maybe they were tired of sticking to Noel's strict no drink and no drugs regime when recording in an attempt to get the best out of Liam's voice in the studio. Noel wanted the band to be more professional and business-like, so there was a changing of the old guard. Noel recorded both Bonehead and Guigsy's parts and, for touring, Gem Archer and Andy Bell were brought in.

Noel was determined to launch this album on his terms, the first on the band's label, Big Brother, after Creation's demise in 1999. The album got to number 1 in the UK and number 24 on the *Billboard* charts but remains the band's least popular in terms of sales. They embarked on an eventful world tour. In 2000, they had to cancel a gig in Barcelona as Alan White had tendonitis and they got drunk instead. Liam and Noel start in fine fettle, but quickly the banter dissolves into violence when Liam questions the parentage of Noel's daughter with ex-wife Meg Mathews. Noel is quickly on top of Liam and beats him up. He then decides he's had enough, again, and would no longer play overseas gigs with the band; if they wanted they could finish the tour without him. After some arm-twisting

Noel was convinced to return for the British and Irish legs of the tour, but only those.

The band released their fifth studio album, *Heathen Chemistry*, in 2002, this time with Bell and Archer in for the recording. It also reached number 1 in the UK and peaked at number 23 on the *Billboard* charts. The critics continued to compare anything Oasis released with their first two albums but the fans were still excited by anything new. They weren't going to reach the sales and the unique successes of *Definitely Maybe* and *(What's The Story) Morning Glory?* but Noel tried and the fans hoped. This was a more back-to-basics rock band. They sounded great, were tight as a unit, and the other thing that stood out was how Liam had a song on the album; in fact, everyone except drummer Alan White had a part in some way with the songwriting. 'The Hindu Times' got to number 1, 'Stop Crying Your Heart Out' to number 2, 'Little By Little/She Is Love' also reached number 2, and Liam's 'Songbird' reached number 3. The band embarked on another world tour with their management praying there would be no self-inflicted histrionics. In the States, Noel, Andy Bell and the band's live keyboard player, Jay Darlington, were involved in a car accident and some shows had to be cancelled.

Later on the tour, in Germany, more shows were postponed after Liam, Alan White and three others in the Oasis camp were involved in a brawl in Munich and arrested. Liam lost two front teeth and would eventually be fined around £40,000 for allegedly kicking a German policeman in the ribs. At the time, I remember the press having a field day on hearing that Liam in particular had got a violent kicking. Another example of how the tide had turned in the media's perception of the band's rags to riches story: now they were practically frothing, eagerly awaiting their demise. The subtext changed from something like 'Go on, Liam! That's it, lad!' to 'Serves the arrogant dickhead right.'

January 2004 started with the shock of Alan White leaving. He was replaced by Zak Starkey. Later in the year, Oasis headlined Glastonbury to mixed reviews, then work eventually commenced, at Capitol Studios in LA, on their sixth album *Don't Believe the Truth*, which finally came out in May 2005. The album was critically received and, like every album thus far, entered the UK album charts at number 1. They also bagged two number 1 singles in the UK with 'Lyla' and 'The Importance Of Being Idle', while 'Let There Be Love' reached number 2. With Starkey, Bell and Archer, the band had found musicians capable of undertaking the responsibility of a mammoth world tour. There's a dedication, stamina and perseverance required to embark on the world tours that bands like Oasis need to undertake to satisfy their fans. They played 113 shows to over 3.2 million people in twenty-six countries and there was no major drama. A rockumentary was made of the tour, entitled *Lord Don't Slow Me Down*.

In 2006 they released an eighteen-track double album, a retrospective collection called *Stop The Clocks*. In 2007 they received a Brit Award for their outstanding contribution to music. Starkey had been officially invited to sign on the dotted line and become a fully-fledged member of Oasis but had to turn the offer down because he had already committed to work with The Who. He left to be replaced by former Icicle Works and Robbie Williams drummer, Chris Sharrock. They recorded and released their seventh album, *Dig Out Your Soul*, which entered the UK album charts at number 1. Their hard work came to fruition in America where the band were rewarded by reaching number 5 on the *Billboard* charts. Again, they embarked on an eighteen-month tour. In June 2009, they played three concerts at Heaton Park in Manchester.

By this time, speculation over the band's future was rife. There were rumours they'd already gone their separate ways and were meeting their contractual commitments to play the remaining shows before concentrating on solo projects. The management moved quickly to officially deny these stories. Obfuscation was the order of the day. Vagueness gave way to clarity. Press releases were skilfully issued but still obscured the real story.

However, in Paris on 28 August 2009, Noel and Liam had yet another row backstage which escalated into a vicious fight, culminating in Liam damaging one of Noel's guitars. You would think by now that Liam knew not to mess with Noel's guitars, or perhaps he knew what he was doing? After the fight, Noel left the group, blaming Liam's 'intolerable level of verbal intimidation and violence'.

Marcus Russell immediately announced that the show in Paris at the Rock en Seine festival was off, as was the remainder of the European tour, and that the band had split, this time for certain. That was it, game over. This might sound slightly surreal, but I remember it because it was my first experience of the power and reach of Twitter (as it was known then). The news came from Scottish singer Amy Macdonald, who was on the bill at Rock en Seine. A friend Chris Crozier followed her and showed me the tweet: *Oasis cancelled again with one minute to stage time. Liam smashed Noel's guitar, huuuge fight!* She then added . . . *Noel's quit*. I don't remember thinking this was the day the music died, I better get home and listen to their albums. I do remember thinking wow, this is amazing, how quickly this has spread on Twitter. I was more impressed by the speed, immediacy and range of reaction to the news. It was bizarre. This had only happened minutes before in Paris. It took another four years before I signed up to Twitter; I don't like rushing into these things.

The music industry, from The Everly Brothers to The Kinks, from The Beach Boys to Oasis has always featured brothers who find themselves in a situation where their relationships are put under the microscope and stretched to breaking point. Oasis weren't the first band to be in this powder keg situation. And it might be the case that most artists could manage their emotions for the greater good and find a way of navigating through the storm to keep the fans happy.

This is a business though, and they aren't doing these lucrative gigs for free; there was plenty of motivation to bite your lip, knuckle down and work it through. However, the situation had become too charged for Liam and Noel to work together. They were travelling separately with their own entourages, not speaking and only seeing each other for a few hours on stage every night. By the end, in 2009, after it was announced they were splitting up, Noel said in *Q* magazine that he didn't like Liam. Liam responded in the *NME* by saying, 'It takes more than blood to be my brother. He doesn't like me and I don't like him.' And at that point, they both moved on to focus on their respective solo projects.

In 2010, *Q* magazine named Liam as the greatest frontman of all time. Liam grew into a commanding lead singer who could dominate the stage, but it's hard to accept that he was better than Jagger. Was he better than Iggy Pop, Jim Morrison or Johnny Rotten? Freddie Mercury or Robert Plant? Liam's guttural, everyman voice struck a chord with millions of fans. His personality and presence wasn't an act; there's nothing false here. He's been banned for life from Cathay Pacific for being 'abusive and disgusting'. So there, he is a genuine bad boy.

Liam's Beady Eye and Noel's High Flying Birds were both a diminished version of Oasis at their best, but they were still welcome projects. When you consider their previous destructive tendencies, there is at least a level of mature professionalism, which ironically has diluted the message and in some ways the excitement. If they had used the professionalism and discipline saved for recording and touring with their respective solo projects for Oasis at their peak, they would've had a genuine claim to greatness. Perhaps that's growing up for you; the difference between being in your twenties and your thirties or forties. Noel may have had the songs but the band lacked the discipline required to move to the stage where they could comfortably play and fill arenas and stadiums and go on a world tour for eighteen months and, more importantly, get on while doing it. Maybe they were too reckless and irresponsible to undertake such a commitment; perhaps they were too busy using all their energy fighting with each other. They were in better shape professionally when the line-up solidified with Gem Archer and Andy Bell and drummers like Zak Starkey and then Chris Sharrock. But it remains true that fate, attacks by fans, car crashes and, well, let's be blunt, at times a sheer loathing of each other, wreaked havoc.

Tellingly, in February of 2010 Oasis won the award for Best British Album of the Last 30 Years as voted for by BBC Radio 2 listeners. Liam thanked everybody but his brother before throwing the award into the crowd. Yet another compilation – this time of all the singles – was released in June 2010, *Time Flies . . . 1994–2009*.

Then, in the summer of 2011, another Manchester band put their differences aside. If The Stone Roses can do it, surely Oasis would always be a hot ticket, having now amassed so many hit singles and albums? They would still be firm favourites if they got back together, especially at a major festival, to play both *Definitely Maybe* or *(What's The Story) Morning Glory?* in their entirety.

One of the upsides to being at King Tut's on that landmark night is that it gives you a unique insight into so many elements of the human condition. It's about luck, fate and . . . yes, I know we have cynics who claim that Oasis were always on Creation's radar. I don't believe they were, but then I'm a dreamer and a hopeless romantic. It's one of the most talked about moments in musical folklore, one forever intertwined with King Tut's and the story of the band. Then you start to think, why was I there? Was it meant to happen? It was a Bank Holiday and we felt like catching some bands. At the time, the way the Oasis story began gave band members hope. Admittedly, we didn't have their stage presence, their cool hair or Liam's cheekbones . . . or his voice, or the band's songs. But apart from that . . .

Oasis were part rock 'n' roll legend, part soap opera saga: *Coronation Street* meets *Shameless* . . . One thing's for sure, they did shine through the mediocrity and leave their mark and they did it with their songs. It's always about songs. Songs last; songs stay alive in our hearts and minds. As some listen to 'Satisfaction', 'Waterloo Sunset' or 'Pretty Vacant' with hazy nostalgia and acceptance that these are the songs that guide us, then future rock 'n' roll generations will listen to 'Live Forever' and 'Cigarettes & Alcohol' and 'Champagne Supernova'. That's what happens when you write majestic tunes. Oasis are an enormous part of our pop and rock culture and heritage.

It's true that they are one of those bands who have always split opinion, but whether you love them or hate them, you can't deny their journey has been a fascinating one. To go from King Tut's to Knebworth in three years? A Hollywood scriptwriter couldn't have dreamt up that as a plot twist. To capture the mindset, the mood and the spirit of the time with songs that fire the imagination, then add in those unpredictable, fiery performances, which could be staggering or calamitous. The way their trajectory went stratospheric and in such an emphatic way. It's a breathtaking achievement. Then there's the biblical fable that runs throughout: the mistrust and antipathy between Noel, the creative force, the renowned songwriter, and Liam, the mercurial frontman – brothers, for good or for bad.

Marcus Russell was determined to distance the band from the petty-mindedness of the Britpop scene and took exception to the tag. He didn't want to commit to anything as frivolous and short-lived as Britpop. He felt the blatant branding was detrimental to the band's ambition. It was too parochial – he wanted the band to be big in the USA, Japan and Europe and felt the term and Oasis's involvement in it was counterproductive. His instinct was that Britpop was a fad, too much of a gimmick; it was a marketing ploy, whereas Oasis were about albums, touring and longevity.

He was also angered when Creation lumped Oasis in with other bands in their Britpop promotional campaigns. His argument has proved prescient. Why should *Definitely Maybe* be on the same shelves for under a fiver beside Menswear, Elastica, Gene, Supergrass or The Bluetones? This always irritated him. You can understand the sales teams saying, it's another 30,000 units, we're in the music business, we're supposed to sell product, but Russell's vantage point has been proved correct over the years. It was better for his band to play the game for a few weeks with Blur but remain committed to the long-term view of album, world tour, album, world tour. He felt Britpop would undermine worldwide sales. When *(What's The Story)*

Morning Glory? had a breakthrough in the States and with Blur's *The Great Escape* nowhere to be found, Russell could be forgiven for thinking Blur were no longer the competition. They would now be competing on the world stage, against acts like U2, the Rolling Stones and Bruce Springsteen, selling millions of albums and playing to enormous crowds on era-defining world tours.

It has been an unbelievable odyssey for McGee, Oasis and Creation and I believe the final chapter has still to be written. If I had only one question for Noel Gallagher regarding his songwriting and any possibility of a future for Oasis, it would be this. 'I know you think every song you write is fantastic but if you write one and, instinctively as an artist, you immediately know this is better than "Live Forever" or "Wonderwall" and is perfect for Liam, do you keep it in a secret file marked *Future Oasis Album*?'

When you consider the internal conflict at the centre of the group it's even more of an achievement that they managed to garner such critical acclaim and commercial success with so many songs that delivered such a sense of connection. In the splendid Paolo Hewitt book, *Getting High: The Adventures of Oasis*, he uses a line that sums up the band and the excitement they generate, especially in their live shows: 'Freedom is in short supply these days. But not at Oasis concerts, their words are about freedom their music breathes it.' I think Lester Bangs, as ever, said it best: 'Rock 'n' roll should make you glad to be alive.'

30

We Are the Resurrection & Reunion

In late August 2024 I was on a much-needed holiday in Ibiza. I was in the old bit of the island, demographically more grave than rave and more arty than party. As we walked into the old town, a couple were settled having a coffee in a café, and on the Spanish newspaper they were reading, I saw a small photo of Noel Gallagher. My Spanish isn't that good, but I could make out something like: 'Oasis star back on island.' That's interesting. Shouldn't that be former Oasis star, I laughed to myself. Then I realised that I'd forgotten Noel did have a place here. I knew he used to have a villa, previously owned by Mike Oldfield, a stunning property overlooking the Mediterranean, but I thought he'd sold up and moved elsewhere.

After flying home, we opened the duty-free and watched YouTube. First up was a show with John Robb interviewing Noel in the legendary Manchester second-hand record store, Sifters on Fog Lane, Burnage. At first, I was unsure if it was an old or new interview or where it had come from. I double-checked and it was new. The tone was upbeat. Noel was complimentary about Liam. He was speaking ahead of the *Definitely Maybe* reissue (30th Anniversary Deluxe Editions 30.08.24). Noel reflected on Liam's voice. 'When I would sing a song, it would sound good. When he sung it, it sounded great . . . I can't sing "Cigarettes & Alcohol", "Rock 'n' Roll

Star" and all that. I don't have the same attitude as him. If songs were drinks, Liam's is a shot of tequila and mine's a half of Guinness. My voice is half a Guinness on a Tuesday – it's all right. Liam's is ten shots of tequila on a Friday.'

In a revealing and telling chat, Noel suggested that part of the band's appeal was about coming together; their songs were not elitist but all about inclusivity. He felt that came from the acid house scene. He speaks candidly about the Monnow Valley recordings not having a swagger because they weren't recorded as a band but separately.

As for Liam, he had been toying with his followers over the same weekend on social media. He had just played *Definitely Maybe* in full, ahead of the thirtieth-anniversary reissue, at Reading Festival on Sunday 25 August, where he dedicated 'Half A World Away' to his brother, 'Noel f*****g Gallagher'. After the set, on Liam's screens in Oasis branding and font came the date '27.08.24', and the time 8 a.m. After 11 p.m., Liam, then Noel, then the official Oasis account posted to their accounts.

This was happening.

By the following day, the internet was awash with news of a reunion. Initially, Oasis were rumoured to be playing a run of shows at Wembley and Manchester. Typical Oasis, announcing a reunion on a Bank Holiday. Fans would need to wait until Tuesday 27 August for the full dates and news on the availability of tickets. On Tuesday it was confirmed. Their sixteen-year feud was over. The warring brothers were reforming and playing shows across the UK and Ireland in 2025, in Cardiff, Manchester, London, Edinburgh and Dublin.

The world couldn't get enough of that peerless combustible chemistry from the Gallaghers. The press release announcing the reunion was funny and succinct: 'There has been no great revelatory moment that has ignited the reunion – just the gradual realisation that the time is right.' The band followed suit: 'The guns have fallen silent. The stars have aligned. The great wait is over. Come see. It will not be televised.'

It always felt like it had to happen, yet I was caught out by it all. There had been so many false dawns. In 2016, ahead of the premiere of *Supersonic*, the Oasis movie which charts their rise to fame, Liam was positive about a reunion. But the Gallaghers played the public feud like a couple of old boxing pros teasing about a rematch. Liam proved his voice could hold out by playing some killer festival shows. A cynic would suggest he was almost toying with his older brother and performing brilliantly out of badness to let Noel know what he was missing. Liam had also collaborated with Stone Roses guitarist John Squire. Noel enjoyed performing chaos-free shows, his calm professionalism almost came across as going through the motions on his High Flying Birds festival dates. For him the time, and the money, were right.

Unusually, for planet Oasis, it was all going smoothly. Too smoothly. I was amazed at how slick the announcements were. A co-ordinated, targeted campaign. This wouldn't be Oasis without a mighty spanner thrown into the works. Love was all around. The angels were singing. A reunion. Wow. Then the tickets went on sale and, within minutes, everyone hated them.

On the most missed, cherished and celebrated band, the public turned big-style, furious at their treatment at having to wait all day, for hours on end, then paying massively over the odds for tickets. Not only had Oasis fans been waiting since 2009 to see the band back together, but once they were organised and ready to book, they were bombarded with error messages, held in an online queue for hours and then had to deal with Ticketmaster's 'dynamic' pricing strategy with prices becoming increasingly extortionate due to the crazy demand. It was chaotic. It was dispiriting. It was national headline news.

The problem was the unprecedented demand. The entire tour could have been sold out many times over but the technology was unable to deal with the volume and didn't work properly – or fairly. Thankfully, by the end of September ahead of dates in the US, issues with online ticketing were ironed out. Oasis's management intervened and Ticketmaster's dynamic pricing model would not be used for the North American dates.

Experts suggested one of the contributing factors behind a reunion was generational. The kids of those into the band have grown up loving their music. It was noticeable how young the audience at Liam's *Definitely Maybe* shows were and they knew every word. The band's music has lived on and reverberated through the ages. Their numbers, particularly on TikTok, are phenomenal. They have 21.6 million monthly listeners on Spotify and 'Wonderwall' has been streamed over a billion times. This all points to a younger, newer demographic – a whole new fanbase. The band continue to have a real emotional pull and connection. Just like the 1990s, when they were front and centre culturally. They are a voice for so many, and now a new generation connects with their music. As just one example, after the Manchester Arena bombing in May 2017, when twenty-two people were killed, the crowds spontaneously sung a heart-wrenching version of 'Don't Look Back In Anger'.

Bookmakers were offering four to one on the band falling out. For those who have purchased tickets, I would not worry too much. I don't think bookies are fully cognisant of the watertight contracts 'argumentative' bands, prone to falling out, have to sign. These come with catastrophic financial consequences if contracts are not honoured, and high insurance premiums if it all goes wrong. Ask The Everly Brothers, The Eagles, Fleetwood Mac or most famously, Simon & Garfunkel. Maybe separate dressing rooms and flights will do the trick. Catch up at show time.

Noel and Liam have both kept busy. Noel's High Flying Birds, formed in 2010, have released four albums and sold over 1.5 million copies. Liam enlisted three former Oasis members, Andy Bell, Gem Archer and Chris Sharrock, for Beady Eye in 2009 and they recorded two albums before disbanding in 2014. He performed as a solo artist, releasing a critically acclaimed album, *As You Were*, in 2017. In 2024 he performed his thirtieth anniversary *Definitely Maybe* shows. They have both kept match fit, with high-profile shows and the airing of many an Oasis hit.

This Live '25 tour is a serious set of shows. On the news of the first tranche of dates, experts estimated that the band, from the initial fourteen-date UK and Ireland tour, would generate £400 million in tickets, merchandise and other add-ons. The Gallagher brothers would make £50 million each. Being erratic and unpredictable is OK for a gigging stand-up comedian, but not a band like Oasis. There's now far too much at stake.

I remember the hype and excitement around the announcement of one of Oasis's biggest influences, The Stone Roses, reforming in 2011. They proclaimed they were back, reuniting for a Reunion World Tour, including three sold-out homecoming gigs at Heaton Park and Phoenix Park in Dublin. It makes for an easy comparison with a similar hype and fascination; it was also a huge story. But nowhere near the size and reach of Oasis reforming. Let's hope they make it through and perhaps learn from The Stone Roses' reunion, captured by filmmaker and fan of the band, Shane Meadows.

Maybe we should listen to Alan McGee's advice during his PIAS interview. When asked if Oasis would ever get back together he said: 'I hope not. So long as they don't get back together, we're all fucking legends.' Let's hope they continue to be legends throughout this world tour and come out the other side unscathed . . . and still legendary. Hopefully, the fractured relationship has had time to mend and is not being masked by convenient painkillers.

It's their capriciousness that makes them so special. Up until now that unpredictability, however exhilarating, had stood in the way. But the brothers were burying the hatchet. They were reunited. This transcended music. Oasis had reached a surreal level of popularity. The realisation that they'd be on the road again, performing together, became a moment of cultural utopia.

Acknowledgements

Thanks to Sharron for her continued support and to Derek McKee for placing us on the guest list. To Ross Clark for twisting my arm to head to King Tut's for an uneventful evening. I'd also like to thank Birlinn, especially Andrew Simmons, for nudging me towards Polygon's editor Alison Rae. I'm hugely grateful to Alison and Emma Hargrave for their editing, and I would also like to thank Debbie Ellis for our enjoyable blether masquerading as an interview.

SOURCES

Films

1991: The Year That Punk Broke
Supersonic
Upside Down: The Creation Records Story

Books

A Bit of a Blur, Alex James (Abacus, 2008)
Against Interpretation, Susan Sontag (Farrar, Straus and Giroux, 1966)

Creation Stories: Riots, Raves and Running a Label, Alan McGee (Allen & Unwin, 2024)

Getting High : The Adventures of Oasis, Paolo Hewitt (Dean Street Press, 2016)

Mind the Bollocks: A Riotous Rant Through the Ridiculousness of Rock 'n' Roll, Johnny Sharpe (Portico, 2012)

Take Me There: Oasis the Story, Paul Mathur (Bloomsbury, 1997)

The Condition of the Working Classes in England, Friedrich Engels (Penguin Classics, 2009)

Press/Magazines/Sites

Beffshuff Blog Q&A

Dundee Courier

FHM

Glasgow Herald

The Guardian

Loaded

Maxim

Mixmag

Mojo

NME

The New York Times

PIAS

Q Magazine

Record Collector

Rolling Stone

San Francisco Chronicle

Select

Vice Magazine

WalesOnline